Archipelagoes *of* My South

Archipelagoes *of* My South

EPISODES IN THE SHAPING OF A REGION, 1830–1965

J. MILLS THORNTON III

The University of Alabama Press
Tuscaloosa

The University of Alabama Press
Tuscaloosa, Alabama 35487-0380
uapress.ua.edu

Hardcover edition published 2016.
Paperback edition published 2022.
eBook edition published 2016.

Typeface: Caslon

Cover design: Michele Myatt Quinn

Paperback ISBN: 0-8173-6055-9

A previous edition of this book has been cataloged by the Library of Congress.
ISBN: 978-0-8173-1933-5 (cloth)
E-ISBN: 978-0-8173-9067-9

For Ed Bridges,
who suggested this volume

Contents

List of Illustrations ix

Introduction xi

1. The Ethic of Subsistence and the Origins of Southern Secession 1

2. Fiscal Policy and the Failure of Radical Reconstruction in the Lower South 28

3. Alabama's Presidential Reconstruction Legislature 71

4. Alabama Emancipation in the Courts 92

5. Redemption and the Jews in Montgomery 110

6. Senator J. Thomas Heflin and the Expulsion Movement of 1929 123

7. Hugo Black and the Golden Age 148

8. The Structure of White Supremacy in Alabama in the Era of World War II 164

9. Rosa Parks and the Law 186

10. The Montgomery Freedom Rider Riots of 1961 199

Conclusion 216

Index 221

Illustrations

FIGURES

2.1. Receipts and Disbursements, Alabama, Actual Dollars 39

2.2. Receipts and Disbursements, Florida, Actual Dollars 40

2.3. Receipts and Disbursements, Louisiana, Actual Dollars 41

2.4. Receipts and Disbursements, Mississippi, Actual Dollars 42

2.5. Receipts and Disbursements, South Carolina, Actual Dollars 43

2.6. Receipts per White, Disbursements per Citizen, Constant Dollars, Alabama 50

2.7. Receipts per White, Disbursements per Citizen, Constant Dollars, Florida 51

2.8. Receipts per White, Disbursements per Citizen, Constant Dollars, Louisiana 52

2.9. Receipts per White, Disbursements per Citizen, Constant Dollars, Mississippi 53

2.10. Receipts per White, Disbursements per Citizen, Constant Dollars, South Carolina 54

2.11. Receipts and Disbursements, Georgia, Actual Dollars 65

MAP

6.1. Alabama's Black Belt 124

TABLES

2.1. State land tax on a farm of 160 acres, Alabama 46

2.2. State land tax on a farm of 160 acres, Mississippi 47

2.3 State land tax on a farm of 160 acres with smallest land-tax receipts, Alabama 48

2.4. State land tax on a farm of 160 acres with smallest land-tax receipts, Mississippi 49

3.1. Expenditures on public schools, Louisiana 58

3.2. Expenditures on public schools, South Carolina 58

3.3. Median legislative slaveholding 72

3.4. Economic groupings in the legislatures 73

Introduction

"The tourist archipelagoes of my South / are prisons, too, corruptible," writes the poet Derek Walcott. He refers to the actual archipelagoes of the Caribbean. But his South and mine share that in common, imprisoned in an inherited corruption. The tourists who visit, and indeed, too many of the southerners who live their lives there, remain essentially ignorant of the fractured layers of history that lie beneath the landscape they see—and therefore, of the complex capacity of those histories to manifest themselves in what observers take to be the present.

I have adopted Walcott's phrase as the title for this collection in part because these essays seem to me islands in the stream of southern history, independent investigations linked together by the powerful and tortured past of the region. They do not tell the whole story, or even any considerable part of it. But each can serve in some sense as a metaphor, and together they allow us to see the South's history working itself out in a variety of situations.

It is not that they started out that way, I should say. The essays span my entire career as a scholar, from one written as a seminar paper in graduate school to one written only last year and published here for the first time. The unity I attribute to them derives not from any conscious design on my part, but from the persistent region that is their common focus. I have spent the last fifty years puzzling over the South, and particularly over the ever-gathering force of its history in the lives of its people. The essays all represent efforts to understand the sources of the region's power, drawn from various times in my own intellectual life and from various points in the southern past. I do not expect that the essays will come together to provide the reader with a key to the regional conundrum, but I do think they will serve to clarify for the reader why the enormous diversity of the southern experience makes that power so great. I also think that the variety of the articles' subject matter, and the fact that the collection spans much of the nineteenth and twentieth centuries, may allow the reader to see interconnections that would otherwise not be apparent.

I have said that my focus is on the South, but the reader will soon see that, in large part, it is actually on Alabama. I do not mean to imply that the South is merely Alabama writ large. On the contrary, I believe strongly in the significance of the local in the shaping of history, and I therefore accept—indeed, affirm—the elements of uniqueness that separate each southern state, and all of its localities, from one another. At the same time, it is clear that southern states, and their counties and towns, share historical experiences and institutions that mark the region, and more, that the experiences and institutions they share with the rest of America are received into and distorted by the regional historical context. In that sense, I do believe that the study of Alabama can teach us about the region at large, and for that matter, about the dilemmas of humanity.

That may be all the introduction this collection requires. Each article can, I trust, stand on its own bottom, and the lessons to be derived from placing them in conversation with one another I will largely leave to the reader, with the hope that readers may find the process as moving and instructive as I do.

Nevertheless, I have thought that a brief account of my own intellectual biography might help to place the articles in the context that gave immediate rise to them.[1] I was particularly fortunate as an undergraduate at Princeton to work with two superb historians, Professors James M. McPherson and F. Sheldon Hackney. I first undertook the serious study of history in a sophomore seminar conducted by Professor McPherson on comparative reconstructions. McPherson validated my then distinctly sophomoric belief that the investigation of the history of my native Alabama was actually a legitimate enterprise, kindly sharing with me an unpublished seminar paper that he had written on Alabama's Democratic Reconstruction governor, Robert B. Lindsay, and urging me to pursue related topics. Professor Hackney joined the Princeton faculty in my senior year, and I wrote my senior thesis under his direction, on Alabama's disfranchising Constitutional Convention of 1901.

Both McPherson and Hackney had studied under the eminent C. Vann Woodward, and they each encouraged me to apply for graduate school at Yale to work with him. Doing so was certainly one of the best decisions of my life. As an undergraduate I had read Woodward's *Tom Watson: Agrarian Rebel* (1938), and I was at once fascinated and captured by his portrait of the conflicts of the 1890s as rooted in the antebellum arguments between Whigs, the intellectual ancestors of the New South industrializers such as Henry Grady, and the Jacksonians, the progenitors of Watson's Populists. That insight became the foundation of the dissertation I wrote for Professor Woodward, and that became my first book, *Politics and Power in a Slave Society: Alabama, 1800–1860* (1978). In it I sought to retrieve what seemed to me the profound radicalism and the neglected strength of the antebellum

South's Jacksonian tradition. Elements of that project are to be found also in several of the essays in this volume, especially the initial one.

When I received my doctorate in 1974, I joined the faculty of the University of Michigan. I would remain there until my retirement in 2010. My years in Ann Arbor were enriched by a succession of brilliant students who elaborated, amended, and deepened my own understanding of these arguments. In the meantime, however, my scholarly interests increasingly responded to my desire to examine the working out in the rest of southern history of the great issues that had animated Jacksonian politics, slavery (or, more broadly than they would have understood, white supremacy) and the concentration of economic and social power. That exploration led me forward, through Reconstruction and into the twentieth century, and out of it eventually came my book on the civil rights movement, *Dividing Lines: Municipal Politics and the Struggle for Civil Rights in Montgomery, Birmingham, and Selma* (2002). These preoccupations are to be seen in a number of the articles in this volume, and they account for what other historians may think a curious lack of chronological focus in my scholarship. My principal concern has always been not any one period, but the arc of regional evolution. Thus interrelationships across eras and generations are another recurring theme in many of these essays. A final theme, as I have already noted, is the significance of the local, involving my commitment to the belief that the mechanisms of political and social change are to be sought not usually at the national level but at the level at which the great mass of people live and act.

I will return to some of these reflections at the conclusion of this volume. For the present, however, I trust that these introductory remarks have been sufficient to situate readers amid what may otherwise seem a quite disparate series of essays. I should say that most of the essays have, to one degree or another, been revised and updated for this volume. I have already asserted my confidence that each essay can stand on its own. But I do believe also that together they have a collective force, which I have here sought to intimate. I hope that readers may find it so.

Note

1. I discuss my background and career at greater length in an interview with Joseph W. Pearson, in Megan L. Bever and Scott A. Suarez, eds., *The Historian behind the History: Conversations with Southern Historians* (Tuscaloosa: University of Alabama Press, 2014), and in my preface to the new paperback edition of my *Politics and Power in a Slave Society: Alabama, 1800–1860* (Baton Rouge: Louisiana State University Press, 2014).

Archipelagoes *of* My South

I

The Ethic of Subsistence and the Origins of Southern Secession

In the spring of 1984, the legislature of Maryland undertook to modify the words of the state's famous anthem, "Maryland, My Maryland," written in the far more passionate spring of 1861 by James Ryder Randall. Enraged by the violence that had surrounded General Benjamin Butler's efforts in April to get his frightened Massachusetts militiamen through Baltimore, on their way to Washington, Randall had dashed off his poem as a call to his fellow Marylanders to join the Confederate cause. His summons contained the stirring admonition, "The despot's heel is on thy shore! / His torch is at thy temple door!" These sentiments have proven too strong for the legislators who today guide Maryland's destiny. They have voted their preference instead for the following doggerel: "Oh, join we all to lift a song / To home and state we've loved so long." The author of this sanitized rhyme is a Baltimore schoolteacher, Barbara Klender. Asked by the press to explain her desire to suppress Randall's text, she said that she had found it impossible to explain to her pupils how Abraham Lincoln could have been considered a despot.[1]

Barbara Klender's approach to historical evidence has all too often been the refuge, as well, of professional historians: the document whose words prove inexplicable has an unfortunate tendency to disappear from the record. We should consider, though, what might have been the salutary outcome if Klender had turned her talents from bowdlerizing and had instead asked her students to reflect seriously on the implications of Randall's words. Imagine if she and her students had contemplated the possibility that many hundreds of thousands of Americans might have believed President Lincoln to be a despot. Just conceivably, the exercise might have served to call into question one of America's most enduring and delusory historical myths.

Many antebellum Northern Republicans, just as blind to antebellum Southern realities as Barbara Klender, had expected with the outbreak of fighting in 1861 a rapid Southern social disintegration under the stresses of war. For that matter, many Republicans expected something like a disintegration to arise eventually, whether there was a war or not.[2] They found strong support for their belief in a volume by the North Carolina abolitionist Hinton Rowan Helper, *The Impending Crisis of the South* (1857). Helper argued strenuously that slavery as an institution had the effect of exploiting white nonslaveholders, preventing the development of the Southern economy and elevating white plantation owners to the status of a ruling class. He predicted that these conditions would soon produce an internal crisis in the region. If many Republicans found Helper's claims of inevitable antagonism between white slaveholders and nonslaveholders congenial, essentially all of them were even more certain of general enmity between the slaveholders and their slaves, and particularly so after the powerful fictional portrait of the relationship by Harriet Beecher Stowe, *Uncle Tom's Cabin* (1852).[3]

The Republicans' beliefs about Southern society implied the existence of fissures along which the South might be expected to crack. White nonslaveholders would resist secession; many would refuse to fight for the preservation of the institution that was the source of their degradation, and would desert if drafted; a substantial number would welcome the Northern liberators who promised to deliver the South from feudalism and to bestow upon it the blessings of democracy, free labor, and progress. The backward Southern economy would be unable to sustain the war effort. As the Northern armies approached, slaves promised their freedom would rise in revolt against their masters; this belief was in fact one of the sources of the Emancipation Proclamation. Nonslaveholder opposition, economic dislocation, and slave insurrection all portended a rapid Southern collapse. The South would fall from its own internal contradictions.

In the event, this analysis was not without some objective confirmation. The most important bit of evidence that it contained elements of truth is the state of West Virginia. Populated overwhelmingly by nonslaveholding white small farmers, the western counties of Virginia strongly discountenanced secession, and when the rest of the state forced it upon them, they proclaimed their own secession from Virginia and applied to the Congress for admission as a separate state. It was this path, or one closely resembling it, that many Republicans expected the majority of the South's white yeomanry to follow.

There were echoes of West Virginia's action in the Appalachian counties of Tennessee and North Carolina, but here the situation was a great deal more complicated. As a result of political events whose roots extend back to the Jeffersonian period, the Whig party had emerged in the 1830s and 1840s as a powerful force in this area. Tennessee and North Carolina were the only two Confederate states in which Whiggery had any substantial following in Appalachia. Whigs, in these states as elsewhere in the South, tended to be dubious of secession. The question of secession therefore became a part of long-standing partisan disputes in the states' highlands. The Democratic Party in these counties solidly supported the Southern Rights candidacy of John C. Breckinridge in 1860, while the Whigs rallied to the Tennessee Unionist John Bell. The Unionist Democrat Stephen A. Douglas received only a tiny scattering of votes in the region—indeed, considerably below the quite small percentage he received in each state as a whole. In the secession crisis, probably a majority of the area's Breckinridge Democrats—most prominently, Tennessee's Andrew Johnson—joined the Bell supporters in opposing the dissolution of the Union. But the area's secessionists, though a clear minority, were essentially all Democrats, while very nearly all the Whigs were Unionists, at any rate until the actual outbreak of fighting in April. It seems reasonable to maintain, then, that the opposition to secession in the states' Appalachian counties represented as much a Whig dissent as a yeoman one.[4]

Despite this evidence of nonslaveholders' antipathy to secession, the actions of the yeomanry generally in the South did not accord with Republican expectations. There were indeed committed Unionists among the yeomen, and they would become the backbone of the scalawag Republican faction during Reconstruction. To focus on the dissidents, however, is to focus on the recessive, rather than the dominant theme. The truth about Southern society is that, though its internal divisions were real, yet through four years of war, the fissures failed to widen into fractures; the region retained its coherence substantially as well as did its Northern adversary. The yeomanry showed no widespread hostility to enlisting in the Confederate cause; often yeomen displayed great enthusiasm for the prospect. The Confederate army was composed in great part of yeomen. There were desertions from the Confederate army, as from the Union army. But it was very rare for deserters from either army to join the other side. Usually Southern deserters simply went home to help their families with their farms, and after a period away, they sometimes actually returned to the ranks. There was considerable antagonism toward the conscription laws, in both sections. In the South, as in the North, however, this dispute was in general contained within the bounds of political activity. The South saw individual resistance to conscription but experienced no urban draft riots as the North did. A study of voting patterns in the Confederate Congress, moreover, reveals that the contention over the draft, the tax-in-kind, the suspension of the writ of habeas corpus, and other controversial issues, ordinarily reflected not class or partisan divisions but divisions between representatives of occupied districts, who wanted a maximum military effort to be made to recapture their areas, and those from unoccupied districts, whose constituents would actually have to bear the burdens the acts imposed.[5] As the war dragged on and the Confederate armies suffered important defeats, there was increasing disillusionment with their leadership and war-weariness among Southern voters. But the same can be said of the Northern electorate; indeed, the North, unlike the South, developed a substantial and politically significant peace movement.

It is certainly true that the Southern economy was not as well developed as the Northern one, and considerable economic dislocations developed as the war progressed, particularly as a result of the Union's blockade of Southern ports and the massive inflation of the Confederate currency. There were even small food riots in some Southern cities. Despite these strains, however, the economy was remarkably successful in sustaining the war effort, and Southerners demonstrated great ingenuity in finding substitutes for goods they could not obtain.[6] And, of course, no slave insurrection ever developed. Although slaves very frequently fled within Union lines when the approach of the Northern armies made that action possible, and though there were individual examples of resistance to, as also of genuine cooperation with, their masters, the slaves almost never sought to exact general vengeance in blood.[7]

In short, then, Republican expectations of a rapid Southern internal collapse proved inaccurate in essentially every particular. When the South was finally defeated, it was so not because of its social weaknesses, but because of hard-won and bloody Union victories on the battlefield. The South in wartime betrayed no significantly greater degree of incoherence in its society than the North did. Both societies showed strains. Neither cracked because of them.[8]

Virtually no Republicans were led by the failure of their analysis to reconsider its fundamental presumptions, however. Republicans easily explained to themselves the failure of the yeomanry by and large to oppose the Confederacy by observing that some had done so, and concluding that the majority of them had been so brutalized and beguiled by the slaveholders that they were unable to understand what policies would truly benefit them. And as for the slaves, though Republicans had longed for an insurrection to aid their military effort, they rightly noted that for a slave deprived of weapons to rise in revolt would simply have been foolhardy. Republicans were therefore able to take the recalcitrant reality of the South in stride. Undaunted by events, they pressed on to found their program for Southern Reconstruction upon the very same beliefs about planters, poor whites, and blacks in the region that had so lately miscarried. The results would prove disastrous for all concerned.

Northern Republicans were definitely not wrong, of course, when they noted deep divisions within Southern society. In particular, they were surely correct in observing the existence of profound enmities between white slaveholders and nonslaveholders. And yet the stress of war by and large failed to split white society apart along this seam. This pair of observations inevitably leads us to ask the source of the nonslaveholders' devotion to the Confederate cause. Why did the yeomanry prove in general not to represent the ally of the free labor crusade that the Republicans had anticipated? It is my intention in the present essay to attempt to define the error that lurked at the heart of the Republicans' reading of the Southern situation. To do so requires a brief sketch of the structure of political life in the antebellum South. My goal is to convey some sense of what it was that frightened the mass of the Southern electorate into voting for, and then supporting, sometimes to the death, this war against Republican dogma.

The first step in understanding antebellum Southern politics is to distinguish the Southern reality from the Northern myth about it. The notion took firm root in the North—particularly in Republican Party propaganda—in the late antebellum years, that Southern politics and Southern society were aristocratic. After the Civil War this peculiar idea gained acceptance among Southerners as well—both among Southerners who looked longingly back at the world they had lost and among reformers who wished to prod the South toward their various conceptions of modernity. But before the Civil War, the idea that the South was an aristocratic region was Northern. Southerners conceived of their own section as the citadel of American democracy and believed that the seat of aristocracy in North America was to be found in New England. These rival notions were derived from widely accepted beliefs about the character of the wealthiest groups within the two regions. In the North, Southern planters were very frequently associated with the Tory loyalists who had resisted the American Revolution, and hence were thought to be pro-British and contemptuous of the aspirations of the yeomanry. In the South, New England was quite generally associated with Hamiltonian Federalism, and hence was thought to have been hostile to the rise of the common man and sympathetic to the British in the War of 1812. Moreover, wealthy capitalists and industrialists from the great cities of Philadelphia, New York, and Boston were depicted in the oratory of Jacksonian politicians as conniving to erect a financial oligarchy in America. A great many in each section believed that the wealthy element in the other section held political control of its region. On the other hand, each section ordinarily felt confident that its own electorate had succeeded in holding the incipient aristocracy within it in check. Thus much of the electorate in each section came to conceive of itself—and with increasing conviction in the years after the Mexican-American War—as maintaining the true precepts of the American creed, and to conceive of the other as having diverged along an un-American path.[9]

The Northern portrait of an aristocratic South, enshrined in late nineteenth-century accounts of the causes of the Civil War and ratified by Southern acceptance of it, persists in the popular imagination and in historical literature to this day.[10] But however strong may be its hold, it bears virtually no relation to the facts. Planters (that is, owners of twenty or more slaves) were indeed a majority of state legislators in South Carolina, a state that, uniquely in the region, retained in its constitution significant property qualifications for legislative membership. But in no other Southern state were they more than approximately a third of the lawmakers, even late in the antebellum period. And in many states they were far less than that proportion: 5 percent in Texas, 7 percent in Tennessee, 10 percent in Arkansas, about 20 percent in Louisiana and Virginia, and about 30 percent in Georgia and Mississippi. The median figure for the future Confederate states in 1850 was one-fourth.[11]

But the point to be made is far more than merely that planters were outnumbered among Southern legislators by some three to one. The real point is that Southern politics rested squarely on the exploitation of popular resentment and hostility toward planters and other wealthy citizens. This political style had its roots in early struggles to democratize state constitutions: to correct legislative malapportionment and to alter the basis of apportionment, to eliminate property qualifications for office-holding and for voting, to make more and more officials, including judges, subject to popular election, and often to shorten their terms.[12] But politicians found the warning that the state constitution contained aristocratic features so powerful a charge with the voters that they quickly applied variants of it to virtually every area of political conflict. On the federal level, early antebellum politics focused particularly on questions growing out of public land policy. On the state level, the principal concerns were the regulation of banks and the propriety of governmental assistance to corporations. Each of these subjects depended for its emotional force upon the voters' fears of a growing aristocracy.[13]

The source of these political divisions, and of the fears on which they were founded, is to be sought in large part in the expansion of the market economy in the years between the War of 1812 and the Civil War. Acceptance of the virtues of the national and international marketplace on the one hand and resistance to its requirements on the other implied a conception of the meaning of freedom. For adherents of the Jacksonian or Democratic Party—a party whose appeal to the ordinary voter very much derived from its symbolic defense of the ethic of subsistence agriculture, even if its more cosmopolitan state and national leaders all too often failed fully to comprehend that fact—freedom was something the citizenry had gained in the American Revolution and held by right, but that evil antidemocratic forces were attempting to take away. A man was free when he was self-sufficient, dependent on no one else for his livelihood and welfare. Movements and institutions whose success would diminish the existing autonomy of the individual were thus by definition aristocratic, and inimical to the American experiment. For Whigs, freedom was not something Americans already had, but something for which they were perpetually striving. A man became free by fulfilling his potential, by becoming all that he could be. The fetters of ignorance and poverty were his greatest enemies; the expansion of knowledge and opportunity was his principal security.

These differing definitions of freedom carried with them differing notions of the proper role of government. Whigs sought the enactment of programs intended to break the shackles that, from their perspective, held the mass of Americans in economic, social, or moral bondage: programs such as governmental aid for the construction of railroads, roads, and canals; protective tariffs to encourage the growth of manufacturing; central regulation of the currency supply and the credit and banking system; the establishment of public schools; the prohibition of the sale of liquor; and the creation of hospitals to treat the insane, institutions to train the deaf and blind for usefulness, and penitentiaries to redeem criminals. Jacksonians generally regarded all such efforts as products of paternalistic elitism. That the ordinary citizen should be taxed to benefit railroads, factories, and banks, that his private conduct should be regulated, that his children should be forcibly indoctrinated with alien, urban ideals, they thought intolerable.

Jacksonians campaigned for the abolition of property qualifications for voting and office-holding primarily because they hoped that a broadened electorate would be able to use the government to restrict the growth of corporations, and ultimately to destroy them. They conceived of their political party as a sort of trade union of the electorate, through which ordinary citizens, individually weak, could band together and use their numbers to counterbalance the power of the wealthy. Many Whig leaders, on the other hand, were doubtful that the poverty stricken and the ill educated were capable of appreciating what was actually in their own best interests. Whigs conceived of their party as a sort of evangelical religious denomination, an organization of believers met to convert and to save the society at large. Although practical political considerations soon led Whig politicians to abandon their early defense of wealth restrictions on the suffrage and on qualifications for office, they continued to place hope in public schooling and to insist on examinations for admission to such professions as law and medicine.

In the lower South, the origins of Whiggery lay in the use of nullificationist doctrines to assert the right of each state to expel the Indians within its boundaries. The ease with which these nullifiers embraced the broad-constructionist program of the national Whig party in the later 1830s is an index to the degree to which ideology in the region was an extension of interest. Those merchants and planters who had eagerly sought the opening of Indian lands for speculation and exploitation were just as eager for roads, railroads, and the easy credit promised by a national banking system, however inconsistent the constitutional theories underlying the two positions may have been.

While a great many planters were Whigs, planters were not the cutting edge of the party. This point is very often misunderstood, because the Northern conception of the planter as the dominant figure in the society is now so firmly entrenched in beliefs about it. The reality, however, is that the intellectual leaders of the Whiggery were the urban lawyers, merchants, and factors the planters envied and emulated.[14] Planters in general led an isolated rural existence. The towns and villages of the South were the points of contact with the wider world: the places where the party newspapers were edited, the source of knowledge about changing styles and fashions, the locations in which the planter and his family received their images of status and progress. These notions the planter often absorbed from his annual visits at harvest time to the offices of the factors and commission merchants, and from his subscriptions to urban papers and magazines. It is true that the factors and merchants were the economic dependents of the planters, rather than vice versa. But in a comparable sense, industrialists were the economic dependents of the laborers in their factories, and indeed, planters were the economic dependents of their slaves. Social notions of dependency, it is clear, need not parallel economic relationships. The planter and his family almost always harbored a surreptitious fear of being taken for country bumpkins, and therefore eagerly internalized the values of the towns.

The strength of the Jacksonian party, in contrast, was usually to be found concentrated in those areas that were most insulated from market agriculture. The semisubsistence farm on the fringes of the market economy was even more isolated than was the plantation—in part because roads in the hill counties and the pine barrens were very poor and railroads were only just beginning to penetrate these areas at the end of the antebellum period. But even more importantly, this isolation persisted because semisubsistence agriculture simply did not require the regular contacts with urban centers that were a necessary part of growing primarily for the market.

If the relationship between planters and urban elements is frequently misconceived, the situation of the white small farmers is depicted inaccurately even more often. The first thing to be said about them is that their desire for self-sufficiency was no pipe dream. If we may take figures for the South Carolina upcountry in 1850 as reasonably typical, then the majority of hill country farms in every size classification were self-sufficient. Even among the very smallest farms (49 or fewer improved acres), 54 percent were self-sufficient in grain and 42 percent in meat. And in all larger categories (from 50 to 200 improved acres), 80 percent to 90 percent were self-sufficient in grain and about three-fourths in meat. Among very large farms (those of 200 or more improved acres), self-sufficiency in meat, though not in grain, fell again to 63 percent, reflecting the tendency of many planters to purchase meat from drovers. But with this exception, self-sufficiency was usual everywhere in the hills. Moreover, these figures are calculated exclusively from the farm's productions. They do not reflect the ability of the small farmer to supplement his family's diet through hunting, fishing, and trapping, though his opportunities through these methods were very considerable. And even among tenant farmers, who were some 15 to 20 percent of hill country cultivators, self-sufficiency was not uncommon: 43 percent of them in grain, 28 percent in meat.

In the second place, much of the yeomanry in the antebellum, unlike the postbellum, South, did not participate extensively in the growth of cotton, which was the hallmark of commercial agriculture in much of the region. Thirty percent of nonslaveholding yeomen, and 20 percent even of small slaveholders (owners of fewer than six slaves) grew no cotton at all. And the many small farmers who did grow cotton produced only two or three bales, a level of production indicating that no more than 5 to 10 percent of their improved acreage was devoted to the cash crop. Small farmers, instead, for the most part grew food crops, primarily to feed themselves, their families, and their livestock. If in a given year they produced a surplus after meeting these needs, they might barter it with neighbors who could supply them some service, or with the country storekeeper for "store-bought goods." But the production of a surplus to market was not their principal goal; their goal was to sustain themselves, to avoid dependency, to guard their status as freemen. They practiced what has been called "safety-first agriculture."[15]

The small farmers' substantial herds of livestock, in particular pigs, point to another seldom understood aspect of their social situation. Perhaps two-thirds of all acreage in farms in the region was unimproved, often heavily forested. The law in every lower South state was firm in declaring all unfenced land to be common grazing area. It was the responsibility of all farmers to guard their growing crops with a fence that was, in the colorful language of the Southern statutes, "horse high, bull strong, and hog tight." Small farmers were thus at liberty to brand their livestock—the origin of our term *earmarking* because pigs were branded by making notches in their ears—and to turn them free to graze in the woods and meadows, fattening them in anticipation of the annual roundup. Because so much acreage was unimproved, farmers had access to very large areas that they did not own, even in the generally settled South Atlantic states.

And if the areas were large in the South Atlantic states, they were vast in the Old Southwest. Before the passage of the Graduation Act of 1854, immense stretches of the Gulf states—half the total land area of Alabama in 1850, for instance—remained in the public domain. This land was simply not worth the $1.25 an acre that was the minimum purchase price the United States could accept under the law. Thus in the Gulf states, the small farmer had access to land he did not own not only for grazing but for cultivation as well. Indeed, it was much to his advantage to cultivate the public domain, because under the federal preemption statutes, if he cleared a part of the public domain and planted a crop on it, he thus gained a preemption right to purchase the surrounding 160 acres at the minimum price if later someone threatened to bid on it at auction.[16]

But if the objective economic situation in the hill counties and the pine barrens provided the semisubsistence farmer with a considerable measure of insulation from the vagaries of the marketplace, it by no means gave him a sense of security in his status. On the contrary, the Southern yeomanry was consumed by the stark terror that titanic and inscrutable forces were conspiring to reduce all poor farmers to serfdom. The sources of that terror are both obvious and subtle.

In the first place, the figures I have cited indicate that the overwhelming majority of yeoman farmers were self-sufficient, but they also indicate that about a fifth of them, and among the smallest farmers perhaps two-fifths of them, were not. In a given year, too little rain, too much rain, hailstorms, windstorms, insect infestations, and other such unpredictable occurrences could considerably increase that proportion. Thus the yeomanry unavoidably lived always with the prospect of being suddenly precipitated into want and debt. And what was most frightening was that the individual yeoman farmer's decision each spring on whether or not to plant cotton, and if so, how much of his acreage to devote to the crop, could become the decisive factor in determining whether he retained or lost his self-sufficiency in food. If he guessed right in this annual gamble, then the resultant cash income might enable him to buy his land, if a squatter or tenant, or to pay off a mortgage on it and thus secure his independence, or to provide a dowry for a daughter or a farm for a son of marriageable age. But if he guessed wrong, his family might go hungry while neighboring ones did not. This was the perpetual dilemma of safety-first agriculture: when and to what extent to venture into the market.

When we understand how critical was the decision of the small farmer to raise several bales of cotton, we understand a considerable part of his fear of and hostility toward the forces of international finance that determined the price he would receive for his few bales. The small farmer was sufficiently isolated from the market economy that its operations remained rather mysterious to him. Financial panics, suspensions of specie payment, the oscillations of the Liverpool cotton exchange, all could have the character of the occult from his perspective. But what he did know was that, unlike the rains, winds, and insects, these misfortunes were the work of men—wealthy and, as he was easily led to believe, evil and exploitative men. It was upon these emotions that the Jacksonian crusades against banks, bondholders, and paper money were largely built.

The other source of Jacksonian strength among the yeomanry is a bit more obscure. When the small farmer was deprived by events of the self-sufficiency that, in his mind, constituted the essence of his freedom, he sought to survive through bartering his labor or his skills with a neighbor for a portion of the neighbor's surplus grain or meat. And even when the farmer was in no need of food, the swapping of horses and mules, and bartering with other farmers, with ginners, millers, blacksmiths, or with the country storekeeper for any number of goods not readily made on the farm, was a way of life. Although the farmer might live on the fringes of the international agricultural market, he lived at the very heart of a constantly active local market defined in great measure by barter, reciprocity, and mutual obligation. These relationships were extensive and important. Socially, his world demanded as the price of membership conformity to the community's values, a conformity enforced through gossip and disapproval, confession before or expulsion from his church congregation, and through the jury or the lynch mob if the farmer's transgressions went far enough. In short, the yeomanry's world was intensely and closely bound. It was this fact that caused the small farmer to respond so sympathetically to the Jacksonian warning that America's troubles proceeded from excessively powerful institutions, a lack of individualism, the indefensible inability of each citizen to determine his own destiny, to rule his own life, without interference from society.

There was an analogous pattern in the social experience of the urban Whig. Living as he did in the highly competitive, too often even cutthroat, world of trade and commerce in the cities and towns, he was easily convinced of the accuracy of the Whiggery's diagnosis of America's principal illness: the lack of mutual cooperation and concern; the need for Americans to recognize the mutuality of their interests, to ignore the demagogic politicians who played upon class, ethnic, sectional or other divisions and jealousies, and to pull together to benefit the nation as a whole. The irony of antebellum political culture was that the Whigs advocated programs in effect conducive to urbanization and industrialization in the belief that they were pursuing the cooperative commonwealth, while the Jacksonians' enthusiasm for individualism and hostility to institutions were shaped by the defense of a way of life singularly interdependent and marked by quite rigid social, moral, and intellectual conformity.[17]

These generalizations depend for their validity on the approximate correspondence here asserted between the Jacksonian constituency and semi-subsistence farmers on the one hand, and the Whig constituency and commercial, professional, industrial, and market-oriented agricultural interests on the other. These correspondences, however, are far from exact. No rural county was so isolated that it did not contain a substantial number of Whigs; a desire for upward mobility, as opposed to a passion to be left alone, was the essential factor in creating a Whiggish disposition in a voter, and that desire might be found even in the most hidden coves and hollows. In the cities, the Jacksonians had many supporters; free-trade advocates, and journeymen fearful of those developments in the organization of labor that were increasingly depriving them of independence as workers, moved naturally into the Jacksonian coalition. Membership in certain religious denominations and ethnic groups predisposed a voter to the one or the other party; Roman Catholics, and especially the Irish immigrants among them, were overwhelmingly Democratic, while the Whig advocacy of moral reform movements attracted the adherence of Presbyterians, Congregationalists, and other evangelical Protestants. Other more personal considerations, such as friendship with a particular candidate, could easily determine a voter's preference in a given contest.

Moreover, in certain states the political geography was not fully consonant with the general pattern. For instance, as the introduction to this essay has already noted, in Tennessee and North Carolina the Whiggery had strong support in Appalachia. In North Carolina, many planters of the coastal plain had followed the Old Republican senator Nathaniel Macon in the early years of the century into a firm allegiance to strict constructionist doctrines. This interpretation of the Constitution led substantial numbers of them in the 1820s into the Jacksonian camp. In the meanwhile, the backcountry was becoming more thickly settled, and a portion of the yeomanry of the area came to associate the coastal counties' opposition to state assistance in the building of the transportation facilities that were needed to open the backcountry fully, with supercilious planter hostility to common folk. This yeoman resentment of low-country planters impelled many Appalachian farmers into the Whiggery, a party dedicated to internal improvement, and hence, in the local context, a party that seemed the friendlier one to mountain people. In Tennessee, Andrew Jackson's own state, Jackson had early associated himself politically with wealthy Nashville planters and land speculators. Jackson's identification in the arena of local politics with middle Tennessee planting interests provided Whig spokesmen in east Tennessee with the opportunity to play upon economic and sectional resentments, and thus to gain a significant following among the yeomanry there. Just as the powerful presence of Macon and Jackson in the formative years of the party system affected its structure in North Carolina and Tennessee, the presence of John C. Calhoun similarly distorted the course of its development in South Carolina. There Calhoun's popularity was so great that he became the head of a dominant political machine. The result was that South Carolina, uniquely in this period, became a one-party Democratic state. South Carolina's fidelity to the Democracy, however, represented simply a loyalty to Calhoun as a local leader, rather than to Jacksonianism. Calhoun's control of the Democratic Party, therefore, effectively deprived the state's yeomanry of a distinct political voice.

These variations from the asserted norm, however, even though they may appear at first blush to call the accuracy of that norm into question, actually confirm the presence of the social dynamic underlying it. Irish immigrants, for instance, came to America from exactly the sort of rural and wounded society, on its guard against the domination of a more cosmopolitan and industrialized ruling power, that was likely to provide corroboration in their emotions for Jacksonians' warnings against the presumptuous arrogance of the sophisticated Whig capitalists and reformers. The nativism and anti-Catholicism that were usually more openly avowed in Whig circles than in Democratic ones further fortified Irish suspicions. Similarly, the journeyman artisan who saw his ability to control the pattern of his daily work giving way before the demands of larger-scale production, might respond to the Jacksonian emphasis on the necessity to preserve each citizen's personal independence and autonomy in quite the same way that the semisubsistence farmer would. In North Carolina and Tennessee, though the events of each state's history had shaped the local political geography into an unusual pattern, the rivalry between the yeomanry and the planters was nonetheless at the heart of the process that had produced this novel outcome, just as it was in all the other Southern states. Moreover, a careful study of one

North Carolina Piedmont county indicates that, at the precinct level, the partisan division parallels the one which exists more broadly in the other states: the Democratic Party's strength was centered in the more isolated areas of the county, the Whigs in the more urban and market-oriented precincts. In the Appalachian counties of both North Carolina and Tennessee, the Whig majority was a rather narrow one. It may well be that in these counties generally, those yeomen who did not fall under the Whiggery's influence were likely to be those who resided in the most remote areas. Finally, even in one-party South Carolina, a persuasive investigation has revealed that, though the conflict was not as elsewhere embodied in partisan warfare, nevertheless the politics of the state clearly reflects the clash of the yeoman and planter cultures.[18]

The ethic created by the life of the semisubsistence farmer, then—the ethic of autonomy—was at the heart of the Jacksonian crusade. It is to be found at work in all areas of antebellum American life, whenever the modernizing tendencies of an expanding national economy encountered the more traditional values of those citizens who feared above all else the prospect of being manipulated by powerful institutions and forces beyond their community, of losing control of their lives and destinies to unseen enemies. Even when the formal structures of politics and economics do not immediately appear to exhibit this encounter, a closer analysis will often show its presence. In the South, the particular incarnation of this antagonism was the region-wide political struggle between the planters and the yeomanry. This struggle, ordinarily manifested in the disputes of the parties, antedated the parties' existence, however, and altered only its shape, but not its fierceness, in the final antebellum years, when the parties began to decay.

Events of the 1850s, in fact, further exacerbated the yeoman farmer's fears. The passage of the Graduation Act of 1854 so reduced the minimum price per acre of government land that substantial acreage in the southwestern states that formerly had seemed permanently a part of the public domain, began to be bought up by private individuals. The Democratic politicians who had sponsored this legislation had thought that they were assisting the squatter to become a landowner. In fact, they succeeded chiefly in attracting the interest of land speculators to these sections and reducing the area upon which the small farmer could allow his livestock to forage. Grants of public land to railroad corporations in the 1850s aggravated this situation, and the railroads themselves, as they built into the yeoman areas, brought additional economic pressures to bear upon the small farmer to grow for the market. And wealthy planters and capitalists, the very embodiments of the yeomanry's fears, commenced near the end of the antebellum years to have increasing success in the political arena. All of these developments, but particularly the last one, were frightening ones. It was upon the yeoman farmer's poignant desire to be left alone, and upon his deep-seated dread of manipulative concentrations of power, that Jacksonian politics had always fed. In the 1850s, however, the farmer's position seemed especially insecure.

Through most of the antebellum era, the white yeoman farmer was repeatedly told that he was the king of Southern politics. Solicitous lawmakers rushed to give statutory form to his aspirations and anxieties. The region's tax structure, for instance, was heavily weighted against the farmer's villains, the planters and capitalists. The greatest share of Southern states' revenue was derived from the tax on slaves, a tax paid in any significant amount almost exclusively by planters. And the trappings of the planters' socioeconomic status—pleasure carriages, race horses, gold watches, silver services, private libraries, and household furniture of more than five hundred dollars or so in value—were all subject to specific levies. The activities of capitalists were also taxed; there were levies, for instance, on the stock of banks and manufacturing corporations, on money lent at interest, on the purchase of bills of exchange, drafts, and certificates of deposit, on the income of transportation and insurance companies, on the salaries of corporate officers, and on savings held in cash. The yeoman farmer, in contrast, would pay a small land tax—a tax held to quite low levels by the revenue from the slave tax—if he owned his farm. If he was exclusively a squatter, however, he was subject only to the nominal poll tax.[19] And if he fell into debt, most of his property was protected from his creditors under the "homestead exemption." The fear of concentrations of power was expressed in many other ways, as well. Corporate charters, for example, often contained provisions weighting the votes of small stockholders more heavily in corporate elections. Banks and railroads were objects of particular legislative suspicion and regulation.

But Jacksonianism contained one more supreme irony at the core of its ideology: the citizenry was as frightened of its government as it was of other power centers, and therefore refused to tolerate a level of governmental activity sufficient to check effectively the accumulation of power by the wealthy. As a result, as the antebellum period progressed—and particularly after the return of prosperity that accompanied the Mexican-American War and the discovery of gold in California—the well-to-do in the South slowly began to achieve a measure of political influence, despite all the statutory checks upon them. In Alabama, for instance, large planters (owners of fifty or more slaves) were only 7 percent of the members of the state legislature in 1830 and 10 percent in 1840, but they advanced to 18 percent of the legislators in 1850 and almost a fourth of them in 1860. In addition, the occupations of legislators began to shift away from agriculture and toward law. Attorneys, inevitably professional agents of the world of commerce and contract whatever their own partisan affiliation, had little natural sympathy for the instincts of a yeomanry mistrustful of the demands of the international marketplace. Alabama again provides an index to the dire implications of this change. In the Alabama Secession Convention of 1861, Cooperationists were a majority among those delegates who were engaged in agriculture and among those delegates who were neither in agriculture nor in law. But among lawyer-delegates, immediate secessionists held a majority of two to one. The semisubsistence small farmer, who observed the events of his world with the frightened intensity of a fugitive from impending doom, saw these developments and knew what they portended without having to be told.

The rise of the planters to a share of political power in the 1850s was followed by the state governments' beginning to adopt programs long advocated by the Whigs. This result was only facilitated by the collapse of the national Whiggery in the middle 1850s. By about 1857, the vast majority of state legislators in the lower South called themselves Democrats. From this total victory came the destruction of Democratic Party discipline: without an opposition, party whips had no threat with which to hold the members in line; orthodoxy became passé. These events, and the prosperity of the 1850s that brought rising tax receipts, produced a startling expansion of state government in the final antebellum decade. Expenditures increased rapidly. States adopted general programs to aid railroad construction. They established insane hospitals, schools for the deaf and blind, and penitentiaries. Louisiana and Alabama established statewide public school systems, and all of the states greatly increased state aid to local school districts. Governmental programs multiplied on every hand. In Alabama, for instance, state expenditures in 1847 were about what they had been in 1827, but in the dozen years from 1848 to 1860, state expenditures rose fifteenfold. Many voters, even in the hill counties and the pine barrens, increasingly were tempted away from their devotion to limitations on government by the prospect of riches. Beguiled by "progress," however, they remained suspicious of its larger implications.

Thus with each passing year, the small farmer could see the levees that protected his autonomy eroding, being washed away by the powerful currents of an advancing urbanized and commercialized interconnection. He saw the consequences, but he did not fully understand the cause. He searched for leaders who could explain what was happening to him. He cast about for a crusade that would slay the monsters that beset him. And as it happened, too, there were politicians who believed they possessed an explanation, and who were prepared for a crusade.

In the Jacksonian period, as this essay has sought to argue, the attitudes and programs at issue between the parties in the South were the same as those at issue throughout the nation. The expansion of the market economy was a national phenomenon, and the response was national, encompassing fears and hopes as real in the South as in the North. It is for that reason that Jackson, Clay, and Polk spoke so successfully to national constituencies. There was one institution that did distinguish the North from the South in these years, however: the institution of slavery. In the South, slavery was an integral assumption in the ideology of each party. An understanding of how the parties viewed slavery is essential to an understanding of the electoral success of secession.

The Whig conception of slavery is easier for us today to understand, because the Whig conception of freedom as upward mobility is the more familiar of the two rival definitions of freedom to us. Whigs thought of slavery as a mechanism of social advancement, another of the many happy American institutions that facilitated the efforts of the industrious to achieve economic success. Their attitude toward slavery was, in other words, essentially an extension of their attitudes toward the values of market agriculture, the virtue of hard work, and the moral quality of individual achievement, because their encounters with slavery were almost uniformly in these contexts.

The Jacksonians' view of slavery, on the other hand, seems as odd to us now as does their definition of freedom in terms of individual autonomy. Jacksonians conceived of slavery as protecting the communities of semi-subsistence farmers from being sucked into the vortex of the marketplace. As they saw it, with slaves to supply plantation labor, the white independent yeomanry could not be converted into a proletariat, subservient to those incipient oligarchs, the planters and capitalists. As the resolutions of a Southern Rights convention put the matter in 1852:

> The total abolition of slavery would affect more injuriously the condition of the poor white man in the slaveholding States than that of the rich slaveholder; for the slaveholder, having the means which attends upon the possession of slaves, would be able to maintain his *position*, whilst the poor man would have to doff that native, free-born and independent spirit which he now possesses, and which he prizes above all wealth, and would have to become virtually the slave (barring color) of the rich man. This would be one of the consequences of the abolition of negro slavery, and the poorest white man who walks,

> barefoot, our hills is wise enough to see it; and though he may only leave to his children the heritage of *freedom* and *poverty*, yet he is determined that neither they nor his children's children, to the latest generation, shall ever occupy, through their remissness of duty, the position of *servants*.[20]

This point has not always been understood. An important group of historians, led by the late professor Eugene Genovese, joins many Northern Republicans at the time in believing that, because the nonslaveholding small farmers supported, in many cases with their lives, the institution of slavery, which was the source of the economic and social power of their natural enemies, the planters, therefore the planters must have established an intellectual hegemony over the yeomanry that seduced it, in effect, into supporting its own subordination.[21] Nothing could be further from the truth. As we have seen, farmers on the fringes of the market were acutely aware of their differing interests from the planters; the entire political structure reflected that awareness. The yeomanry's support of slavery in general did not represent its seduction by plantation values, but rather its desire to maintain its independence of the plantation system. Professor Genovese and his followers unconsciously assume, I suspect, the Whig conception of freedom as upward mobility, that the farmers were "condemned" to subsistence agriculture, and ought to have wanted to "rise" into the market economy. But for the majority of Jacksonian yeomen, subsistence was not something to which they were condemned. It was the material reflection of an ethic, the ideal of autonomy, the status of self-sufficiency, the meaning of freedom. Thus they supported slavery not because they had accepted the values of planters, but because they had not done so. From their perspective, slavery insulated them from becoming the economic dependents of the wealthy. Their motives for supporting slavery were wholly distinct from, even antithetical to, the motives of the slaveholders for doing so. And their motives proceeded quite as much from a conception of their own interests as did the motives of the planters. The study of what happened to yeoman farmers after the Civil War indicates that they may well have been wiser in this regard than have many later commentators. Deprived of the insulation from involvement with the market that slavery had afforded them, and increasingly deprived as well of the use of the public domain and unimproved farmland, which had often contributed decisively to their self-sufficiency, they slipped inexorably into the dependency that had always been their greatest terror.[22]

Democrats and Whigs, then, because they differed in their understanding of freedom, therefore differed in their understanding of slavery. But because each party regarded its conception of freedom as the essence of the meaning of America, therefore both regarded slavery as essentially American, a bulwark of the liberty and democracy that were the republic's distinguishing characteristics. As a result, when proposals to exclude slavery from the Western territories gained popularity in the North, both Jacksonians and Whigs in the South concluded that the absence of slavery from the territories would lead to the establishment in them of a hierarchical, un-American society, on the Northern model. The final antebellum years, therefore, found Jacksonians and former Whigs throughout most of the region united in desiring permission for slavery to go West—the Jacksonians saying that it would permit a society there in which the yeomanry could be secure from the encroachments of dependency, and the Whigs concluding that it would promote the settlers' material advancement. Very few Southern slaveholders actually wanted to risk taking their own slaves to the territories. But virtually all white Southerners, slaveholders and nonslaveholders, regarded any national law forbidding them from taking slaves into the territories if they wished to do so, as a mortifying declaration that Southerners were not equals of other Americans.

If, however, the South was united in its opposition to free soil, it was by no means united on the question of how far to go in resisting the free soilers. Former Whigs and Know-Nothings continued dubious of the radical solutions promoted by the Southern Rights leaders, while the Democrats moved in increasing numbers to embrace extremist positions. In Mississippi, about two-thirds of the supporters of John Bell who voted in the Secession Convention elections cast their ballots for the Cooperationists; in Louisiana about three-fourths of them did so; and in Alabama, a majority of Bell voters abstained in the convention election. Meanwhile, the Democratic supporters of John C. Breckinridge in November who voted in the convention elections some six weeks later overwhelmingly backed immediate secessionists—by an overall margin of two to one, and virtually unanimously in Louisiana and Mississippi. Those Democrats who had voted for Stephen A. Douglas were equally unanimous in supporting the Cooperationists, but they constituted only some 15 percent of the electorate in Alabama and Louisiana, and just 5 percent of it in Mississippi.[23] Thus, though substantial numbers of former Whigs did embrace the secessionist cause, and significant numbers of Democrats continued to resist it, it is clear that, in general, it was the Democratic constituency and not the Whig one that eventually came to accept the necessity for revolution. A glance at the nature of the Southern Rights propagandists' case reveals why.

The exclusion of slavery from the territories, wrote one fire eater, was a declaration "that a free citizen of Massachusetts was a better man and entitled to more privileges than a free citizen of Alabama." To the voters it presented the question, "Will you submit to be bridled and saddled and rode under whip and spur" or affirm, alternatively, "the great doctrine of *Equality*: Opposition to ascendancy in any form, either of classes, by way of monopolies, or of sections, by means of robbery." The Northern political hegemony was manipulating its power to abridge the freedom of Southerners, to bar them from settling on the new lands, to mark them as second-class citizens. Serfdom threatened. Southern Rights congressman David Hubbard informed the voters,

> It is clear that the power to dictate what sort of property the State may allow a citizen to own and work—whether oxen, horses or negroes; or what religion he may preach, teach or practice, on account of its morality, is alike despotic and tyrannical, whether such power is obtained by conquest in battle or by a majority vote and is equally galling and oppressive upon those whose consciences are made to conform to the standard of morality which the majority sets up; and was never surpassed by the British crown during the reign of her most absolute and despotic kings.

Another writer described the providential functioning of the South's slave-based economy in Whiggish terms:

> Under this system of things all thrived and all were happy. From father to son, through a long succession of years, they progressed, and have gone on accumulating at a steady rate until, without apparently being aware of the fact, we, their posterity, have become a prosperous and wealthy people—not in the sense in which these terms are applied in England and the North—not by the concentration of capital in the hands of a few enterprising individuals, to whom the many are the mere "hewers of wood and drawers of water"—but by a general diffusion of wealth and happiness over the whole community.

Meanwhile, Democratic congressman Sampson W. Harris proclaimed, "The peace that tyranny imposes can have no charms for a freeman. The measure of his rights, injustice may not limit. . . . Better, far better, a never-ending resistance to wrong, than the cold and joyless repose which awaits on conscious inferiority, and humbles the proud man's spirit to the lessons of obedience." It was because the Southern Rights men conceived the sectional conflict in these terms that an editor could write that, should the conflict be decided in favor of the South, "the people may continue free, united and happy, bearing steadily aloft the beacon-light of liberty, to conduct the wayfaring, the oppressed and downtrodden of other nations to the haven of freedom; but if decided the other way, the sun of liberty, as regulated by the eternal principles of justice, will have set in darkness, and the bright hopes of man will be extinguished forever."[24]

Northerners generally failed to understand the implications of the Southern Rights argument. After all, they frequently noted, it was only the slaveholder, not poorer Southerners, who would be excluded from the territories by a free-soil policy, and even the slaveholder only if he insisted on retaining his slaves. But if the Northern free labor system generated hierarchy, oligarchy, and relationships founded upon economic dependency, then inviting Southerners to move to such a world was inviting them to surrender their American birthright in order to become a part of a crypto-European order. It was an invitation that was no invitation at all.[25] Moreover, free soil was a policy founded upon the assumption, explicitly stated, that the Northern system was the truly American one, to be fostered, and Southern society an aberration, subject to restriction and, in the long run, extinction. It was therefore a policy ready made for the warning that it branded Southerners as second-class citizens, that it reduced them to intolerable inferiority in their own country, that it mocked their pretensions to equal partnership in the American experiment.

All of these arguments resonated with the fears and resentments of a yeomanry visibly losing the initiative in its struggle to preserve its way of life. And yet it doubtless is the most somber irony in a collection of ironies that, at this crucial moment in its long battle to survive, the yeomanry should have turned its antagonism outward, away from the planters and merchants against whom its antipathy had been so long directed, and toward the Republicans of the North. The reason for this development is to be found in the changing nature of Southern political leaders.

The yeoman farmers' hostilities had always had a national component. The crusade against the Bank of the United States, for instance, had paralleled and coexisted with crusades against banks and other corporations at the state level. The 1850s, however, saw not only the increasing political success of Whiggish programs and interests, but also the increasing absence of Democratic politicians who wished to launch crusades against them. Leadership in the Democratic Party was passing to younger men, ambitious attorneys, eager for social advancement and attuned to urban values, who became Democrats not because they understood the Jacksonian creed—they called the Jacksonians "Old Fogies"—but because the Democrats were the majority party and therefore offered the easier path to office. The Democratic Party not only lost its discipline in the 1850s; under the leadership of Young America, it lost its soul.

The farmers searched eagerly for an explanation of the developments so readily apparent to them. Their world was closing in on them; a national society was gelling around them; forces were at work that were reducing them to dependency and thus to servitude. They turned to their political leaders for an explanation. The only political leaders who had an explanation, however, the only politicians who also detected an impending despotism, were the Southern Rights radicals. The farmers listened as the Southern Rights men told them that the guarantee of their freedom lay in their equality of citizenship under the American Constitution, but that the Republicans were intent on stripping them of that equality, on refusing them access to the territories, the common property of all Americans, on marking them as moral and political inferiors. The farmers listened, and tragically a majority of them believed. They voted for the Southern Rights politicians for the same reasons that earlier they had voted for the enemies of the Bank of the United States. Aristocracy could not be tolerated; the victory of tyranny appeared imminent. An entirely sectional majority had been able to force on them a president who had not been a candidate in their region and who was committed to the notion that their region was un-American. The provocation demanded vengeance. The time had now come, as it had in 1776, when if they were to keep their freedom and equality, they would have to fight for their rights. Secession followed.

This is the understanding of Lincoln's election to which James Ryder Randall's poetic battle cry appealed, and which Barbara Klender found so difficult to explain to her students. Marylanders, unlike their fellow citizens in the more southerly slave states, chose in the end to close their ears to Randall's emotional plea. If Klender's pupils are ever to understand the circumstances that required the lives of 600,000 Americans in the four terrible years after Randall wrote, however, they ought to hear his words, and ponder them.

Notes

This article initially appeared, in a somewhat different form, in the *Tennessee Historical Quarterly*, summer 1989. It was awarded the Tennessee Historical Society's Moore Prize, and is reprinted here with the kind permission of the Society.

1. *Montgomery Advertiser*, March 18, 1984.

2. An excellent summary of Republican Party ideology in the period is Eric Foner, *Free Soil, Free Labor, Free Men: The Ideology of the Republican Party before the*

Civil War (New York: Oxford University Press, 1970); see especially 40–72. On Republican expectations of Southern Unionists and nonslaveholders, see David M. Potter, *Lincoln and His Party in the Secession Crisis* (New Haven, CT: Yale University Press, 1942).

3. The relationship was in fact vastly more complex than Republicans imagined, however; see Eugene D. Genovese, *Roll, Jordan, Roll: The World the Slaves Made* (New York: Pantheon Books, 1974).

4. On Virginia, see William A. Link, *Roots of Secession: Slavery and Politics in Antebellum Virginia* (Chapel Hill: University of North Carolina Press, 2003). On North Carolina, see Marc W. Kruman, *Parties and Politics in North Carolina, 1836–1865* (Baton Rouge: Louisiana State University Press, 1983), and Harry L. Watson, *Jacksonian Politics and Community Conflict: The Emergence of the Second American Party System in Cumberland County, North Carolina* (Baton Rouge: Louisiana State University Press, 1981). On Tennessee, see Jonathan M. Atkins, *Parties, Politics, and the Sectional Conflict in Tennessee, 1832–1861* (Knoxville: University of Tennessee Press, 1997); Charles G. Sellers, *James K. Polk, Jacksonian, 1795–1843* (Princeton, NJ: Princeton University Press, 1957); and E. Merton Coulter, *William G. Brownlow, Fighting Parson of the Southern Highlands* (Chapel Hill: University of North Carolina Press, 1937).

5. Thomas B. Alexander and Richard E. Beringer, *The Anatomy of the Confederate Congress: A Study of the Influences of Member Characteristics on Legislative Voting Behavior, 1861–1865* (Nashville: Vanderbilt University Press, 1972).

6. See Frank E. Vandiver, *Ploughshares into Swords: Josiah Gorgas and Confederate Ordnance* (Austin: University of Texas Press, 1977; orig. pub. 1952); Mary Elizabeth Massey, *Ersatz in the Confederacy* (Columbia: University of South Carolina Press, 1952); and Drew Gilpin Faust, *Mothers of Invention: Women of the Slaveholding South in the American Civil War* (Chapel Hill: University of North Carolina Press, 2004).

7. See Bell Irvin Wiley, *Southern Negroes, 1861–1865* (New Haven, CT: Yale University Press, 1938).

8. James M. McPherson, *Battle Cry of Freedom: The Civil War Era* (New York: Oxford University Press, 1988), restores the genuine contingency of the battlefield to its proper place in determining the Civil War's outcome. Gerald F. Linderman, *Embattled Courage: The Experience of Combat in the American Civil War* (New York: Free Press, 1987), correctly emphasizes the great similarity in the attitudes of soldiers in the two armies.

The Republican expectation that the Confederacy would be destroyed by its internal social contradictions, despite its having proved chimerical at the time, has nevertheless recently obtained a good deal of historical currency. See Paul D. Escott, *After Secession: Jefferson Davis and the Failure of Confederate Nationalism* (Baton Rouge: Louisiana State University Press, 1978); Michael P. Johnson, *Toward a Pa-*

triarchal Republic: The Secession of Georgia (Baton Rouge: Louisiana State University Press, 1977); Richard E. Beringer, Herman Hattaway, Archer Jones, and William N. Still Jr., *Why the South Lost the Civil War* (Athens: University of Georgia Press, 1986); and Steven Hahn, *The Roots of Southern Populism: Yeoman Farmers and the Transformation of the Georgia Upcountry, 1850–1890* (New York: Oxford University Press, 1983), 116–33. For the reasons here stated, I do not find these arguments convincing.

9. On the origins of antebellum sectional stereotypes, see William R. Taylor, *Cavalier and Yankee: The Old South and the American National Character* (Cambridge, MA: Harvard University Press, 1979).

10. A particularly aggressive statement of it, for instance, may be found in Emory M. Thomas, *The Confederate Nation, 1861–1865* (New York: Harper and Row, 1979), 1–66.

11. A convenient tabular statement is in Kruman, *Parties and Politics in North Carolina*, 49–50. In South Carolina, state representatives had to own a freehold estate worth 150 pounds sterling and state senators a freehold estate worth 300 pounds sterling. On South Carolina's political structure, see James M. Banner Jr., "The Problem of South Carolina," in *The Hofstadter Aegis: A Memorial*, ed. Stanley Elkins and Eric McKitrick (New York: Knopf, 1974), 60–93.

12. On these struggles, see Fletcher M. Green, *Constitutional Development in the South Atlantic States, 1776–1860: A Study in the Evolution of Democracy* (Chapel Hill: University of North Carolina Press, 1930).

13. Much of what follows is argued at greater length in my *Politics and Power in a Slave Society: Alabama, 1800–1860* (Baton Rouge: Louisiana State University Press, 1978). See also Michael F. Holt, *The Political Crisis of the 1850s* (New York: Wiley, 1978); Kruman, *Parties and Politics in North Carolina*; Watson, *Jacksonian Politics and Community Conflict*; and Lacy K. Ford Jr., *Origins of Southern Radicalism: The South Carolina Upcountry, 1800–1860* (New York: Oxford University Press, 1988). On the political significance of public land policy, see Daniel Feller, *The Public Lands in Jacksonian Politics* (Madison: University of Wisconsin Press, 1984). An excellent brief summary of antebellum land legislation, in both provision and practice, is Thomas Le Duc, "History and Appraisal of U.S. Land Policy to 1862," in *Land Use Policy and Problems in the United States*, ed. Howard W. Ottoson (Lincoln: University of Nebraska Press, 1963), 3–27. On the state-level conflicts over banking, see James Roger Sharp, *The Jacksonians versus the Banks: Politics in the States after the Panic of 1837* (New York: Columbia University Press, 1970).

14. On this point, see Charles G. Sellers, "Who Were the Southern Whigs?" *American Historical Review* 59 (January 1954): 335–46. On the antebellum Southern bourgeoisie, see Jonathan Daniel Wells, *The Origins of the Southern Middle Class, 1800–1861* (Chapel Hill: University of North Carolina Press, 2004).

15. Instructive analyses of the economic and social position of the Southern

yeomanry are in Ford, *Origins of Southern Radicalism*, 44–88, 244–63, and Hahn, *Roots of Southern Populism*, 15–85; the statistics in this section are adapted from Ford. Hahn, unlike Ford, greatly understates the extent of the antebellum yeomanry's political influence (86–116), thus marring an otherwise admirable study. Two other very fine investigations that, to my mind, tend to err similarly are Orville Vernon Burton, *In My Father's House Are Many Mansions: Family and Community in Edgefield, South Carolina* (Chapel Hill: University of North Carolina Press, 1985), and J. William Harris, *Plain Folk and Gentry in a Slave Society: White Liberty and Black Slavery in Augusta's Hinterlands* (Middletown, CT: Wesleyan University Press, 1985). Also very useful on the economy of the yeoman areas are Lewis E. Atherton, *The Southern Country Store, 1800–1860* (Baton Rouge: Louisiana State University Press, 1949); Sam Bowers Hilliard, *Hog Meat and Hoecake: Food Supply in the Old South, 1840–1860* (Carbondale: Southern Illinois University Press, 1972); and Gavin Wright, *The Political Economy of the Cotton South: Households, Markets, and Wealth in the Nineteenth Century* (New York: Norton, 1978).

Much of what current scholars argue about the status of the yeomanry was suggested initially, and quite correctly, by the so-called Owsley school, though because of certain methodological flaws in their work, the contentions of these historians were widely dismissed until recently. See Frank L. Owsley and Harriet C. Owsley, "The Economic Basis of Society in the Late Ante-Bellum South," *Journal of Southern History* (February 1940): 24–45; Frank L. Owsley, *Plain Folk of the Old South* (Baton Rouge: Louisiana State University Press, 1949); Blanche H. Clark, *The Tennessee Yeomen, 1840–1860* (Nashville: Vanderbilt University Press, 1942); and Herbert Weaver, *Mississippi Farmers, 1850–1860* (Nashville: Vanderbilt University Press, 1945).

16. On the open range, see R. Ben Brown, "The Southern Range: A Study in Nineteenth-Century Law and Society" (PhD diss., University of Michigan, 1993).

17. My understanding of these points has much benefited from Lawrence Frederick Kohl, *The Politics of Individualism: Parties and the American Character in the Jacksonian Era* (New York: Oxford University Press, 1989); see also John Ashworth, *"Agrarians" and "Aristocrats": Party Political Ideology in the United States, 1837–1846* (London: Royal Historical Society, 1983), and Rush Welter, *The Mind of America, 1820–1860* (New York: Columbia University Press, 1975). On the conflicts of the era, see Charles G. Sellers, *The Market Revolution: Jacksonian America, 1815–1846* (New York: Oxford University Press, 1991), which tells the story from the Jacksonian perspective, and Daniel Walker Howe, *What Hath God Wrought: The Transformation of America, 1815–1848* (New York: Oxford University Press, 2007), which tells it from the Whig one.

18. On ethnocultural and religious divisions between the parties, see, e.g., Ronald P. Formisano, *The Birth of Mass Political Parties: Michigan, 1827–1861* (Princeton, NJ: Princeton University Press, 1971), and Paul Kleppner, *The Cross of Culture: A So-*

cial Analysis of Midwestern Politics, 1850–1900 (New York: Free Press, 1970). Both of these studies, and others of their school, err, however, in overstating the extent to which the divisions were causes of, as opposed to correlates of, partisan allegiance. The divisions were less relevant to Southern politics, in any case, because European immigrants formed a considerably smaller proportion of the electorate there than in the North. On the changing status of journeyman artisans, see, e.g., R. Sean Wilentz, *Chants Democratic: New York City and the Rise of the American Working Class, 1788–1850* (New York: Oxford University Press, 1984). On politics in North Carolina and Tennessee, see the works cited in note 4; I have reference in the text particularly to Watson, *Jacksonian Politics and Community Conflict*, and Ford, *Origins of Southern Radicalism*.

19. On Southern state tax policy, see my "Fiscal Policy and the Failure of Radical Reconstruction in the Lower South," in *Region, Race, and Reconstruction: Essays in Honor of C. Vann Woodward*, ed. J. Morgan Kousser and James M. McPherson (New York: Oxford University Press, 1982), 349–94 (which is the next essay in this volume).

20. *Montgomery Advertiser*, March 9, 1852.

21. See Eugene D. Genovese, *The Political Economy of Slavery: Studies in the Economy and Society of the Slave South* (New York: Vintage Books, 1967), and his "Yeoman Farmers in a Slaveholders' Democracy," *Agricultural History* 49 (April 1975): 331–42. Although Professor Genovese's notion of "cultural hegemony" leads him to accept, in effect, the Republicans' explanation for the behavior of the white yeomanry, yet in his *Roll, Jordan, Roll* (note 3 above), he has been in the vanguard of the effort to move historians beyond the Republicans' simplistic explanation for the absence of a slave insurrection, to appreciate the many and emotionally complicated levels of the relationship between masters and slaves. The result of Professor Genovese's work, therefore, has been to challenge the Republicans' naive view of slavery, while at the same time lending the Republicans' equally unsophisticated understanding of relations among whites a powerful, if specious, rationalization.

22. On this point, see Hahn, *Roots of Southern Populism*, 137–289; see also Orville Vernon Burton, *The Age of Lincoln* (New York: Hill and Wang, 2007), 234–369.

23. Peyton McCrary, Clark Miller, and Dale Baum, "Class and Party in the Secession Crisis: Voting Behavior in the Deep South, 1856–1861," *Journal of Interdisciplinary History* 8 (Winter 1978): 429–57. In Alabama, the Secession Convention election was complicated by a fusion of the secessionist Democrats and the Know-Nothings in the southern part of the state, and internal Democratic rivalries that led many Breckinridge supporters in the hill country to cooperate with the Douglasites. As a result, dissent in South Alabama was necessarily expressed chiefly as abstention, while in North Alabama the Breckinridge vote, uniquely, was fragmented. The failure of the McCrary group to take account of the very special political alliances in the Alabama Convention election makes many of the summary data for

the three states in their article less useful than the data they give for each state individually, I believe. In the three states, four-fifths of those who had voted in the presidential election of 1856 and who abstained in the Secession Convention elections were Know-Nothings.

24. *Montgomery Advertiser*, June 25, 1851; February 6, 1850; May 7, 1851; August 28, 1850; January 15, 1851.

25. Although the Northern yeomanry was perhaps a bit more generally involved with market agriculture, its position was in quite important ways analogous to that of the Southern yeomanry, and therefore its attitude toward the extension of slavery into the territories was, not surprisingly, virtually a mirror image of the Southern one. Moreover, the belief that slavery encouraged aristocracy shaped attitudes everywhere in the North. Of the Northern working class, Eric Foner tells us, "Free white laborers of the North would never migrate to a land where labor was held to be disreputable, where social mobility was all but non-existent, and where they would have to labor in close proximity with Negro slaves" (Foner, *Free Soil, Free Labor, Free Men*, 57). On the status of the Northern yeomanry, see Christopher Clark, "The Household Economy: Market Exchange and the Rise of Capitalism in the Connecticut Valley, 1800–1860," *Journal of Social History* 13 (Winter 1979): 169–89; Martin J. Hershock, *The Paradox of Progress: Economic Change, Individual Enterprise, and Political Culture in Michigan, 1837–1878* (Athens: Ohio University Press, 2003); Richard F. Nation, *At Home in the Hoosier Hills: Agriculture, Politics, and Religion in Southern Indiana, 1810–1870* (Bloomington: Indiana University Press, 2005); John Mack Faragher, *Sugar Creek: Life on the Illinois Prairie* (New Haven, CT: Yale University Press, 1986); and Don Harrison Doyle, *The Social Order of a Frontier Community: Jacksonville, Illinois, 1825–1870* (Urbana: University of Illinois Press, 1978). On the territorial question in national politics, see Michael A. Morrison, *Slavery and the American West: The Eclipse of Manifest Destiny and the Coming of the Civil War* (Chapel Hill: University of North Carolina Press, 1997).

2

Fiscal Policy and the Failure of Radical Reconstruction in the Lower South

One of the most pernicious difficulties afflicting the historiography of Reconstruction is that few historians of Reconstruction have done much research on the antebellum period that preceded it. White Southern voters who judged Reconstruction policies at the polls viewed those policies from the perspective of a lifetime's experience with their state government; history did not begin for them in 1867. But too many historians approach Reconstruction as the carpetbaggers at the time did: devoid of any thorough knowledge of what the earlier policies of Southern governments had been, relying instead on a few facts and hostile legends. This absence of an accurate conception of the antebellum context is arguably a principal reason that the carpetbaggers were so markedly unsuccessful in their efforts to hold the allegiance of native white voters. And it is the principal reason, I believe, that recent historians have so misunderstood the factors underlying white small farmers' desertion of the Republican cause.

In his first book, published three-quarters of a century ago, Professor C. Vann Woodward laid much stress upon the necessity of appreciating the connections between antebellum political assumptions and postbellum discontent among white small farmers. He sought to show that the lines of descent in Southern history join antebellum policies and the attitudes of the Populists.[1] But that lesson has still not been learned. Recent historians of Reconstruction, displaying little sensitivity to the worldview of nineteenth-century white Southern small farmers, have therefore been unable to offer any compelling explanation for small farmers' behavior during the decade. Small farmers' increasing distrust of the Republicans, and their eventual cooperation with the Redeemer Democrats in overthrowing Reconstruction, have been attributed simply to racism.[2]

I would certainly not wish to question the power of racial antipathies in shaping the course of Southern history. Racism cannot serve, however, as an all-purpose explanation for white small farmers' electoral behavior. Another essential concern of the work of Professor Woodward has been his effort to demonstrate that lower-middle- and lower-class whites have often been willing to rise above their racial attitudes when presented, as in Populism, with a political or economic movement that offered real hope of ameliorating their hard lot.[3] As depicted in much of the recent historiography, Republicanism ought to have been just such a movement. Republicans, we are told, established or greatly increased support of public schools. They aided the building of railroads into the hill counties. They looked with favor on a wide variety of eleemosynary institutions. If white small farmers were not wholly averse to cooperating with blacks in the Populist effort to make the government the defender of the masses, one must wonder why their racism had so inhibited such cooperation only twenty or so years earlier.

The answer is that Republicanism was not at all like Populism. One important difference between them, I should admit, reinforces the notion that racism was at the root of small-farmer behavior. The Populists did not take nearly so strong a stand in favor of legal guarantees of equal rights for blacks. But the Populist experience seems to me to indicate that the small farmers might even have tolerated on practical political grounds the passage of state and federal civil-rights acts, if the Republican Party had otherwise been vigorously espousing policies that promised small farmers important benefits. Far from promising them benefits, however, Republican policies may actually have seemed to be inimical to their interests. Many poorer whites did indeed support the Republicans early in Reconstruction, even though doing so meant working with blacks and Yankees. But the fiscal policies that the Republicans implemented, once in power, drove, I think, white small farmers into the arms of the Redeemers. And the final irony of this process is that many Republicans, particularly those who were carpetbaggers, never really comprehended why the small farmers were so hostile to these policies.

The explanation I would offer for the white small farmers' perception of Republican fiscal policies turns upon an understanding of the fiscal policies they replaced. The principal source of tax revenue in all of the lower South states during most of the antebellum period was the tax on slaves.[4] The slave tax constituted some 60 percent of the total receipts in South Carolina and 30 to 40 percent in the others. The substantial revenues from this source allowed the states to hold their land taxes at quite low levels. Even toward the end of the antebellum period, when the land tax rose somewhat to meet greatly increased expenditures, it generally remained under two mills on the dollar. In addition, the states levied a variety of specific taxes on luxuries and capital. Only the modest land tax and a small poll tax—a levy of from 25 cents to one dollar on white males between twenty-one and forty-five—were broad-based taxes. The result of this tax structure was in large measure to exempt poorer whites from direct taxation. It would appear that the wealthiest third of the citizenry in the lower South paid at least two-thirds, and probably substantially more, of its taxes.

The abolition of slavery brought dramatic changes to the Southern tax structure, as to all areas of Southern life. Reconstruction legislators turned to the land tax to make up for the loss of the slave tax; the land tax produced some two-thirds, and in a few cases an even larger proportion, of the state revenues during the decade. At the same time, disbursements rose far above those of antebellum levels. The greater reliance on the land tax and the increase in disbursements together forced extraordinary increases in the millage rates. In Mississippi, for instance, the tax rose from 1.6 mills near the end of the antebellum years, to 9 mills in 1871 and 12 1/2 mills in 1873. Alabama taxed at a rate of 2 mills in 1860 and 7 1/2 mills in 1870. In Louisiana the millage rate was 2.9 in 1860, but 20 1/2 in 1872, and 14 1/2 in 1874. In Florida the millage rate went from 1 2/3 mills in 1860 to 7 mills in 1870 and 13 mills in 1874. These rates reflect only state taxes, of course. In Florida in 1874 the counties assessed an additional 11 1/2 mills, for a total rate of 24 1/2 mills. These large new taxes fell on every property owner. For the first time in Southern history the burden of taxation came home to the white small farmer. Largely exempted from taxation throughout the antebellum years, he was suddenly called upon to support a very active government.

It might be said that in return for this new contribution the small farmer received much in disbursements for social-service programs. But such a contention would, I believe, misrepresent the small farmer's own perspective. Because the citizenry to be served had been virtually doubled by the emancipation of the slaves, and because the inflation of prices caused by the war required, until the panic of 1873, the expenditure of more money in order to purchase the same amount of goods and services, so that disbursements for many programs were apparently but not really larger, white small farmers had in many cases in the antebellum period actually received benefits equal to or greater than those they received during Reconstruction, and for a great deal less in taxes. Recent historiography, for instance, has emphasized Republican generosity to the public-school systems in the South. However, public-school expenditures per eligible child, measured in constant dollars, remained about the same in one state, rose in two, but still only to quite modest levels, and actually declined in two others.[5] I need hardly add that the freedmen, because they owned very little property, paid directly only a small proportion of the taxes: 2.3 percent of the property-tax receipts and 7.4 percent of the total tax receipts in Georgia in 1874, when they composed some 46 percent of the population. As the white small farmer could well have seen his situation, therefore, he was paying far more in taxes, but his contribution was in considerabre measure state-enforced altruism; he was getting back little more in services than he had received earlier.

Having advanced these arguments in a preliminary way, I shall now turn to a more detailed examination of each of them. I shall then conclude with some remarks on the possible implications of my findings for Reconstruction politics.

I

In his inaugural address in 1841, Governor Benjamin Fitzpatrick of Alabama announced, "The essence of modern oppression is taxation. The measure of popular liberty may be found in the amount which is taken from the people to support the government; when the amount is increased beyond the requirement of a rigid economy, the government becomes profligate and oppressive."[6] This attitude was widely shared in the antebellum South, and as a result of it, both legislators and voters paid close attention to questions of tax policy. Historians who have failed to appreciate the extent of small farmers' political power in the antebellum South may be surprised at the extent to which taxes were borne by the wealthy. But if taxation was oppression, politicians could be counted on to know which of their constituents it was safe to oppress. Not only did planters pay almost all the slave tax and much of the land tax, in several states they were also faced with a variety of taxes on luxuries, directed at the external marks of their social position. Taxes were levied on pleasure carriages, race horses, private libraries, furniture worth more than $500 or so, gold watches, gold or silver plate worth over $50 or so, pianos, and similar property—which planters were likely, and poorer whites exceedingly unlikely, to own. These taxes were greater in both number and amount in the more Democratic states, but even Whiggish states taxed some of these items. At the other end of the scale, farmers' and mechanics' tools, livestock below a certain number, usually 100 head, and a variety of necessities were in most states exempted from taxation—and often also from execution for debt.

The Southern states generally also taxed capital. Money lent at interest or held in savings and capital invested in the stock of banks and other corporations were taxed in all the states.[7] The practice of levying income taxes on professionals was not infrequent, though some states levied fixed license fees instead. There were also taxes on the gross receipts of insurance companies, on commissions received by factors and auctioneers, and, in Louisiana and Florida, on capital invested in steamboats. And trade was taxed in the form either of a percentage of total sales—that is, a sales tax—or of a percentage of the capital invested in merchandise offered for sale. These latter taxes were, presumably, borne indirectly by consumers.

All of the states levied poll taxes on free males. In all of them except Louisiana, the poll tax on free Negroes was substantially higher than that on whites, reflecting a conscious policy to discourage the settlement of free Negroes in the South. Because the poll tax was the one tax that reached those who did not own property as well as those who did, it was often in the later antebellum years—and always in the postbellum years—dedicated to the support of public schools. As a rule, only males between twenty-one and forty-five, that is, those likely to have children eligible for school, were subject to it. Georgia was the single state in this period that required the payment of the poll tax as a prerequisite for voting; that practice became universal only in the twentieth century.

These taxes—on land, slaves, luxuries, capital, trade, and polls—essentially constitute the limits of antebellum taxation. It was a tax structure whose principal result was to protect the less well-to-do from any but the most nominal exactions. As I have said, a crude estimate would indicate that the wealthiest third of the citizenry paid at least two-thirds, and very likely much more, of the taxes. In order to avoid misunderstanding on this point, I should enter two caveats. First, the total amount of taxes assessed by the Southern states in the antebellum years was small; indeed, the maintenance of a "rigid economy" was one of the articles of the antebellum creed. As a result, any redistributive effect this tax structure might otherwise have had was effectively nullified. It is, I think, one of the profoundest ironies of Southern Jacksonianism that while it succeeded in giving concrete expression to poor-white resentments through a tax structure directed at the rich, its fear of an active government at the same time prevented the levying of taxes sufficient to alter the distribution of wealth in the society.

Second, though the richest third of the citizenry paid fully two-thirds of the taxes, it may well have owned more than two-thirds of the region's total wealth. One scholar concludes, for instance, that owners of slaves held more than 90 percent of the lower South's agricultural wealth, at a time when the value of farms and farm implements and machinery accounted for a bit less than a third of the total value of the area's real and personal property.[8] The fact that equity might have dictated an even more progressive tax structure, however, does not dim the significance of the fact that the tax structure was as progressive as it was.[9] Few, if any, states today can claim, I would venture, that their wealthiest citizens bear even that proportion of the support of their government. The tax structure certainly points to important aspects of public sentiment and political reality in the antebellum South that are not always emphasized. And, material to our present purpose, it created for white small farmers a body of experience and assumption about public finance that was to receive a rude shock during Reconstruction.

Having said so much about the hostility to the wealthy—and particularly to planters—that the antebellum tax structure appears to reflect, I cannot leave the subject without noting an equally salient aspect of the story: the decline of the proportion of state revenue produced by the slave tax near the end of the antebellum period. I have elsewhere argued, in regard to one of the lower South states, that the 1850s witnessed the emergence of planters as holders of a substantial—albeit still a minority—share of state legislative power for the first time.[10] The increasing legislative power of the planters in the South is, not surprisingly, the source of the relative decline of the slave tax. I shall not attempt to detail the process by which the decline occurred. I do want to give the outline of the story.[11]

South Carolina, Georgia, and Louisiana entered the depression of the 1840s with anachronistic methods of assessing the land tax, methods that had remained unchanged from the late eighteenth century. The values assigned to land in the various parts of the three states had doubtless at one time borne some relation to true prices, but by the mid-nineteenth century they were wholly arbitrary and discriminated particularly against the areas of the states that had been settled earliest. In the three younger states—Mississippi, Alabama, and Florida—the early antebellum tax laws reflected a much stronger effort to collect a land tax that was proportioned to real value. Land was divided into three or four grades by local assessors, the statutes fixed a value per acre to be assigned to land in each grade, and the tax was figured as a percentage of the value thus obtained.

However, though the classification method Mississippi, Alabama, and Florida employed was vastly fairer than were the archaic nonmethods of South Carolina, Georgia, and Louisiana, the different practices of the six states had one thing in common: all held land values for tax purposes considerably below actual market values. This reality apparently fed the notion among slaveholders that their slave property was being taxed in a disproportionately heavy way, and during the depression of the 1840s it moved them to begin demanding the adoption of the ad valorem general property tax. On paper, slaves were not grossly disproportionately taxed in any state except Louisiana. The land tax in the other states was in the neighborhood of two mills; a two-mill tax on a slave valued at $300, an average value in the 1840s, is 60 cents, which is about what the slave tax per head was in most states. But it is not too hard to understand why many slaveholders did not see it that way. The slave tax, as a flat sum per head, was easily assessed and was evaded with great difficulty, and on the whole it was a not inaccurate reflection of market value. The land tax, on the other hand, was based on a value considerably below—in South Carolina, Georgia, and Louisiana, absurdly far below—market value. And the allegedly inequitable result of this system was clear for all to see in the larger total receipts from the slave tax compared with those from the land tax.

It is hardly surprising that nonslaveholding farmers looked with doubt and disfavor on the planters' proposals for ad valorem taxation. The controversy over these proposals was a main theme in Southern state politics in the late antebellum period, and the struggle became a principal testing ground for the emerging political power of the planters. The small farmers had on their side a long tradition of politicians' seeking to outdo each other in boisterous crusades against the machinations of the wealthy. But the final dozen years of the antebellum period saw the dawning of a new day in Southern politics. The planters had two powerful arguments on their side. The first was the seeming justice of their complaint. The second was that a great many of the young politicians of the 1850s desired their states to adopt social-welfare and internal-improvement schemes. Given the failure of many of the sources of nontax revenue after the panic of 1837, such schemes were feasible only if state tax receipts could be greatly increased; the general property tax gave promise of doing precisely that.

The first great triumph of the advocates of the ad valorem general property tax came in the Louisiana Constitutional Convention of 1846. The constitution that body produced mandated both the adoption of an ad valorem general property tax and the establishment of a public school system; the state legislature complied with both of the mandates the next year. But in 1856 Louisiana retreated somewhat from the principle of the general property tax by, for all practical purposes, removing slaves from the ad valorem system. Slaves were divided by age into six categories, a value for each category was fixed by statute, and all tax assessors were required to use this statutory value, rather than the actual market value, in their assessments.

The tax provisions of both the constitution of 1846 and the statute of 1856 represented victories for the planters, at the expense of small farmers and of New Orleans capitalists. As a result of the ad valorem general property tax, Orleans Parish's share of state tax receipts rose from 18 to 38 percent. Tax revenues more than trebled. But nonslaveholding farmers saw their taxes increase even more than that; receipts from the land tax increased three and a half times, while receipts from the slave tax only doubled. The slave tax, half of all tax revenues in 1845, made up only 29 percent of them a decade later.

Alabama and Mississippi also fell under pressure to adopt the ad valorem general property tax in the 1840s. But both states—Alabama in 1847 and Mississippi in 1850—adopted instead a halfway conversion to the new system. Each abandoned classification in favor of ad valorem assessment for the land tax, but each retained specific taxes for all other objects of taxation, including slaves. Alabama made a bow in the direction of ad valorem taxation of slaves by erecting a variety of age classifications and by prescribing different head taxes in each category, the least for children and the elderly, the most for young adults. Mississippi quieted its planters more directly; it retained the flat-rate head tax but considerably reduced the amount. In Alabama, proceeds from the slave tax fell from 46 percent of the total tax receipts in 1849 to 39 percent in 1855 and 32 percent in 1860, at which point the land tax passed it as the state's principal source of revenue. In Mississippi, the slave tax fell from 40 percent of tax revenue in 1850 to 34 percent in 1856 and 31 percent in 1859. But that percentage was too low for Mississippi's legislators to tolerate. Early in 1860, they increased the slave tax from 40 cents a head to 75 cents, a tax comparable to the two-mill land tax enacted at the same time.

The outcome, then, of the tax wars in Alabama and Mississippi—though not the clear planter victory found in Louisiana—appears to have been closer to a planter victory than not. In Florida and Georgia, however, the tax wars produced something of a draw. In Florida in 1850, the land tax and the slave tax were each producing 38 percent of the state's revenues. The land tax on rural property, however, yielded only 30 percent of the taxes; the additional 8 percent came from towns. The decade after statehood in 1845 saw the usual agitation for conversion to the ad valorem general property tax. Florida's legislators resisted, however, until the rapid escalation of slave prices and the considerable increase in the number of slaves in the state—an increase of more than 50 percent between 1845 and 1855—had greatly advanced the value of slave property. In 1855 Florida adopted an ad valorem general property tax, extending to slaves, just as Louisiana was about to remove slaves from the ad valorem assessment system. Florida thus became the only one of the six lower South states making a real effort to assess slaves on a market-value basis at the outbreak of the Civil War. Unfortunately, no figures have survived that would allow the student to determine what percentage of the tax receipts was attributable to slaves after 1855. But a state census of 1855 reported that the value of slave property in the state was almost double that of land. And the federal census of 1860 reported that of the total assessed value of property in the state in that year, 68.5 percent was personal property and 31.5 percent real estate. It appears, therefore, that because Florida's legislators insisted on the inclusion of slaves in the general property tax, the adoption of ad valorem taxation in that state, uniquely, had the effect of greatly increasing the proportion of revenues derived from slaves.

In Georgia, planters had long wanted the abandonment of the state's outmoded tax system. In 1847, rural land produced only 18 percent of the tax revenue, while slaves produced 42 percent of it. And the assessment system was such that most of the land tax was paid by just a few areas of the state, particularly along the coast. But those who profited from this situation—especially nonslaveholders and inland residents—strongly resisted any alteration in it. Finally, in 1852, Georgia adopted a compromise. The legislature enacted a thoroughgoing ad valorem general property tax, as inclusive as Louisiana's. But it also provided that the taxpayer was to value his own property on oath, and it forbade any official to question the taxpayer's value. The functionary who in most states was called the tax assessor was in Georgia to be called simply, and accurately, the receiver of returns. It could hardly have been a surprise to anyone that this self-assessed ad valorem tax did not create in Georgia's tax structure the massive changes that the adoption of ad valorem taxation usually wrought. The general property tax had trebled Louisiana's receipts and would almost double Florida's, but in Georgia it increased receipts by only a third. The percentage of taxes derived from the tax on slaves declined slightly, from 42 percent to 40 percent, and the percentage derived from the tax on rural land rose from 18 percent to 24 percent. Most of the tax increase that occurred, however, resulted from the more inclusive taxation of capital. Taxes on capital were only 4 percent of tax receipts in 1847, but were 17 percent of them a decade later. Near the end of 1864, by which time it was much too late to matter, the legislature enacted a system to compel the assessment of slaves—but no other form of property—at true market value.

Only in South Carolina did agitation in favor of ad valorem taxation fail to develop. Progressive state officials sometimes called for reform, but there was no mass constituency favoring a change. The reason is close at hand. Residents of the backcountry in South Carolina escaped with virtually no taxation of their farms under that state's eighteenth-century assessments, and as a result they were unlikely to seek any alteration in the system. Large slaveholders, and particularly those who resided in the coastal parishes, did have to pay substantial taxes. But under an 1808 amendment to the state constitution, each parish and district received one member in the state house of representatives for each one-sixty-second part that its white population had of the total white population, and one member for each one-sixty-second part of the total state taxes that it paid. The coastal parishes, which had very small white populations, were thus rewarded for bearing a great part of the tax load by receiving a disproportionate voice in the state legislature. Under this arrangement, planters were also unlikely to seek a different tax structure. Although they could not use their legislative power to reduce their tax burden, they were in a position to protect their interests in other ways. And low-country legislators themselves were exceedingly unlikely to favor a change that would eliminate their legislative seats. South Carolina therefore retained its archaic tax laws throughout the antebellum period. The slave tax produced about 60 percent of tax revenues. The land tax produced between 20 and 25 percent of tax revenues, but only about 12 percent of tax revenues came from the tax on rural land; the remainder came from urban property.

The antebellum tax wars give clear evidence of the most important—and the least noted—single development in the political history of the time: the rise of planter political power during the final decade of the antebellum period. The increasing political influence of the planters in the 1850s has been so little noted because its earlier absence has been so seldom recognized. But the nature of tax policy before about 1847 and the strong efforts of the planters to alter that policy as soon as they gained the capacity to do so provide as strong evidence of the planters' earlier weakness as their subsequent successes do of the planters' emerging strength. Nor, of course, do the new tax systems adopted after 1847 indicate that planters were now able to dominate their political world. Rather, they indicate that nonslaveholders and small slaveholders were still able to give planters a substantial battle. Although planters were able during the final antebellum years to reduce the portion of the tax load they were compelled to bear to a level that seemed to them more nearly equitable, the slave tax nevertheless remained throughout the antebellum period one of the principal sources of state revenue. And each new tax act, to the very end of the period, meant the renewal of the war.

These observations bring us at last to the significance of the tax wars for the chief subject of this essay, Reconstruction. The general inattention to emerging planter power in the 1850s has inhibited historians from appreciating the true significance of the struggle over ad valorem taxation.[12] And the failure to appreciate its significance has led to a failure to emphasize its existence. It was thus easy for historians of Reconstruction, seldom also specialists in the antebellum period, to be unaware of the earlier importance of the question. But white small farmers were acutely aware of it. They entered Reconstruction painfully sensitive to the implications of tax policy, accustomed to thinking of taxation as a matter crucial to their political and social well-being, and prepared to listen with great respect to political leaders who stressed the subject.[13]

II

It does not seem to me that the recent historiography of Reconstruction has shown a sufficient awareness of just how large the receipts and disbursements of the Southern state governments during the decade were, in comparison with the figures from preceding and following years. They dwarfed the totals from the 1850s, though the 1850s had been a period of massive expansion in governmental activity in most of the lower South states. The graphs on the following pages, showing state receipts and disbursements in actual (current) dollars between 1840 and 1885, illustrate clearly how much greater the Reconstruction totals are.[14] I do not, of course, mean to endorse the implicit assumption in much of the work of the Dunning school that the size of the figures is prima facie evidence of wastefulness. On the contrary, I believe that the heart of the Republicans' political dilemma, to which I shall return later in this section, is that the vast social needs of a devastated region peopled with millions of destitute citizens, black and white, clearly justified the states in undertaking expenditures on a scale equal to the problem. Indeed, one can make a persuasive argument that the expenditures, far from being excessive, were insufficient. But such an argument looks at the matter from the perspective of an administrator seeking to deal with the demands of a difficult situation. The reality of democracy requires that the politician look at matters from the perspective of the voter as well, and the two perspectives are by no means always congruent. In the case of Reconstruction, however great the social needs apparent from the capital may have been, it would not have been irrational for the white small farmer to have felt himself overtaxed and underserved by Republican policies. In this section I shall attempt to suggest what may have been the white small farmer's viewpoint on what was happening to him, as opposed to the viewpoint of his governors, which dominates the current secondary literature.

In the first place, it is necessary to underscore, as the graphs of rising receipts have already indicated, that taxes increased rapidly in this decade. I previously cited a sampling of Reconstruction millage rates, a sampling that shows increases over antebellum levels of from four- to eightfold. I need not belabor this point further; it in any case is generally acknowledged. Far less often recognized is the apparent shift in tax incidence that accompanied the abolition of slavery. Slaves had been a very large part of the total wealth in the antebellum South. One index to their value is that in nine of the fifteen slave states in 1860, according to the federal census of that year, the assessed value of personal property exceeded that of real estate, whereas this situation obtained in only three of the nineteen free states.[15] Slaves

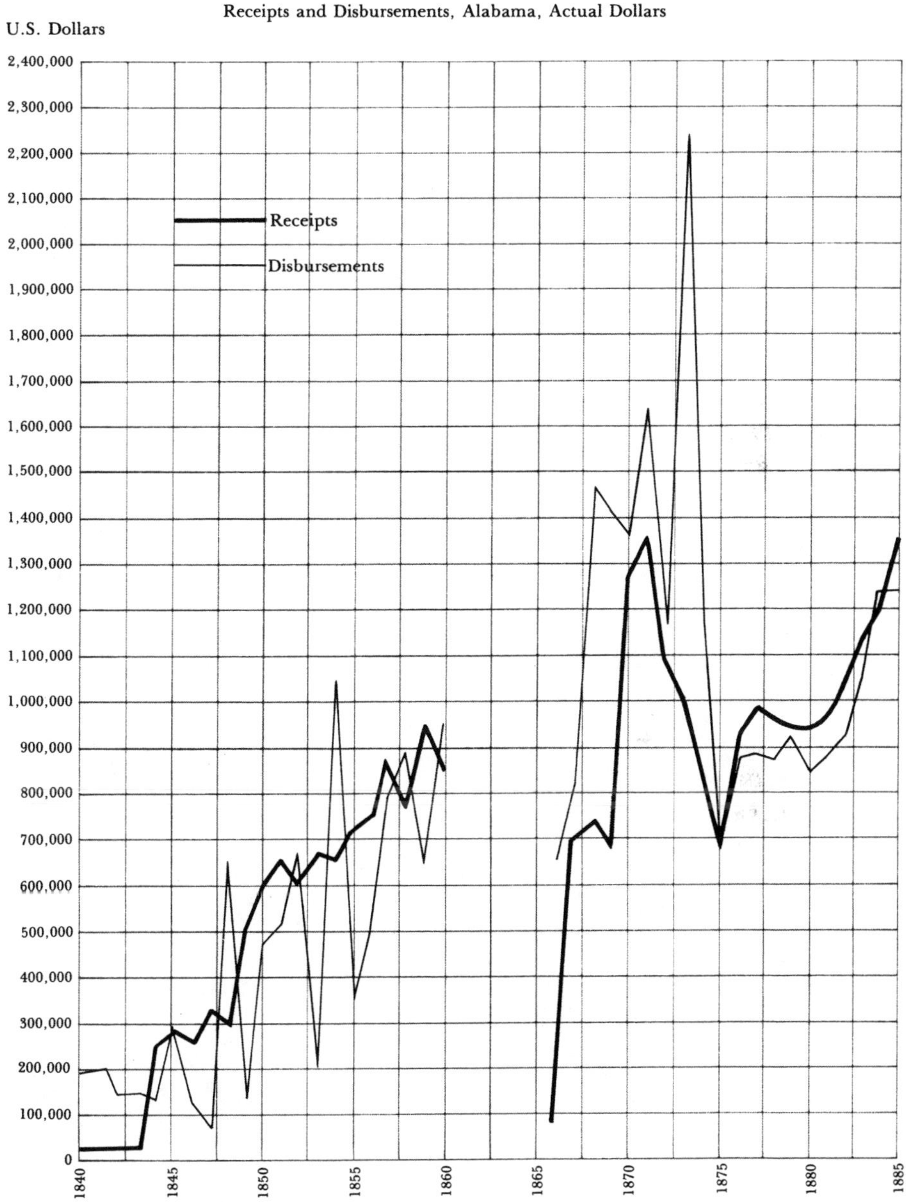

2.1. Receipts and Disbursements, Alabama, Actual Dollars

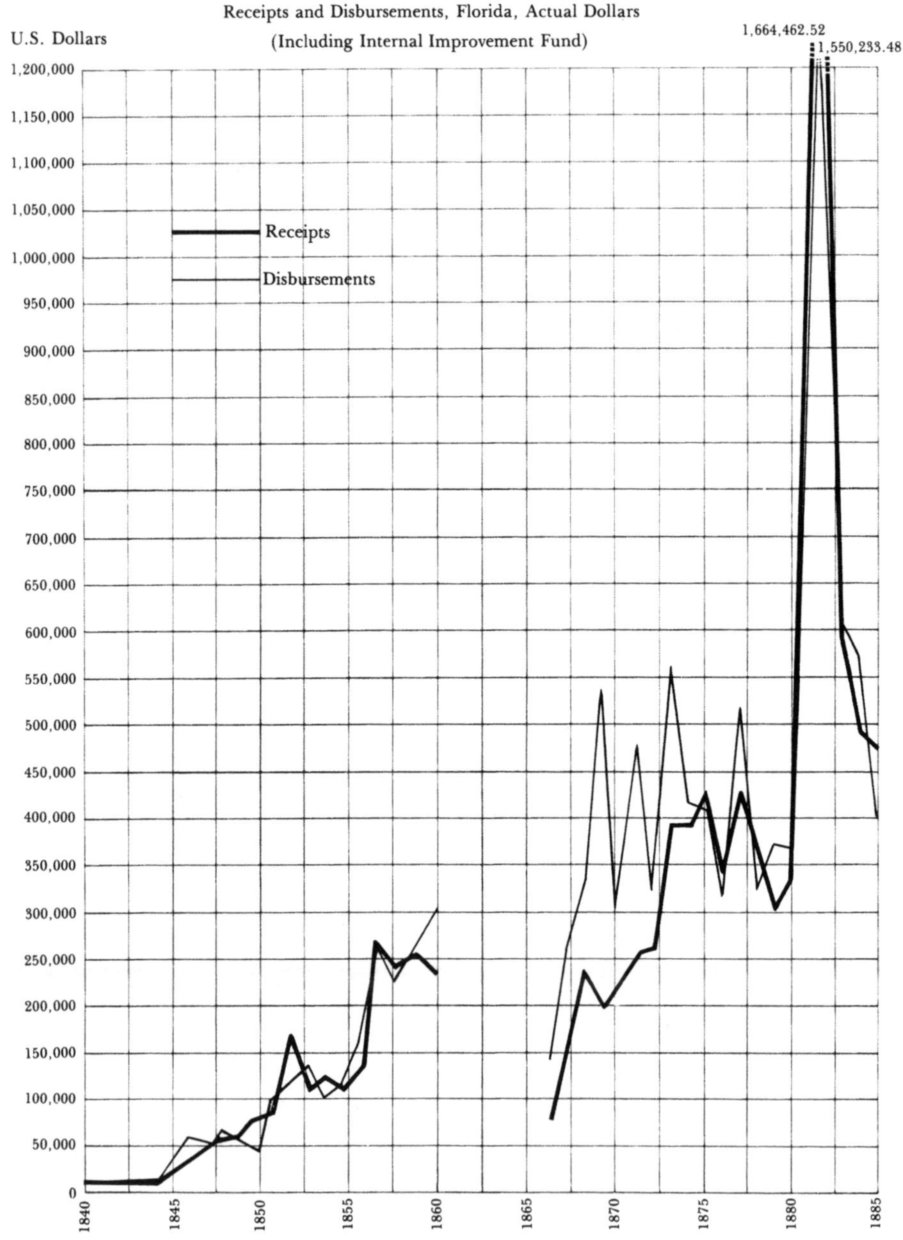

2.2. Receipts and Disbursements, Florida, Actual Dollars

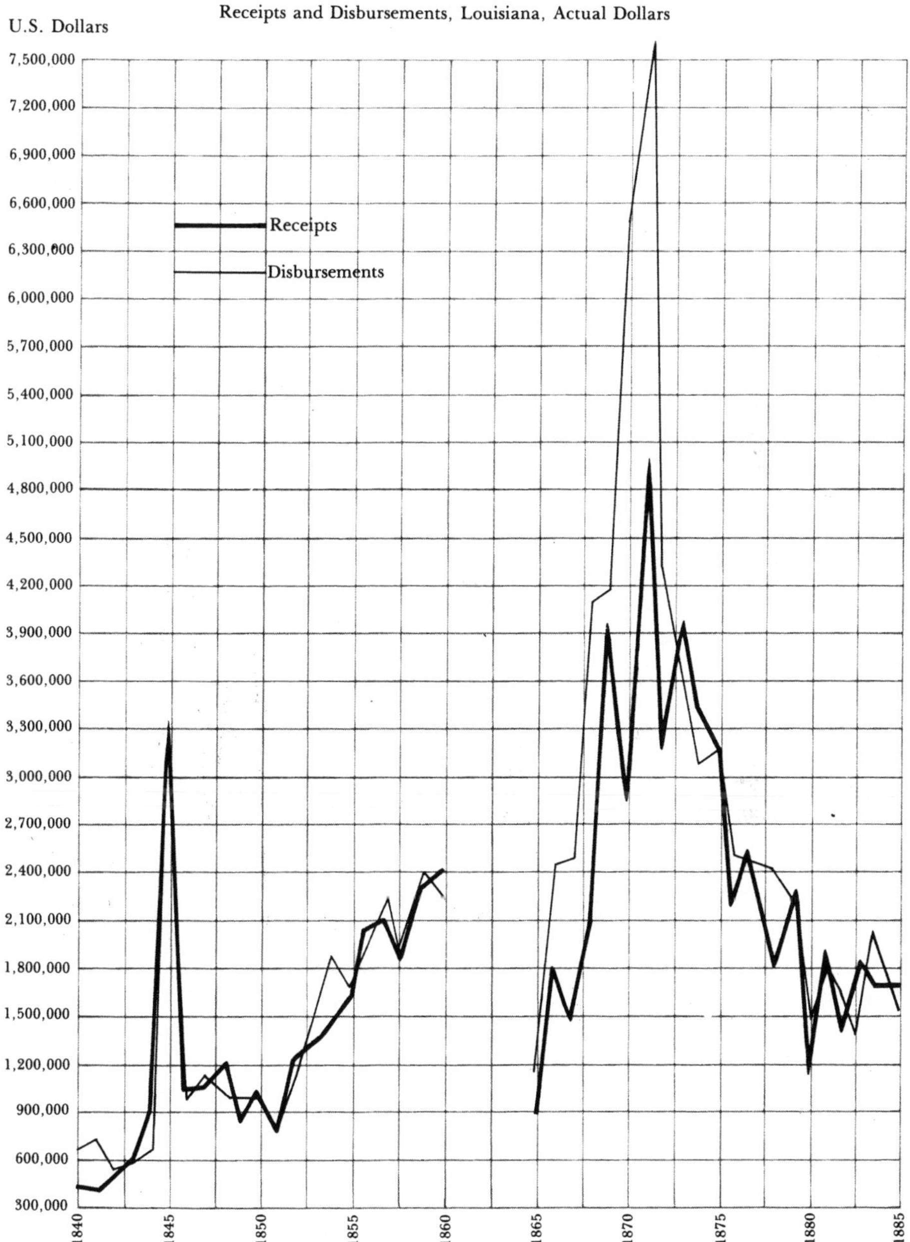

2.3. Receipts and Disbursements, Louisiana, Actual Dollars

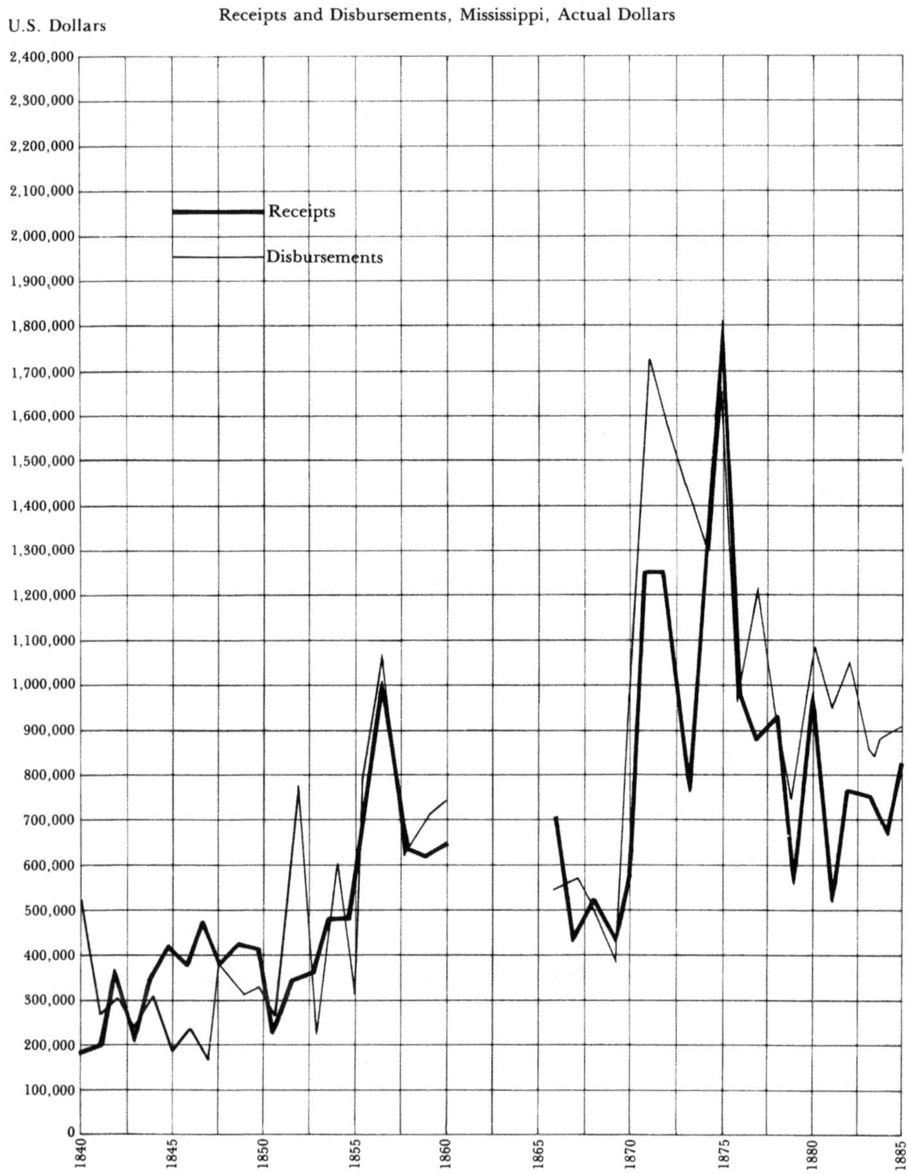

2.4. Receipts and Disbursements, Mississippi, Actual Dollars

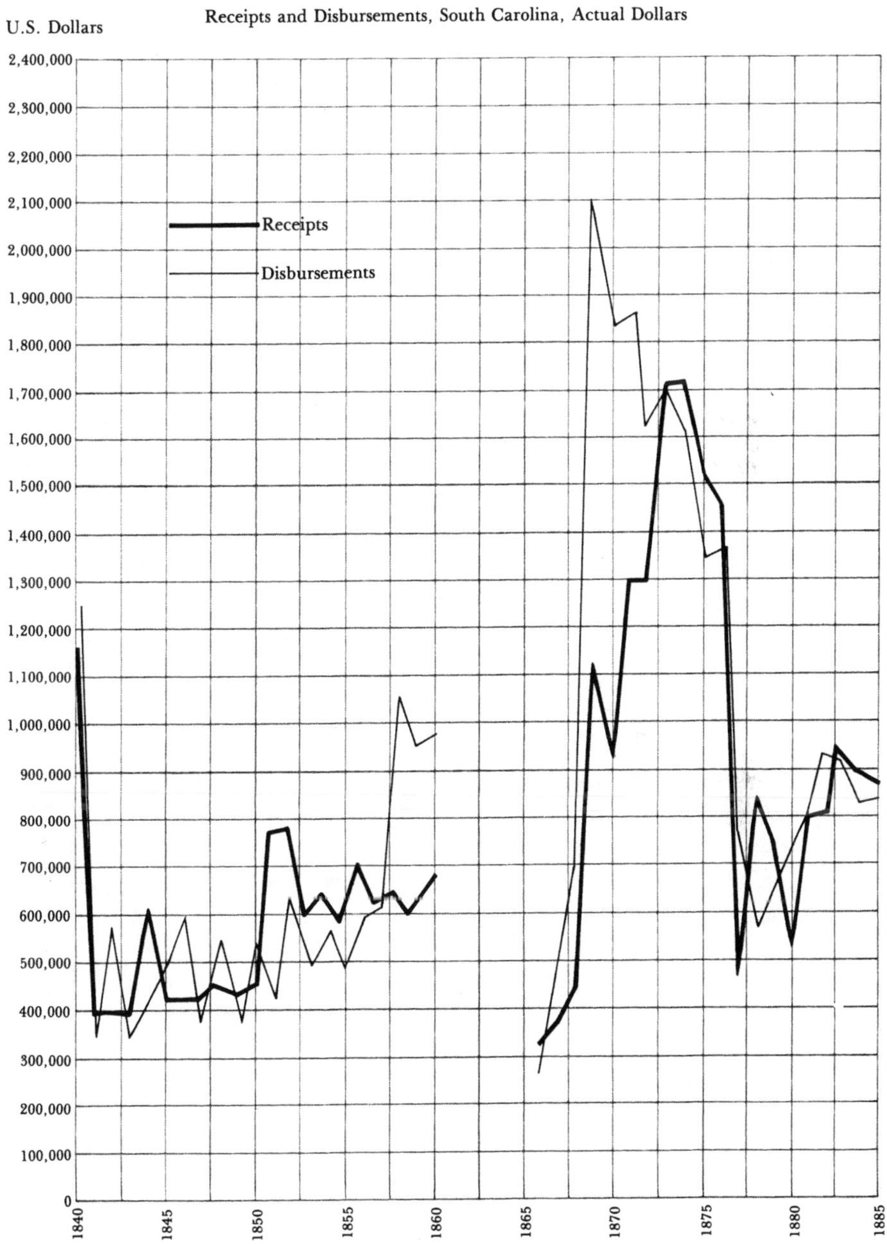

2.5. Receipts and Disbursements, South Carolina, Actual Dollars

were a form of property whose ownership was concentrated almost exclusively in the hands of wealthier citizens. And slaves were an obvious and readily assessable asset. The slave tax had therefore been chiefly responsible for the progressive features of the antebellum tax structure.

After the abolition of slavery, only intangible personal property—stocks, bonds, notes, money at interest—remained as a form of property whose ownership was essentially limited to the wealthy. A property tax on intangibles is, however, notoriously easy to evade, and intangibles did not constitute a substantial part of Southern wealth in any case. Nor is the property tax a very effective method of taxing a business corporation. The Reconstruction statutes insisted that capital and the property of corporations had to be taxed, of course. But receipts from these sources were never very large, perhaps 15 percent of the totals. An additional 15 percent came from other personal property, including wagons, farming implements, furniture, and livestock. The poll tax usually contributed another 5 to 10 percent. It was not the taxes from these sources, however, that really sustained the rapidly expanding Reconstruction governments. Sixty percent or more of this burden fell on a single object of taxation—land.

In the antebellum period, the land tax had seldom exceeded a third of the tax receipts. The presence of the slave tax had allowed legislators to keep land-tax rates low. Just as governmental activity and the consequent need for revenue soared to levels unexampled in peacetime, however, the states faced a newly, and markedly, constricted tax base. It was the decision of Republican legislators to let the land tax alone bear the burden formerly divided between the land and slave taxes.

The value of real estate in the South during this unsettled period had declined markedly from the late 1850s, returning to the levels of the early 1850s. Therefore, the fact that tax rates increased by four to eight times does not imply that actual taxes rose so much. Still, the increase in taxes was steep enough. The following tables illustrate the taxes due on a 160-acre farm in Alabama and Mississippi in various years, assuming that the farm was worth the average assessed value per acre in the year. In Alabama, though the value per acre had declined by a third between 1860 and 1870, the tax on the farm had multiplied by almost two and a half times, and the average tax in the Reconstruction years was double the level of 1860. In Mississippi, the tax in 1871 was three and a half times what it had been in 1857, and in 1873 it was almost five times the figure for 1857, though in 1873 the value of the farm was almost 40 percent less than in 1857.

It might be argued, on the other hand, that the actual tax, in dollar terms, was still a modest one. But such a contention misunderstands the situation of a small farmer operating on the edge of the cash economy. For him these taxes were significant, because his cash income was so small. We may form a rough estimate of what the cash income of the owner of a 160-acre farm was in these two states. The federal censuses of 1860 and 1870 inform us that approximately two-thirds of the farm was unimproved acreage; let us assume that our farmer has 60 of his 160 acres in cultivation. Perhaps two-thirds of the improved acreage was given over to the growth of food crops for use by the farmer's family. On the remaining 20 acres, he might plant cotton to be marketed for cash. During Reconstruction, and we may assume also during the 1850s, the average yield of cotton was a bit less than four-tenths of a bale per acre. Thus our farmer marketed some eight bales. In the marketing years 1855–56 to 1860–61, the weighted average of ordinary-grade cotton sold at New Orleans was 8.445 cents a pound. In the marketing years 1870–71 to 1875–76, the comparable figure was 12.9 cents a pound. These figures, after we deduct 5 percent for factorage fees and transportation costs, produce a cash income for the farmer of about $257 a year in the late 1850s and about $392 a year in the early 1870s. The latter amount is, incidentally, less than 18 percent greater than the former one in constant dollar terms, because of the postwar inflation of prices. If these estimates are reasonable, then the state land tax alone represented 1 percent or more of the farmer's total cash income in Alabama during the Reconstruction years, except for the brief period in 1871–72 when the Democrats regained power. And it was some 1 1/2 to 2 percent of his income in Mississippi during the period. The Alabama percentage is nearly double that for 1855 and 50 percent above that for 1860. The Mississippi percentage in 1873 is more than treble that for 1857.

To the state land tax must be added the county and school district taxes, the personal property tax on livestock, farm implements, and similar possessions, and the poll tax, which in Alabama was $1.50, and in Mississippi was $2.00 in 1870 but $1.00 in 1873. It is not at all unreasonable, therefore, to estimate that our owner of a 160-acre farm paid some 2 to 4 percent of his total cash income to the tax collector during Reconstruction. And when we reflect that a considerable part of the farmer's cash income necessarily went to pay the immediate expenses of his farming operation—to pay for seed, supplies, and very probably, interest on his debts—then it becomes apparent that the taxes would have been an even larger percentage of his discretionary income. If a fourth of his cash income remained after the payment of unavoidable farming expenses, he would have paid some 8 to 10 percent or more of that remainder in taxes. Taxation at this level would most certainly not have been inconsequential for the small farmer. Nor are we reduced to mere speculation about its effect, in Mississippi at least. We need only

Table 2.1. State land tax on a farm of 160 acres, valued at the average per acre, Alabama

Year	Average Value per Acre (dollars)	Tax Rate (mills)	Value (dollars)	Tax (dollars)
1848	3.71	2.0	593.60	1.19
1855	4.81	2.0	769.60	1.54
1860	6.41	2.0	1,025.60	2.05
1868	3.89	3.0	622.40	1.87
1869	4.08	7.0	652.80	4.57
1870	4.11	7.5	657.60	4.93
1871	3.84	5.0	614.40	3.07
1872	4.67	5.0	747.20	3.74
1873	3.52	7.5	563.20	4.22
1874	3.39	7.5	542.40	4.07
1875	2.81	7.5	449.60	3.37
1876	2.85	7.5	456.00	3.42
1877	3.09	7.0	494.40	3.46
1878	2.86	7.0	457.60	3.20
1879	2.32	7.0	371.20	2.60
1880	2.74	6.5	438.40	2.85

note that by the spring of 1871, that state was reporting nearly 3,330,000 acres—14 percent of its entire taxable acreage—as having been forfeited to the government for nonpayment of taxes.

The abolition of slavery, then, because it moved so much of the burden of taxation to land, apparently brought about in the lower South a marked shift in tax incidence downward in the social scale. At the same time, rapidly rising tax rates brought taxes to a level at which they became genuinely onerous to the white small farmer. But, it might be said, if the small farmer was paying large taxes for the first time, he was also receiving substantial governmental services for the first time. Although at first glance this position looks very plausible, it does not, I think, accurately depict the small farmer's situation as he may well have perceived it. As an initial step toward understanding what I believe may have been the white small farmer's own sense of the Reconstruction governments, let me offer a series of what may appear to be quite idiosyncratic graphs.

The graphs on the following pages portray Southern-state receipts and disbursements in an unusual way. In the first place, I have converted the fig-

Table 2.2. State land tax on a farm of 160 acres valued at the average per acre, Mississippi

Year	Average Value per Acre (dollars)	Tax Rate (mills)	Value (dollars)	Tax (dollars)
1848	3.82	2.5	611.20	1.53
1850	4.54	1.25	726.40	0.91
1852	5.70	1.6	912.00	1.46
1853	5.67	1.6	907.20	1.45
1854	5.57	1.6	891.20	1.43
1857	6.97	1.6	1,115.20	1.78
1871	4.38*	9.0	700.80	6.31
1872	4.33*	8.5	692.80	5.89
1873	4.26*	12.5	681.60	8.52
1875	4.01	7.25	641.60	4.65
1876	4.04	6.5	646.40	4.20
1877	4.03	5.0	644.80	3.22
1878	4.07	3.5	651.20	2.28
1879	2.72	3.5	435.20	1.52
1880	2.76	3.0	441.60	1.32

*Assuming the total taxable acreage of 1875.

ures into constant dollars, using the Consumer Price Index.[16] This conversion is essential for Reconstruction because, though prices remained fairly stable for much of the nineteenth century, in the years between the Civil War and the panic of 1873 prices maintained quite high levels. Thus the expenditure in 1870 of the same number of dollars disbursed in 1860 would have purchased for the government significantly less in goods and services. Reconstruction legislatures could do nothing about this problem; just to maintain antebellum levels of services, they had to spend more, and fairness to them compels us to take account of this fact.

Having put the figures into constant dollars, I have then chosen to display them as I believe the white small farmers perceived them. Receipts are shown in constant dollars per white inhabitant. Whites paid almost all of the direct taxes both before and after the Civil War. In the antebellum period the only blacks who were taxpayers were, of course, the handful of free Negroes. But even after the war, the freedmen owned virtually no property, and therefore for all practical purposes they were subject directly only to the poll tax. Beginning in 1874 Georgia reported tax receipts seg-

Table 2.3. State land tax on a farm of 160 acres, valued at the average per acre, in the one-third of the counties with the smallest land-tax receipts, Alabama

Year	Average Value per Acre (dollars)	Tax Rate (mills)	Value (dollars)	Tax (dollars)
1848	2.81	2.0	449.60	0.90
1855	2.63	2.0	420.80	0.84
1860	3.64	2.0	582.40	1.16
1870	2.15	7.5	344.00	2.58
1871	2.04	5.0	326.40	1.63
1872	1.89	5.0	302.40	1.51
1873	1.60	7.5	256.00	1.92
1874	1.71	7.5	273.60	2.05
1875	1.55	7.5	248.00	1.86
1876	1.40	7.5	224.00	1.68
1878	1.41	7.0	225.60	1.58
1879	1.12	7.0	179.20	1.25

regated by race. The returns for 1874, as I have already noted, indicate that blacks, who made up some 46 percent of the population in that year, paid only 2.3 percent of the property taxes. The addition of the poll taxes brings the black percentage of the total tax receipts to 7.4. Indeed, it was precisely the ability of the poll tax to extract a contribution from the propertyless that made it seem to Southern legislators—during Reconstruction, as before and afterward—the ideal tax for the support of the public schools. It was the one tax paid by a significant minority—and just after emancipation probably the majority—of the parents whose children used the schools. This attitude among the legislators is connected with the general view among white voters that they were being taxed to provide services to nontaxpayers. Now, this attitude was in part a misconception. Blacks who were renters or sharecroppers contributed to tax receipts indirectly by providing a part of the income out of which the white property owner paid the tax on the farm. But however unfair the attitude was, it was certainly real. After Redemption it produced a vigorous campaign throughout the South to expend on black schools only those school taxes actually paid by black citizens.

I thus come to my display of disbursements. I have shown them in constant dollars per white inhabitant until 1865, and in constant dollars per

Table 2.4. State land tax on a farm of 160 acres, valued at the average per acre, in the one-third of the counties with the smallest land-tax receipts, Mississippi

Year	Average Value per Acre* (dollars)	Tax Rate (mills)	Value (dollars)	Tax (dollars)
1850	1.96	1.25	313.60	0.39
1852	2.98	1.6	476.80	0.76
1853	2.86	1.6	457.60	0.73
1854	2.55	1.6	408.00	0.65
1857	3.86	1.6	617.60	0.99
1871	1.53**	9.0	244.80	2.20
1872	1.56**	8.5	249.60	2.12
1873	1.58**	12.5	252.80	3.16
1875	1.36	7.25	217.60	1.58
1876	1.42	6.5	227.20	1.48
1877	1.42	5.0	227.20	1.14
1878	1.42	3.5	227.20	0.80
1879	0.99	3.5	158.40	0.55
1880	0.91	3.0	145.60	0.44

*Acreage of missing counties in various years is taken from lists of other years.
**Assuming the total taxable acreage of 1875, with two missing counties filled in from 1879.

capita thereafter. It is essential to remember that while the number of taxpayers remained essentially constant after emancipation, the number of citizens needing state services was doubled at a stroke. Disbursements expressed in aggregate terms seem quite small in the antebellum era and much larger during Reconstruction. But the reality is almost the reverse. Because the citizenry was half as large before the Civil War, disbursements per citizen actually declined during Reconstruction. Republicans were well aware of this distinction; it was their standard reply to Democratic charges of profligate waste.[17] But we must note that it was the Democratic charge rather than the Republican reply that appears to have struck home with the white small farmers. As I have said, the Republican argument looked at the problem from the point of view of the administrators, of those in charge of the government. It was necessary for expenditures to expand rapidly even to maintain services at their former levels, they said, because prices were higher and because twice as many people had to be served. But such an ex-

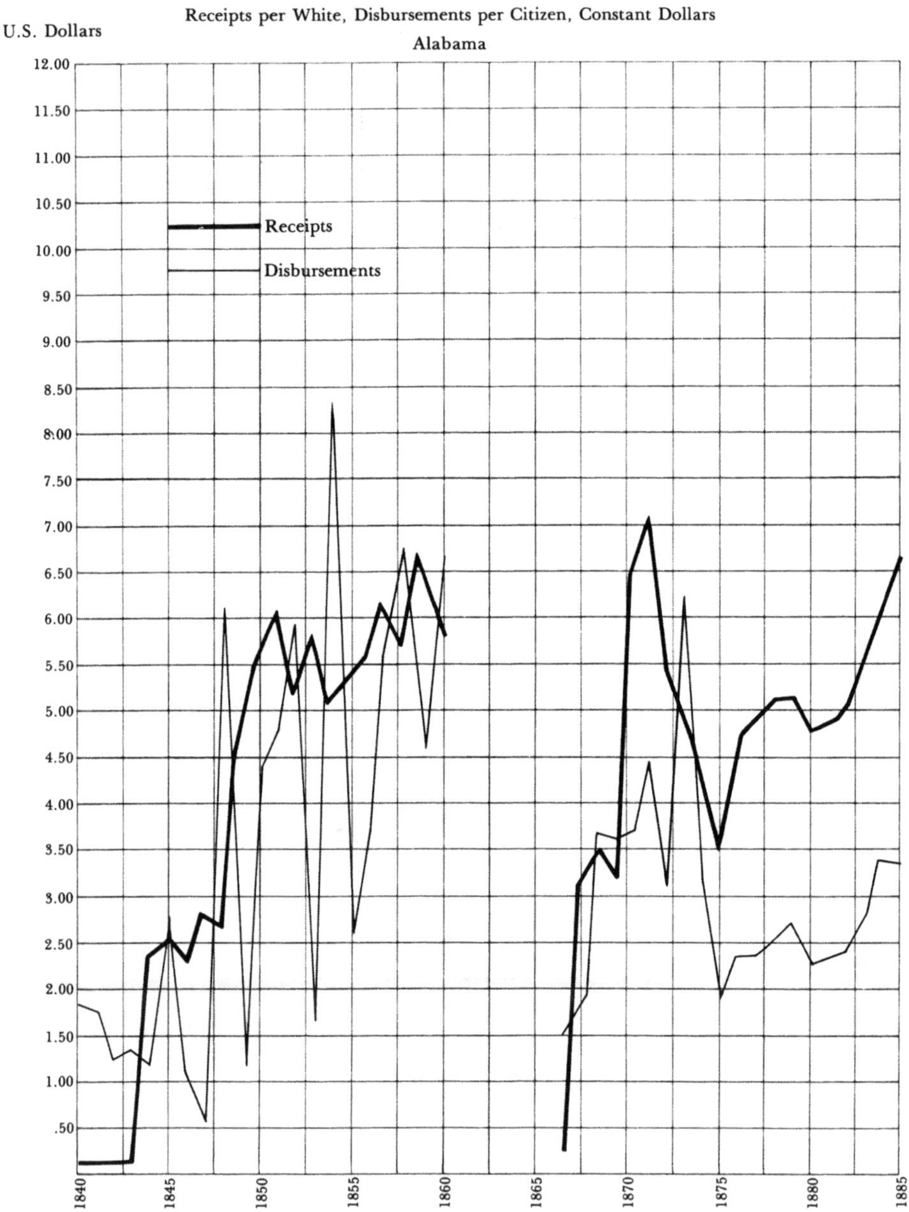

2.6. Receipts per White, Disbursements per Citizen, Constant Dollars, Alabama

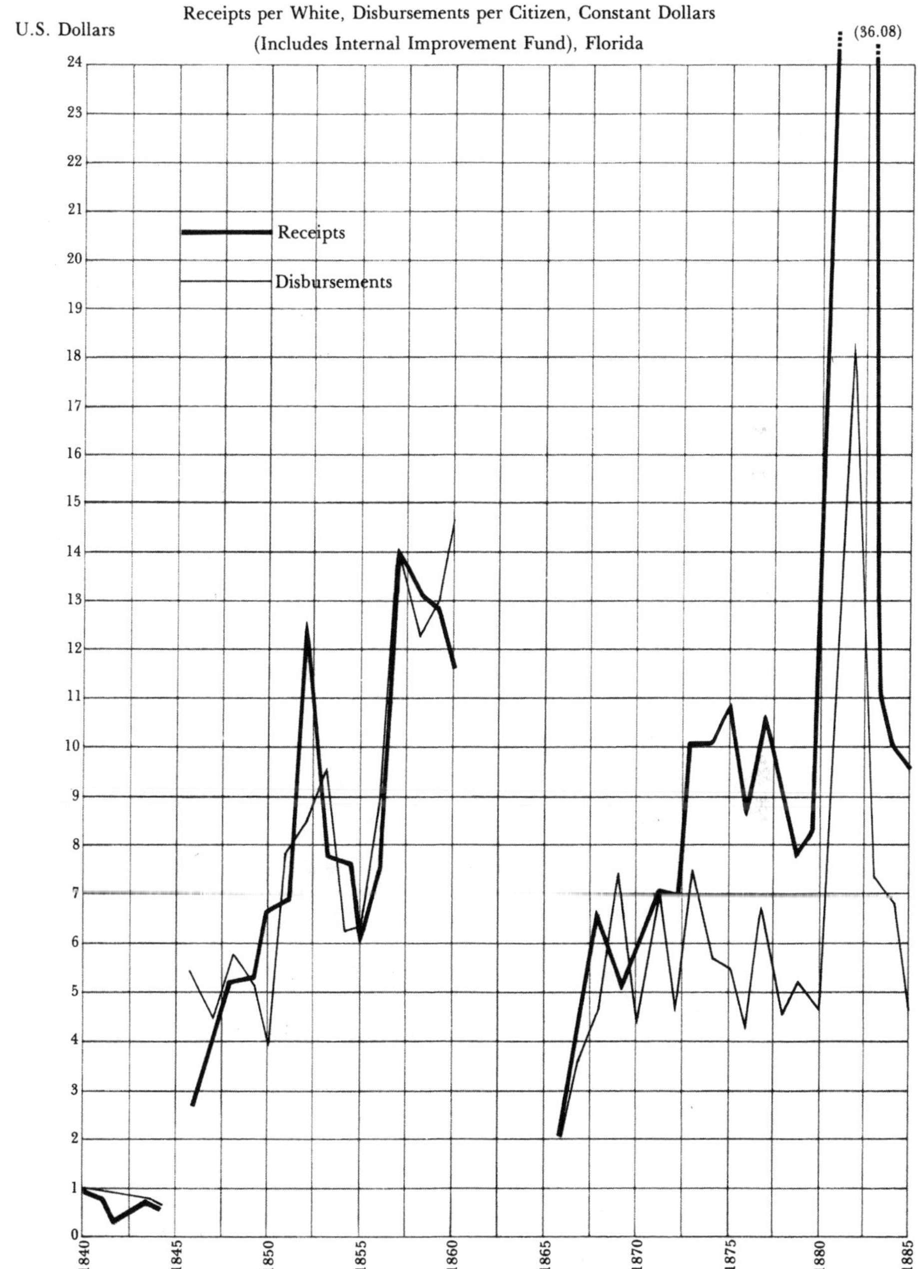

2.7. Receipts per White, Disbursements per Citizen, Constant Dollars, Florida

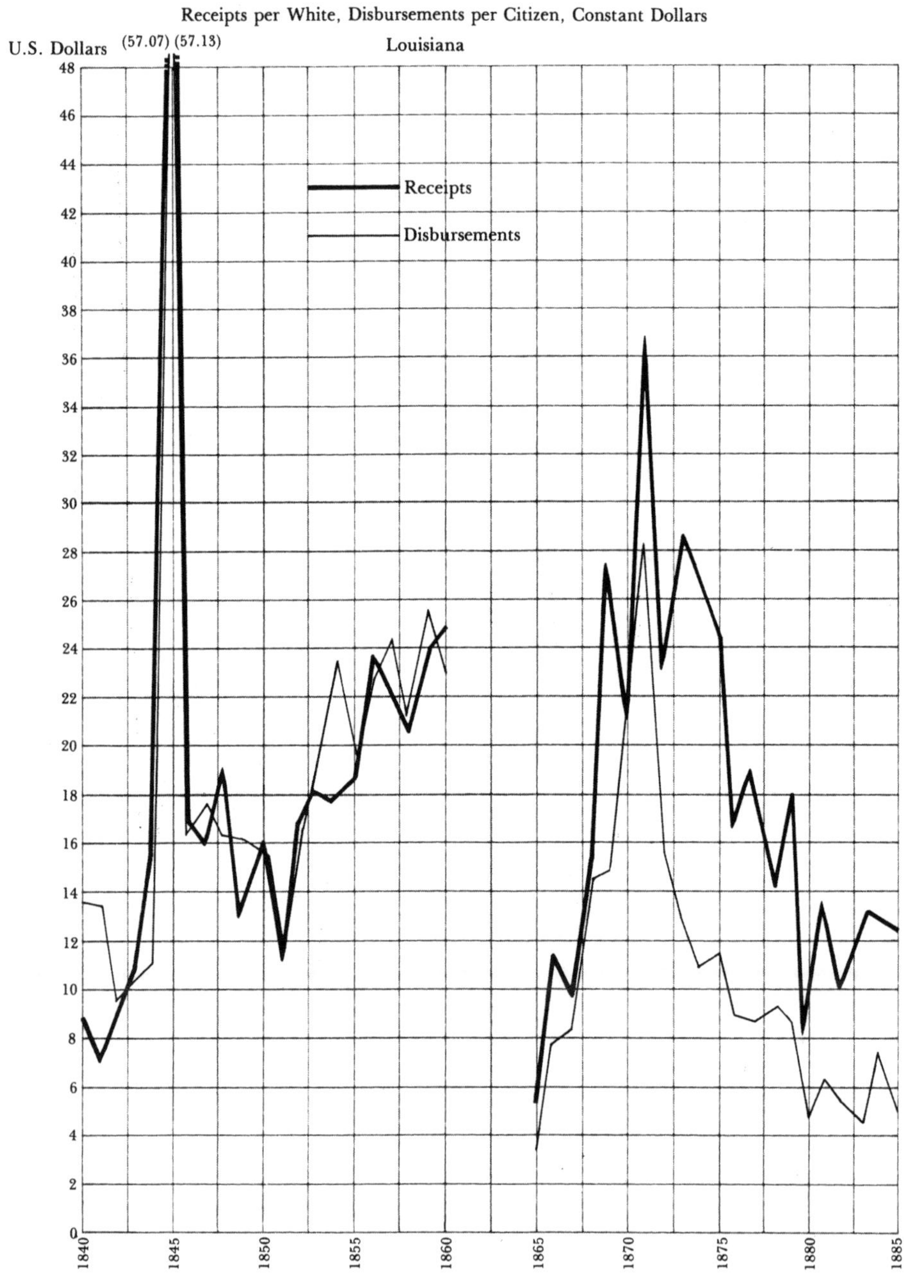

2.8. Receipts per White, Disbursements per Citizen, Constant Dollars, Louisiana

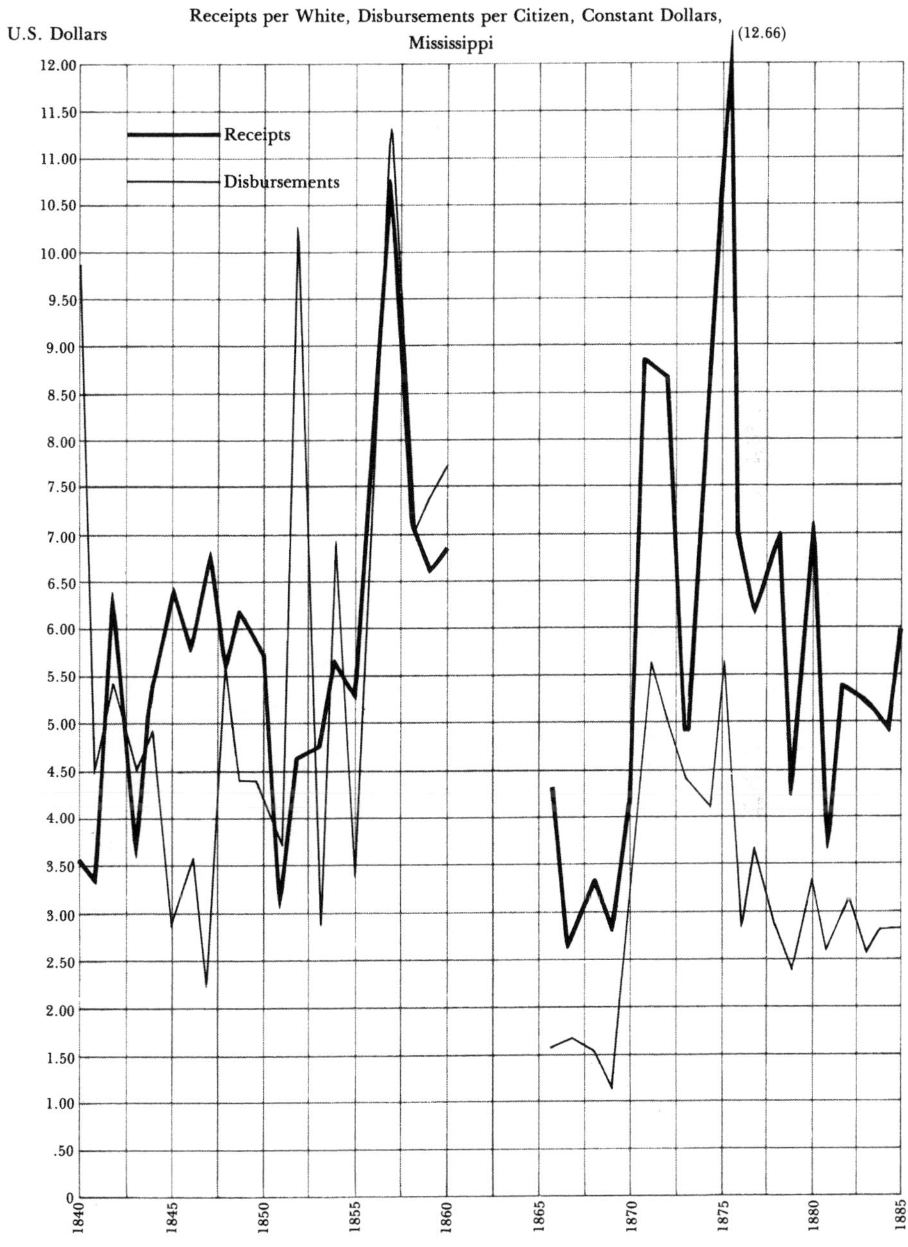

2.9. Receipts per White, Disbursements per Citizen, Constant Dollars, Mississippi

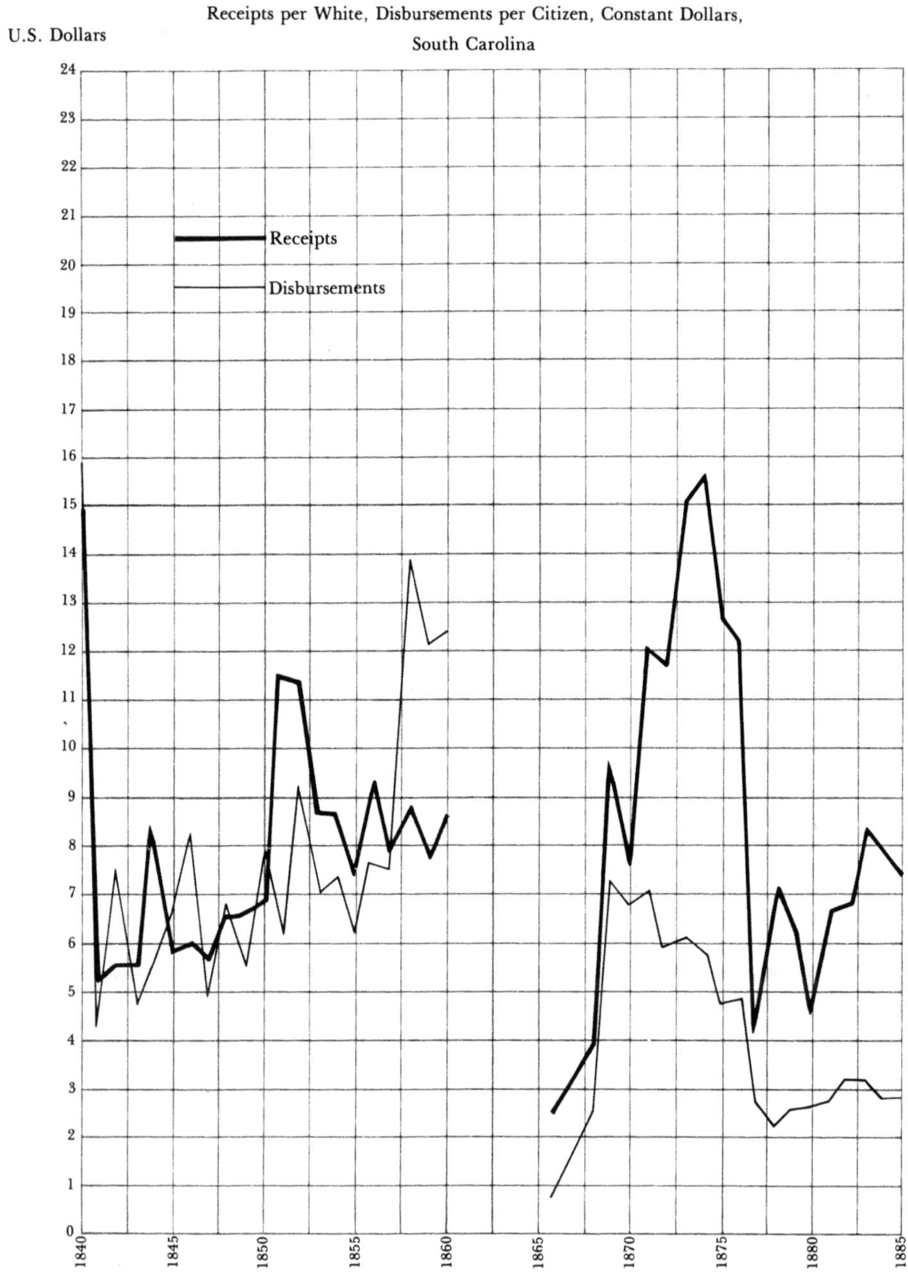

2.10. Receipts per White, Disbursements per Citizen, Constant Dollars, South Carolina

planation, however cogent it was in fact, would probably have seemed to the white farmer only an elaborate rationalization for a gross injustice. As the graphs indicate, the reality for the white farmer was a sharp increase in taxes and a decline in services. From this perspective, it was quite natural that the notion that the large new taxes were going into the pockets of corrupt officials—bolstered as the notion was by a number of cases of genuine corruption among the Republicans—was convincing. And even if it had not been, the simple fact of high taxes and small returns, produced by dividing the tax receipts between hard-pressed whites and "nontaxpaying" blacks, would probably have been damning enough.[18]

One striking example of the way in which small farmers experienced Reconstruction policies is found in state support for the public schools. It has become something of an article of faith in the recent historiography of Reconstruction that state-supported public school systems in the South were largely a product of the Reconstruction period. But such a contention distorts the actual story. State support for public schools had been considerable in the region even in the early antebellum period. Beginning in 1821, Georgia contributed approximately $40,000 annually to its schools and academies, and in 1837 created a full-fledged public school system. Alabama did likewise in the same year. In Louisiana after 1819 the state began distributing $45,000 a year in aid to the public schools. South Carolina adopted in 1811 a program under which it contributed $37,500 a year to public schools. The South Carolina aid continued without interruption into the 1850s, but the public-school programs in Georgia, Alabama, and Louisiana were all disrupted by the panic of 1837 and the depression that followed. Georgia and Alabama repealed their public-school acts, and Louisiana its state-aid act, in the early 1840s, and five or six years followed in which the schools were generally reduced to local support. With the return of prosperity toward the end of the 1840s, however, legislative attention once again focused on education.

Louisiana led this movement. As we have seen, the Louisiana constitution of 1846 had coupled the conversion to an ad valorem general property tax with the command to the legislature to create a state-supported public school system. The legislature of 1847 had complied, and by 1848 the state could claim to be funding its schools quite handsomely: at about $260,000 a year between 1848 and 1852, and at about $320,000 a year between 1853 and 1859. In 1859 the legislature increased the appropriation still further, to about $550,000 a year.

Other states followed Louisiana's example, though not on so lavish a scale. Alabama initially adopted a program of state payments to local schools that amounted to some $30,000 a year in the late 1840s and to more than $50,000 a year in the early 1850s. Then in 1854 Alabama created a state-supported public school system. The funding of this enterprise was placed on a solid foundation in 1856. The state was spending almost $225,000 a year in the middle of the decade and more than $280,000 a year by the end of it. Georgia, which was heavily involved in attempting to complete the state-owned Western and Atlantic Railroad, reinstated its program of state aid to schools quite hesitantly in the late 1840s. By the early 1850s Georgia was spending about $20,000 a year, and later in the decade the figure reached $30,000 a year. Then, at the end of 1858, when the Western and Atlantic was completed and paying dividends, the legislature finally adopted an extensive program of state school aid. State expenditures on public schools quintupled, from about $30,000 in 1859 to almost $150,000 in 1860. The Civil War cut short this promising new beginning.

Florida, which had entered the Union in 1845, at first sought to join the other Southern states in their interest in public schools. In 1849 it created a public school system, but one financed largely at the local level. In 1851, it offered to pay a sufficient amount from state funds to enable each school district to expend at least two dollars per eligible child, but in 1853 it pulled back from this commitment. In the later 1850s it devoted most of its slender resources to an extensive program of state aid to railroad construction. In the meantime, however, its common school fund, which was derived from the proceeds of public-land sales that had been invested in state bonds, had begun to produce income. Thus in the period from 1856 to 1860, Florida was able to distribute almost $5,000 a year in aid to local school districts—a modest sum but, given the state's small school-age population of 20,000 to 30,000, not an inconsequential one. South Carolina, thanks to the fact that the prudently managed Bank of South Carolina had weathered the panic of 1837, had been able to continue its annual school-aid payments throughout the 1840s. In 1854 legislators felt sufficiently confident of the state's financial position to double the annual appropriation, bringing it to $75,000. This doubling of funds increased the percentage of children in school who were receiving state aid from 23 percent to 41 percent.[19] Only in the case of Mississippi is the notion of antebellum state inactivity in regard to public schools a relatively accurate one. Mississippi, alone among the six lower South states, had no program of regular state assistance to the schools. Even Mississippi, however, made several large distributions to local schools on a one-time basis in the early 1850s. If these distributions are averaged over the entire decade, they are the equivalent of aid at the rate of a bit less than $30,000 a year.

It is against this antebellum background, then, that we must judge Reconstruction efforts with the public schools. As a first step, we should emphasize the massive problems that war and emancipation created for the Southern public school systems. Reconstruction legislators did their best to meet these problems, but the fiscal barriers to their doing so were almost insuperable. In the two states, Louisiana and Alabama, that had established centralized state-financed public school systems before the Civil War, there was really no hope of duplicating antebellum levels of support. Expressed in constant dollars of 1967, Louisiana was spending an average of $11.53 per eligible child in the decade from 1850 to 1859, and $17.90 in 1860. In the six years from 1870 to 1875, Louisiana spent $4.86 per eligible child, on the average, measured in the same terms—which is less than a third of the final antebellum figure. In 1871, the single year in which disbursements approximated antebellum levels, the expenditures appear to have included a large sum to pay for deficits from previous years. Similarly, in Alabama, which was spending an average of $4.34 per eligible child, in 1967 dollars, during the late 1850s, and more than $4.90 in 1860, Reconstruction expenditures fell to an average of $2.85. In the early 1870s Alabama did for a brief time manage to regain antebellum levels of expenditure per child, but public discontent with the disbursements necessary to do so—between two and a half and three times the usual totals from the 1850s, in actual dollars—compelled reductions to more modest levels. Even in the states that during the antebellum period had merely provided supplementary aid to local school districts, however, the quandary of Reconstruction legislators is evident. In South Carolina, state aid had averaged $2.52 per child, in constant dollar terms, in the years between 1854 and 1860. During Reconstruction, South Carolina gained a state-administered public school system. But constant-dollar expenditures per child in the years 1870 to 1876 rose one penny, to $2.53. In only three years, from 1873 to 1875, did expenditures per child exceed the average for the 1850s. And yet total disbursements for schools during Reconstruction were, on the average, treble those of the 1850s, and in two years were four and a half times the 1850s figure, in actual dollars. In Florida, school disbursements per eligible child, in constant dollars, averaged 65 cents in the years 1856 to 1860. The comparable figure for the years 1871 to 1876 is $1.74; if we exclude 1871, a year of abnormally high disbursements, we obtain an average of $1.44. Thus Florida school expenditures in constant dollars per child increased by a factor of between two and a quarter and two and two-thirds, a substantial growth. But the Reconstruction expenditure level remained distinctly modest. And to achieve it, Florida had to increase its total annual school expenditures, in terms of actual dollars, some eightfold. In Mississippi, the distributions made to local school districts in the early 1850s were the equivalent of an annual expenditure per eligible child in constant dollars of 86 cents. The comparable figure for the years 1871 through 1875 is $1.09, an increase of about a fourth. But as in the case of Florida, this level of expenditure is quite modest indeed, and achieving it required a nearly fourfold increase in total annual outlays, expressed in actual dollars.

Table 3.1. Expenditures on public schools per eligible child, Constant Dollars (Consumer Price Index), Louisiana

1848	4.83	1858	10.12	1872	4.37
1849	20.11	1859	10.66	1873	4.10
1850	12.65	1860	17.90	1874	3.90
1851	11.94	1865	1.81	1875	3.92
1852	12.43	1866	1.59		
1853	14.38	1867	1.57	1877	2.57
1854	12.04	1868	1.53	1878	3.53
1855	9.66	1869	0.70	1879	2.73
1856	10.74	1870	1.51	1880	1.38
1857	10.65	1871	11.38		

Table 3.2. Expenditures on public schools per eligible child, Constant Dollars (Consumer Price Index), South Carolina

1848	1.27	1856	2.62	1870	1.30
1849	1.40	1857	2.53	1871	2.26
1850	1.38	1858	2.64	1872	1.41
1851	1.31	1859	2.49	1873	3.81
1852	1.33	1860	2.44	1874	3.22
1853	1.76	1866	0.05	1875	3.45
1854	2.53	1867	0.26	1876	2.23
1855	2.53	1868	0.13	1877	1.33
		1869	0.56		

These statistics bring the Reconstruction dilemma into sharp focus. Reconstruction legislators were correct in believing that the schools needed the money being spent on them. Given the demands being placed on the school systems, they were in most states clearly underfunded. But the white farmer-taxpayer was also correct in believing that he was paying much more in taxes, and was generally receiving no more—in fact, often less—in return than he had received before the war. For the Republicans, there was no way out. Black voters badly needed greater social services, and because they paid virtually no taxes, at least directly, they did not immediately feel the effects of the rising tax rates that were necessary to pay for the services; they therefore demanded more. White small farmers, living on the edge of the cash economy, found far more of their disposable incomes going to pay taxes and were unable to discern any increase in services for their greatly increased contribution; they demanded a reduction of the tax rates and an explanation for the seeming disappearance of the state's receipts. And then, on the back of this acutely embarrassed camel was loaded one final straw—the panic of 1873. The price of cotton had been falling throughout Reconstruction, placing greater and greater stress on the small farmer. The weighted-average price of ordinary-grade cotton sold at New Orleans declined from 18.743 cents a pound in 1871–72 and 15.306 cents in 1872–73 to 12.516 cents in 1874–75 and 9.162 cents in 1875–76. But it was a less obvious effect of the panic that was to prove crucial to the fortunes of Southern Republicans. The panic considerably exacerbated the problem of the public debt. At the outset of Reconstruction, several states issued bonds for state purposes, such as for the repair of levees in Louisiana and for an ill-fated land-redistribution scheme in South Carolina, and most of them agreed to endorse large amounts of the corporate bonds of railroads under construction, promising to pay them off if the railroads defaulted. One can easily understand the motives that moved the legislators to take these actions: the repair of the levees was essential; the completion of railroads in the South gave promise of restoring the devastated region to prosperity; and the bonds of an uncompleted railroad could not, of course, be sold at an acceptable interest rate without additional security. But the principal amounts issued, quickly mounted to totals that were beyond the capacity of the fragile, essentially agricultural Southern economies to sustain—particularly if any substantial number of the railroad companies defaulted.

The day of reckoning as to the public debts was postponed in all the states except Louisiana. In Mississippi and in Alabama, the amount of the bonds issued for state purposes, and for which the states were responsible even before the panic, was comparatively small. In South Carolina and in Florida, the state debt became involved in litigation,[20] and the states essentially suspended the payment of all interest while the courts decided the questions at issue. In Louisiana, however, interest payments mounted quickly and alarmingly. Debt service had represented less than 10 percent of Louisiana's disbursements in the 1850s, amounting to an average of about $130,000 a year. But as early as 1869, Louisiana's debt service exceeded $400,000; it rose beyond $1 million in 1870, and beyond $1.3 million in 1871. In 1872, debt service represented 30 percent of the state's total disbursements. This pattern was repeated a bit later in the other states. The settlement of the litigation in South Carolina and Florida was followed quickly by the panic and by the consequent defaulting of most of the railroads whose bonds had been endorsed. Mississippi, one of the most conservative of the lower South states in issuing bonds, nevertheless saw its debt service leap from $110,000 in 1873 to $287,000 in 1875, when the amount was 16 percent of its disbursements. South Carolina's debt service rose from about $190,000 in 1871—and from only $10,000 in 1872 and $4,000 in 1873, years in which it had largely suspended interest payments—to $250,000 in 1875 and almost $300,000 in 1876, by which time debt service made up nearly 22 percent of its total disbursements. In Alabama, interest payments rose from $337,000 in 1871 to more than $540,000 in 1873, when they constituted some 28 percent of disbursements. In Florida, interest payments, including those from the state and those from the internal-improvement fund, rose almost two and a half times between 1872 and 1876, to more than $100,000, or almost 32 percent of total disbursements.

In response to the rapid increases in debt service, Republicans in Florida, South Carolina, and Louisiana pioneered methods of debt reduction that subsequently became favorite devices of the Redeemers. In February 1873, even before the panic, Florida adopted a readjustment statute that swapped outstanding bonds for new ones at a lower interest rate but payable in gold; this statute repealed all taxes for interest on the older bonds, and in effect largely repudiated the massive endorsements of railroad bonds in which the state had indulged in 1870 by forbidding the swapping of railroad bonds for the new bonds. Under the terms of this act, the state negotiated a settlement with one of its largest creditors for 80 cents on the dollar of the face amount due.[21] After the panic, South Carolina and Louisiana took even more forceful action. In December 1873, South Carolina called in all of its outstanding bonds, exchanged them for new bonds bearing lower interest, at the rate of 50 cents on the dollar, and forbade the levying of any tax to pay for any of the older bonds; it thus reduced its state debt by half at one blow. In January 1874, Louisiana called in all its outstanding bonds and swapped them for new bonds at lower interest. It also amended the state constitution to authorize this action, to limit the state debt and total state taxes in the future, and to forbid deficit financing. And it repealed and forbade the collection of all taxes to pay for the older bonds. The next year, Louisiana sought to repudiate $14 million of its bonds, though in the end the courts validated all of them except for one issue of levee bonds from 1866 that suffered from a technical imperfection. In 1876, Louisiana flatly repudiated some of its railroad bonds.[22]

Louisiana's maneuvers succeeded in reducing its annual debt service from more than $1.3 million to about $800,000. But because South Carolina and Florida had ceased to pay interest in the early 1870s, the actual effect of their readjustments, as we have seen, was to divert 20 to 30 percent of their disbursements to debt service. And even in Louisiana, debt service was still some 26 percent of disbursements in 1875. For that reason, the white farmer-taxpayer probably allowed the Republicans little credit for their efforts. From the perspective of Republican legislators, the readjustment doubtless represented a conscientious effort to put their states' financial house in order. From the perspective of the white small farmer, however, it more likely seemed clear proof that the Republicans were beginning to tighten their belts in preparation for a long period of high expenditures to pay off the still outstanding state bonds. In all five of the lower South states controlled by the Republicans, the period after the panic saw the levying of sizable taxes to meet substantial—and in most cases, substantially increased—interest payments, and the general reduction of disbursements for state services. These steps portended at least a decade, and probably more, of austerity.

The Democrats easily answered any claims the Republicans could make for their debt reduction. The repudiation of certain bond issues had forced the Republicans to acknowledge Democratic charges of corruption and mismanagement. The readjustment implicitly conceded that the issuance of so many bonds had been profligate and ill-advised, just as the Democrats had argued. And as to the fact that the public debt and debt service had been reduced, the Democrats simply observed that if interest could be cut from $1.3 million to $800,000, it could be cut still further, that if the face amount of the debt could be halved at a blow, it could be halved again. In the end, therefore, the Republicans' efforts appear merely to have focused the voters' attention even more sharply on the debt question, without blunting it.

The Redeemers' position on the debt has not always been accurately portrayed. During the 1880s they often devoted a large percentage of the sharply reduced state expenditures to paying interest on the sharply reduced public debts. As a result, the Dunning school of historians tended to depict them as honorable statesmen sternly committed to discharging in full, and at great sacrifice, the legitimate portion of the states' obligations. But the usual campaign pledge of the Democrats had been to repudiate as much of the debt as possible, to reduce taxes to the lowest possible level; this was the same program with which their Jacksonian predecessors in many states had sought to meet the panic of 1837. Using highly dubious legal arguments, the Redeemers declared large segments of the outstanding bonds void. Only in South Carolina did a Redemption government permit the bondholders to test these decisions in court—and the South Carolina courts rejected most of the Redeemers' rationalizations out of hand.[23] Following the precedents set by the Republicans themselves, immediately after the panic, the Redeemers in several states also compelled the holders of the remaining bonds to exchange them for new ones at lower interest rates, by the simple expedient of repealing the taxes necessary to pay the interest on the older issues. The effect on the states' debt service was dramatic. In Louisiana, interest payments fell from $827,000 in 1877 to $174,000 in 1881. In Alabama, they fell from $540,000 in 1873 to $236,000 in 1878. Mississippi's interest payments fell from $287,000 in 1875 to $26,000 in 1878, and were eliminated altogether by 1881. South Carolina, under the compulsion of the state-court decision, became the single state in which debt service continued at an undiminished level.

The Redeemers also enacted substantial reductions in tax rates. In Alabama, the Democrats had captured the governorship and one house of the legislature in 1870, and almost their first action had been to reduce the tax rate from 7.5 mills to 5 mills. But when the Republicans returned to power in 1872, they promptly restored the 7.5 mill rate. After Redemption in 1874, the Democrats reduced the millage rate, to 6.5 mills by 1880, and in compliance with the provisions of the new constitution of 1875, also cut assessments almost in half. The average assessed value per acre fell from $4.11 in 1870 and $4.67 in 1872, to $2.85 in 1876 and $2.32 in 1879. In Mississippi, assessments fell almost as much, from a $4.38 average per acre in 1871 and $4.01 in 1875, to $2.72 in 1879. And the millage rate fell precipitously, from 12.5 mills in 1873 through various stages to 3 mills in 1880. In Florida taxes were reduced from 13 mills in 1874 to 8 mills in 1878 and 4 mills in 1884. In Louisiana the Republicans had themselves reduced taxes from their high point of 20.5 mills to 12.5 mills, but the Redeemers slashed the rates even further, to 6 mills after the ratification of the constitution of 1879. And even in South Carolina, saddled as it was with the necessity of paying its Reconstruction debt by its state courts, the Redeemers managed to reduce the tax rate from 12 mills in 1873 to 5 mills in 1880. This reduction was facilitated in several states by the Redeemers' efforts to diminish the Republicans' excessive reliance on the land tax for revenue. The addition of specific taxes, such as license fees for retailing liquor in Mississippi, produced a decline in the percentage of tax receipts derived from real estate. In Louisiana, for instance, real estate produced 77 percent of revenues, excluding the poll tax, in 1874, but 68.5 percent, with the same exclusion, in 1880. In Mississippi, the decline was quite significant, from 61 percent in 1872 to 51 percent in 1876 and only 33 percent in 1879.

The Redeemer governments of the late 1870s and the 1880s are firmly linked in historical literature—and for most states, deservedly so—with their extraordinarily parsimonious fiscal policies.[24] But the extent to which these policies are a product of the Redeemers' ideological commitments may be overstated. In considerable measure the Redeemers were kept from increasing expenditures by the political necessity of maintaining the ground that they had assumed in the crusade against the Republicans during Reconstruction. There were laissez-faire ideologues among the Redeemers, of course, inflexibly dedicated to Social Darwinist notions and hostile to any but the most minimal social services. But there also was a proto-Progressive element among them that persistently sought increased funding for educational and eleemosynary institutions. Most Redeemers occupied a middle ground between these extremes.

Because the Redeemers were divided in their attitudes toward governmental activity, the determining factor in the legislatures was very often the position of the Democratic Party's agrarian wing. In the years immediately after Reconstruction the agrarians, badly scarred by Republican policies, were outspoken advocates of the Redeemers' efforts to repudiate Republican bonds and to reduce tax rates to the lowest possible level. Indeed, they sometimes sought to go further in the process of repudiation than other Redeemers thought wise. But in the late 1880s, after the memory of Reconstruction had faded a bit, the interest of many citizens, including many white small farmers, in increased state services began to reassert itself. This development strengthened the hand of the proto-Progressives among the Redeemers. In the late 1880s and the 1890s, expenditures—and taxes—therefore edged upward again. The efforts of legislators to satisfy the demands of the Farmers Alliance and the Populists furthered this process. Although virtually the entire quarter of a century after 1875 is a period of comparatively low expenditures, the era of genuinely penurious disbursements thus spans no more than a decade. And the attitudes that produced that decade were a result of the political trauma of Reconstruction as much as they were a reflection of a consistent Redeemer ideology.

An interesting test case of this proposition is provided by the one lower South state that Reconstruction had not really wounded, Georgia. The Republicans managed to hold legislative power in Georgia only for a single two-year term. During their brief tenure they had, as in other states, authorized the endorsement of a large quantity of railroad bonds. When the Democrats regained control of the legislature in 1871, they suspended, and subsequently repudiated, most of these endorsements. But bonds had also been issued to fund state operations and to meet outstanding debts, by the Republicans and by the presidential Reconstruction legislature, and a considerable increase in the state debt was therefore unavoidable. Debt service accounted for a bit less than half of the state's total disbursements during the late 1870s and more than 60 percent of them in certain years. Moreover, Georgia, like South Carolina but unlike the other lower South states, continued to bear large interest payments throughout the nineteenth century. In the period between 1880 and 1900, Georgia's interest payments amounted, on the average, to more than $600,000 annually.

These events—the shrill controversy over the railroad bonds and the continued burden of a large debt service—allowed Georgians to believe that their Reconstruction experience had been quite similar to that of their neighboring states. In truth, however, in all areas except that of the public debt, Georgia's Reconstruction was unique. The Republicans did not substantially modify the state's antebellum tax law, with its self-assessment provisions. Georgia established machinery to compel assessment of property at market value only in 1874. And because the Republicans adopted no significant additional spending programs, they had no need to increase the state's millage rate. They passed a new public-schools act that, if they had remained in power, would eventually have cost a great deal of money. But before the law could go fully into operation, the Democrats recaptured the legislature and altered its provisions fundamentally.[25] Although the tax on slaves had accounted for 40 percent of the state's revenues at the end of the antebellum period, the loss of this tax was made up primarily, it appears, by taxes on urban property, not ones on farm property.[26] In short, the features characteristic of Republican tax and fiscal policies elsewhere simply did not appear during the brief period of Radical rule in Georgia.

The implications for the pattern of Georgia's fiscal history of the brevity and mildness of its Reconstruction are unmistakable. The state's receipts and disbursements in the years before the Civil War show the developments common to all of the lower South states. But their course after the war is sui generis. In the other states generally, the figures for the late 1860s and early 1870s reach extremely high levels, then plunge downward in the late 1870s and remain quite low through most of the 1880s. In Georgia, the figures remain relatively stable through the 1870s and actually show steady growth through the 1880s and 1890s. Redemption in most of the South had been preceded by years of fervid Democratic oratory attacking the Republicans' allegedly prodigal expenditures. The response of the electorate to these appeals had made parsimony a political necessity once the Democrats had gained power. But the ease of Redemption in Georgia meant that its Redeemers were not nearly so committed by their past to a niggardly attitude. Georgia's disbursements, measured in constant dollars per capita, remained well below those of any other lower South state in the early 1870s. In large measure for that reason, there was much less resistance to relatively rapid increases in the 1880s and 1890s. At a time when South Carolina, Alabama,

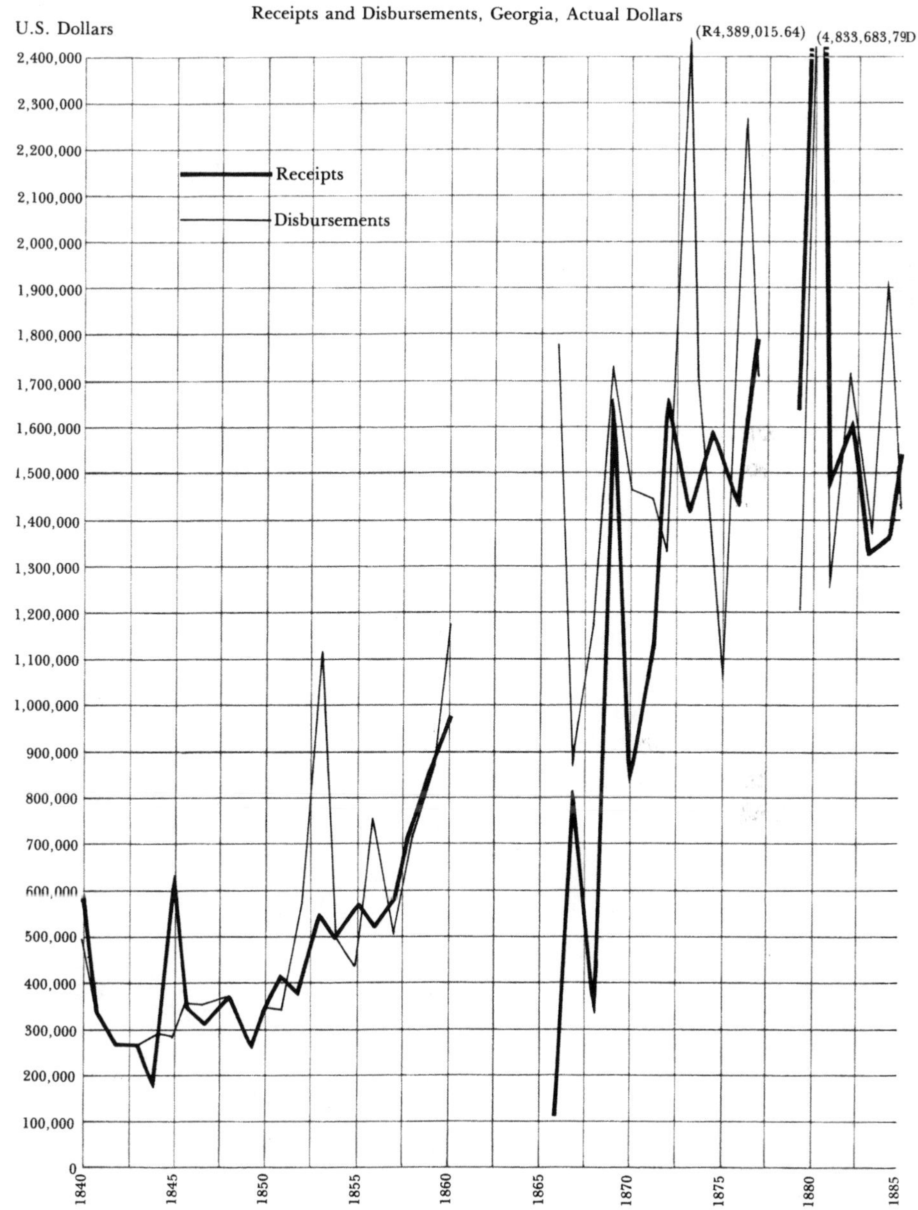

2.11. Receipts and Disbursements, Georgia, Actual Dollars

and Mississippi were still mired in penury, Georgia already showed clear signs of moving toward more liberal policies.[27] The extent of the scars left by Reconstruction, then, appears to have been an exceedingly significant element in defining what was politically possible under the Redeemers.

I do not claim to have proven the validity of the explanation for the course of Reconstruction that I have here advanced, although the evidence offered in this paper is, I trust, at least suggestive. In order to establish the case beyond cavil, the student would need to explore the particular politics of the individual Southern states to detail the precise manner in which fiscal issues were debated in each and to define the ways in which electoral constituencies responded to the various appeals. Such an enterprise is far beyond the scope of the present study. I have sought simply to draw attention to an aspect of the Reconstruction South that has heretofore attracted little attention, in the anticipation that I might move others to look into the matter further. It appears to me that Republican tax policy adversely affected the white small farmer, and that Republican disbursement policies afforded him benefits that may well have struck him as incommensurate with his sacrifices. That the white small farmer was increasingly reluctant to support the Republicans does not, therefore, seem to me too difficult to understand. To my mind, these observations offer a persuasive explanation for small farmers' behavior during Reconstruction alternative to the explanation founded merely on unvarnished racism. But, lacking the evidence that meticulous investigations of this component of Reconstruction political warfare would provide, I must for the present rely on the plausibility of my account. It is my hope that its plausibility will prove sufficient to elicit such investigations.

Notes

This article initially appeared in J. Morgan Kousser and James M. McPherson, eds., *Region, Race, and Reconstruction: Essays in Honor of C. Vann Woodward* (New York: Oxford University Press, 1982), 349–94, and is reprinted here by permission of Oxford University Press, USA.

1. C. Vann Woodward, *Tom Watson: Agrarian Rebel* (New York: Macmillan, 1938).

2. Among the studies that are more or less enamored of the explanation of racism are Alan Conway, *The Reconstruction of Georgia* (Minneapolis: University of Minnesota Press, 1966); James Haskins, *Pinckney Benton Stewart Pinchback* (New York: Macmillan, 1973); Lillian A. Pereyra, *James Lusk Alcorn: Persistent Whig* (Baton Rouge: Louisiana State University Press, 1966); Joe M. Richardson, *The Negro in the Reconstruction of Florida, 1865–1877* (Tallahassee: Florida State University Press,

1965); Loren Schweninger, *James T. Rapier and Reconstruction* (Chicago: University of Chicago Press, 1978); Jerrell H. Shofner, *Nor Is It Over Yet: Florida in the Era of Reconstruction, 1863–1877* (Gainesville: University Presses of Florida, 1974); Kenneth M. Stampp, *The Era of Reconstruction, 1865–1877* (New York: Knopf, 1965); Joe Gray Taylor, *Louisiana Reconstructed, 1863–1877* (Baton Rouge: Louisiana State University Press, 1974); Vernon Lane Wharton, *The Negro in Mississippi, 1865–1890* (Chapel Hill: University of North Carolina Press, 1947). In a well-known article, Michael Les Benedict states flatly that historians "now agree that racial rather than economic issues determined the course of Reconstruction" ("Southern Democrats in the Crisis of 1876–1877: A Reconsideration of *Reunion and Reaction*," *Journal of Southern History* 46, 1980: 491).

3. Woodward, *Tom Watson*; C. Vann Woodward, *Origins of the New South, 1877–1913* (Baton Rouge: Louisiana State University Press, 1951); C. Vann Woodward, *The Strange Career of Jim Crow* (New York: Oxford University Press, 1955).

4. The states with which I shall deal are Alabama, Florida, Georgia, Louisiana, Mississippi, and South Carolina. All figures in this study are taken from the annual reports of the state treasurers, auditors, and comptrollers, unless otherwise stated.

5. In the sixth state, Georgia, the briefness of Republican rule creates a special case. I shall discuss it at the conclusion of this paper.

6. Alabama, *House Journal*, Sess. of 1841–42, p. 93.

7. The taxation of capital stock was more effective before the adoption of the general property tax. Throughout most of the antebellum years, the tax on capital stock was levied against the corporation and was borne by the stockholders only indirectly. After the adoption of the ad valorem general property tax, the individual stockholder was expected to report his stock as part of his personal property, and the opportunity for evasion was thus greatly increased.

8. Gavin Wright, *The Political Economy of the Cotton South: Households, Markets, and Wealth in the Nineteenth Century* (New York: Norton, 1978), 35–36. On the question of the distribution of wealth in the antebellum South, however, the truth is still clouded; see ibid., 24–42, and the works there cited.

9. I should say that I do not use the term *progressive* in its proper technical sense here. That is, the tax rates did not increase as the value of the property increased. I merely mean to characterize the social effect of the tax structure.

10. J. Mills Thornton III, *Politics and Power in a Slave Society: Alabama, 1800–1860* (Baton Rouge: Louisiana State University Press, 1978).

11. The following discussion is based on an examination of the session laws of the six states.

12. My account of this subject, for instance, differs considerably from that offered in George Ruble Woolfolk, "Taxes and Slavery in the Ante-Bellum South," *Journal of Southern History* 26 (1960): 180–200.

13. In this connection, I might note that of the 490,601 potential white voters

in the six lower South states in 1870, almost 66 percent were old enough to have voted in 1860 and almost 42 percent were old enough to have voted in 1850.

14. Casting the figures in constant dollars would alter the pattern shown in the graphs, but graphs of constant dollars per capita would restore the pattern revealed by actual dollars, as I shall shortly demonstrate. In order to emphasize the pattern under discussion, I have excluded from the graphs the abnormal figures from the war years. But perhaps I should say a brief word about receipts and disbursements during the war. These years saw relatively little experimentation with the states' tax structures, except in Georgia, which adopted a state income tax. Expenditures, however, even adjusted for inflation, rose to levels that would not be equaled again in the nineteenth century. The principal cause for these enormous disbursements was a massive program of relief for soldiers and their families. Because expenditures rose sharply and taxes lagged behind, the disbursements were necessarily financed by the creation of extremely large public debts. Later in the century, Democratic politicians founded careers on passionate denunciations of the large state debts created by the Republicans during Reconstruction. It is therefore an irony of considerable proportions that if the Confederacy had succeeded in winning its independence and the Southern states had thus been compelled to pay the debts created during the war, Southern taxpayers would have incurred debt service far exceeding anything that Reconstruction produced.

15. *Preliminary Report of the Eighth Census*, p. 194 (table 35).

16. The Consumer Price Index (CPI) for the nineteenth century may be found in US Bureau of the Census, *Historical Statistics of the United States* (Washington, DC, 1975), Series E 135–166, pp. 210–11. I should perhaps say a word about my choice of the CPI as the index for deflating the state budgets. Because the commodity composition of the CPI is heavily weighted toward food and housing, whereas the Wholesale Price Index (WPI) gives more weight to, for instance, construction materials, it might be said that the CPI is the appropriate one for dealing with such components of state budgets as salaries, but that the WPI should be used for expenditures on construction and related activities. This point is without doubt technically correct. Similarly, it might be noted that because there were real differences between regional price levels in this period, a national index may not accurately reflect the Southern situation. Again, the objection is well taken. Finally, it might be said that the Implicit Price Deflator (IPD) would have been a better choice than either of the other two indices. Unfortunately, the IPD has never, so far as I know, been calculated for the first three-quarters of the nineteenth century. In any case, my answer to all three objections is that I believe that any broad index will serve the purpose of correcting for the major historical price swings. Therefore I do not believe that the CPI is misleading in the present instance. The WPI—and the IPD, for the years for which it is available—indicate essentially the same pattern as that

which the CPI produces. I have benefited greatly from discussing these questions with my former colleague, Professor Gavin Wright.

17. See, e.g., "Reply of the State Central Committee of the Union Republican Party of South Carolina to the Memorial of the Tax-Payers' Convention," in *South Carolina Reports and Resolutions of 1873*, pp. 983–90.

18. It is by no means self-evident that the mass of the white electorate would have desired state services. For the years before about 1850, I would regard that notion as an anachronism, a product of our own twentieth- and twenty-first-century assumptions about the proper role of government. But beginning in the middle of the nineteenth century, the old hostility to governmental activity began to erode in the South, and by the end of the century a belief in at least certain doctrines of the positive state—particularly that it ought to provide schools—had gained widespread acceptance. Reconstruction was thus a time of transition in respect to these ideas. For my present purposes, however, the problem is not a crucial one. Those whites who continued to hold Jacksonian attitudes would have been hostile to Republican tax policies, and those who wanted increased state services would have found Republican efforts inadequate.

19. The state paid for the education of 9,122 children in 1849 and 18,915 in 1860. The federal census reported that 40,373 children attended school in 1850, and 46,590 in 1860.

20. Vose v. Reed, 28 Fed. Cas. 1298; Vose v. Internal Improvement Fund, 28 Fed. Cas. 1286; Morton, Bliss and Co. v. Comptroller General, 4 S.C. 430.

21. *Acts of Florida*, Sess. of 1873, pp. 12–15; Cheney and Wife v. Jones, 14 Fla. 587. In 1876, the Florida Supreme Court declared that the bulk of the railroad endorsements had been unconstitutional (Holland v. State, 15 Fla. 455).

22. *South Carolina Statutes at Large*, vol. 15 (1871–75), pp. 518–23; *Acts of Louisiana*, Sess. of 1874, pp. 39–43, 94–95, Sess. of 1875, pp. 110–12, Sess. of 1876, pp. 130–31; State ex rel. Forstall v. Board of Liquidation, 27 La. 577.

23. Walker v. State, 12 S.C. 200.

24. See, e.g., Woodward, *Origins*, 58–66.

25. *Acts of Georgia*, Called Sess. of 1868, pp. 152–55; Sess. of 1869, pp. 159–61; Sess. of 1870, pp. 49–60, 506–7; 1st. Sess. of 1872, pp. 275–77, 279–83; 2nd Sess. of 1872, pp. 64–75; Sess. of 1874, pp. 108–9.

26. Statistics on the sources of taxation are not, unfortunately, available for Reconstruction proper. The statement in the text is based on a comparison of the sources of taxation in 1858 and in 1874. However, the tax laws in effect in 1874 are quite similar to those of Reconstruction.

27. Louisiana's expenditures at all times in the nineteenth century remained far above those of the other lower South states, reflecting the presence of a great city within its borders. But in comparative terms its disbursements in the 1880s were as

low as those elsewhere—no higher on a per capita basis, in fact, than they had been in the early antebellum period, and far below Reconstruction levels. In Florida, expenditures during the 1880s were sustained by a large source of nontax revenue, the proceeds from the sale of state-owned swamplands in the peninsula, which were first drained and brought into production during these years. I might note that as this nontax revenue declined in the 1890s, the growth of Florida's expenditures essentially ceased.

3
Alabama's Presidential Reconstruction Legislature

The South's Presidential Reconstruction state legislatures have not had a good press. Suspicious Radical Republicans at the time thought them dominated by the former slavocracy and secessionists. The Black Codes a number of them enacted seemed to Radicals—and not without good reason—to represent an effort to recreate slavery in another form. Modern scholars, beginning with W. E. B. Du Bois, have echoed these charges, and have joined the Radicals in regarding the legislatures' membership and actions as proof of the fecklessness and racism of President Andrew Johnson's postwar policies. Yet few of these scholars have subjected the legislatures to close scrutiny. An examination of the personnel and proceedings of Alabama's legislature, for instance, must cause one at least to question many of the Radicals' suspicions, and may even lead the student to doubt the wisdom of the Radicals' response to President Johnson's endeavors.[1]

I

Studies of Presidential Reconstruction have universally failed to note the marked decline in the wealth and social standing of the men elected to the initial postbellum legislatures. In Alabama, at any rate, nothing is more significant than this fact, however.

Until the final dozen years of the antebellum period, Alabama's legislators had generally been men of relatively modest means. I have elsewhere explored the changing socioeconomic composition of the legislature before the Civil War.[2] In 1830 the median legislative slaveholding was 9, and in 1840 it was 9.5. In 1830 half of the legislators were in the middle class of small slaveholders (owners of five to nineteen slaves), while planters (owners of twenty or more slaves) and members of the lower-middle and lower grouping (nonslaveholders and owners of one to four slaves) were each a fourth of the members. Large planters (owners of fifty or more slaves) were only 7 percent of the total. By 1840 the increased social polarization that came with the advent of two-party competition had eroded the middle

Table 3.3. Median legislative slaveholding

	Total	House	Senate	% Large Slaveholders
1829–31	9	8	12	7%
1839–41	9.5	8	19	10%
1849–50	12.5	11	16	18%
1859–60	17	14	19.5	23%
1865–67	8	7	13	13%

class's numbers from both above and below, so that planters, the middle class of small slaveholders, and the lower-middle and lower-class members were each a third of the legislators. The economic and geographical divisions within the state upon which the party system was built—focused as it was primarily on questions of banking and internal improvements—are apparent in the legislators' slaveholdings; throughout this period, the median slaveholding of Whig legislators was double that of Democrats. But large planters were still only 10 percent of the membership.

The rise of the Young America movement within the Democracy in the years after the Mexican-American War had a marked effect on the wealth of Alabama legislators in the 1850s. The exacerbation of sectional tensions in national politics that flowed from Young America's enthusiasm for territorial aggrandizement, and Young America's openness to internal improvements and economic modernization, showed themselves in an increasing representation of planters among Alabama's lawmakers in the final antebellum decade. By 1850 the median legislative slaveholding had risen to 12.5, and by 1860 it had reached 17. In 1850 the lower-middle and lower class and the middle class were again about a third of the legislators, as they had been in 1840. But the proportion of large planters advanced from 10 percent of the members to almost 18 percent. And by 1860, the lower-middle and lower grouping and the middle class had fallen in each case to about a fourth of the legislators, while planters were now half of the membership, and large planters a fourth of it.[3]

The devastation wrought by civil war effectively burst the bubble of increasing legislative wealth that had characterized the 1850s and returned the lawmakers to the humbler status they had occupied for most of the antebellum era, even if measured in antebellum terms. This development seems to have begun in the general election of 1863, when secessionists suffered a widespread electoral repudiation.[4] The median legislative slaveholding for the legislators chosen in November 1865 (derived from the Census of 1860)

Table 3.4. Economic groupings in the legislatures

	1829–31	1839–41	1849–50	1849–50
	% By Slaveholding	% By Slaveholding	% By Slaveholding	% By Real Estate
Lower Middle/Lower	25	34	35	21
Middle Class	50	34	29	34
Small Planters	18	22	18	28
Large Planters	7	10	18	18

	1859–60			1865–67		
	% By Slave-holding	% By Real Estate	% By Personal Property	% By Slave-holding	% By Real Estate	% By Personal Property
Lower Middle/Lower	31	22	30	41	34	43
Middle Class	25	28	21	31	36	27
Small Planters	21	21	24	15	16	15
Large Planters	23	29	25	13	13	15

fell from 17 to 8, even less than it had been in 1830. The median among representatives was 7 and among senators was 13. The lower-middle and lower grouping now formed some 40 percent of the legislators, and the middle class perhaps 30 percent. The percentage of members in the lower-middle and lower classes was their largest proportion of any legislature for which I have developed figures. The percentage of large planters, from 13 to 15 percent, depending on the data used, was a bit above the comparable figure from 1840, but was substantially less than proportions from the 1850s. In general, the legislators of Presidential Reconstruction were poorer than they had been since the early antebellum years.[5]

The legislature did still contain a significant number of wealthy members. The counties of the eastern Black Belt seem to have been especially unchastened. Montgomery representative Tristram B. Bethea had held over 221 slaves, and his colleague, Henry M. Caffey, had owned eighty-nine.

Senator Americus C. Mitchell of Barbour had owned 220 slaves. Macon County representative John C. Judkins had owned eighty-four slaves, and senator James W. Castens of Russell had owned eighty-three. Representative Gardner H. Davis of Barbour had owned fifty-three slaves, and representative Nathan L. Brooks of Lowndes had owned fifty-four. In the western Black Belt, Wilcox County also returned a wealthy delegation; senator Aaron B. Cooper had owned ninety-one slaves, and representative J. Richard Hawthorn had owned 110. Two of Perry County's representatives had owned thirty slaves and the third had owned thirty-six. But other counties in the area showed new doubts about planter leadership. Dallas County elected two Selma physicians, Drs. Albert G. Mabry and James T. Reese, each of whom had owned four slaves—although when Dr. Reese resigned, voters selected a young attorney, William Craig, whose father had owned ninety slaves.[6] Greene County, a center of the state's plantation agriculture, returned Senator Caswell C. Huckabee, a farmer who had owned eleven slaves, though his two colleagues in the House were both from large slaveholding families. The plantation counties of the Tennessee Valley, where the war had been particularly destructive, showed similar ambivalence. One of Limestone's representatives, attorney William Richardson, had owned thirty slaves, but the other, Charles W. Raisler, was a cabinetmaker who had owned only one. Morgan County was represented in the Senate by Dr. James M. Jackson, a physician who had owned fourteen slaves, and in the House by Zenas F. Freeman, a nonslaveholding schoolteacher who was born in New York. Franklin County's senator was future governor Robert B. Lindsay, an attorney born in Scotland—the legislature's only foreign-born member—who had owned fourteen slaves; its representatives were young attorney F. LeBaron Goodwin, who owned no slaves, and farmer Thomas Thorn, who had owned eleven. Madison County was represented in the Senate by farmer John N. Drake, who had owned eighteen slaves, and in the House by planter William D. Humphrey, who had owned forty-four slaves, and Huntsville merchant J. W. Ledbetter, who had owned three.

The bulk of the legislature's poorer members came from the hill country and the Wiregrass. Henry R. McCoy of Tallapoosa had been an archetypal yeoman farmer; a nonslaveholder, he had owned real estate valued at $425 and personal property worth $250. It was very likely the events of the war that elevated McCoy to the legislature; he had become a major in the Confederate Army. But other members of the yeomanry had no such claims: Henry McBee of Calhoun, Winston Steadham of Marion, Joseph D. McCann of Talladega, Henry F. Smith of Jackson, and W. C. Menefee of Pike had all been nonslaveholding farmers with property values comparable to McCoy's. All of the delegation from Randolph County, where resistance to the war had been strong, were nonslaveholders. Dr. Middleton R. Bell, who represented it in the Senate, was a physician and a close associate of Wedowee attorney William H. Smith, who in 1868 would become Alabama's first Radical governor; Dr. Bell too became a Republican. Randolph's three House members were a store clerk, a schoolteacher, and a farmer, all of them with very modest property holdings. The representative from Winston County, where resistance to the war had been even more intense, was also a nonslaveholder, carpenter John Wilhite, who also would become a Republican. Two other future Republicans were Elba physician Dr. John G. Moore and Rockford minister the Reverend James Vansandt, both of whom were also nonslaveholders. George P. Plowman, who would become the leader of Talladega County's Republicans and the county's probate judge, had been the operator of a leather tannery and the owner of eight slaves. Fayette County's delegation consisted of Senator Elliott P. Jones, a lawyer and farmer who owned three slaves, and a merchant and two farmers in the House, the merchant a nonslaveholder and the farmers the owners, respectively, of one and two. Cherokee County's delegation was typical of the Appalachian counties. Senator Augustin L. Woodliff was a farmer who had owned two slaves. Thomas B. Cooper, an attorney who had owned ten slaves, became Speaker of the House. His colleagues were farmer John Lawrence, who had owned fourteen slaves, farmer John W. Brandon, a nonslaveholder, and Methodist minister John Potter (grandfather of the distinguished historian David M. Potter), who had owned two. Blount County, similarly, was represented in the Senate by William H. Edwards, a schoolteacher who had owned no slaves, no real estate, and only $500 in personal property, and in the House by attorney A. M. Gibson and young schoolteacher Solomon Palmer Jr.—a future state superintendent of education—both of whom were also nonslaveholders. The legislature was, in short, more fully representative of the general white population of the state in economic terms than any had been in perhaps two decades.

Another instructive insight into the effect of war and defeat on the electorate is the legislators' occupations. In the early antebellum decades, attorneys had been no more than 12 to 16 percent of the legislators, as against 70 percent or more who were engaged in agriculture. But by the 1850s this balance had changed. In the final antebellum years, farmers fell to some 57 to 59 percent of the legislators and lawyers rose to 26 or 27 percent of them. This tendency reached its highpoint in the Secession Convention, when only 43 percent of the delegates were in agriculture and 37 percent were attorneys. And this rise in the proportion of lawyers had a most baleful effect: opponents of immediate secession were a majority among delegates who were farmers and also among delegates who were neither farmers nor attorneys; lawyer delegates favored immediate secession by two to one.[7] This differential reflected the extensive tendency of ambitious young attorneys to associate themselves with the increasingly influential faction within the Democratic Party led by William Lowndes Yancey, unquestionably in part in an effort to further their careers.

It was a disposition that did not escape public notice. The same resentment that led to a decline in the wealth of the legislators chosen in November 1865 led also to new suspicions of attorneys. Although lawyers continued to be almost 29 percent of the Senate, they fell to only about 15 percent of the House, returning to a proportion comparable to that usual before the 1850s. However, doubts about planter influence kept legislators engaged in agriculture to only about half of the members in each house, far below their early antebellum proportion. The result, especially among the representatives, was a sharp increase in the diversity of the occupations to be found among the members. Physicians were 8 percent of the House and 14 percent of the Senate. Ministers were another 8 percent of the House, and merchants and related occupations were 9 percent of it. Despite the continued power of the bar in the Senate, its influence in the lower house was less than it had been for many years, and the diversity of occupations represented there was greater than at any previous time in the state's history.

One final aspect of the legislature's membership is also significant. Essentially all of the members were Southerners. Only five representatives and three senators had been born in nonslaveholding states. Georgians and native Alabamians together constituted a majority of each house, and the addition of the Carolinas and Tennessee accounted for more than 80 percent of the legislators in each body. Thus virtually all of the members had grown up amid slavery and had known no other world. This fact is an essential point to remember as we turn to the legislature's struggles to adjust to emancipation, which had come to Alabama just seven months before the members' election.

II

The Constitutional Convention that had met in September had formally abolished slavery in Alabama. But ironically, it was this fact that formed the principal argument against the ratification of the proposed Thirteenth Amendment once the new legislature convened in November. As Senator John N. Drake of Huntsville, who led the Senate opponents of ratification, told the upper house, because slavery had already been abolished in the South by the various state constitutional conventions, abolition could not have been the real goal of Congress in proposing the amendment. The actual intention of the congressional sponsors of the amendment, he argued, was to gain for the Congress, through the amendment's enforcement clause, the power to enact federal legislation governing the status of the freedmen. The result would be to "establish the black race on a firmer and broader basis than will be allowed to the white race."[8] To deal with this objection, the House amended the ratification resolution by adding a reservation specifying that in ratifying, the legislature did not intend to confer on Congress the power to legislate upon the political status of the former slaves. With this proviso, the ratification resolution passed the House 75–17 and the Senate 23–5. Alabama completed its ratification on December 9, and North Carolina and Georgia followed later that same week, bringing the number of states ratifying to three-fourths, and thus making the amendment a part of the Constitution.[9]

The fifteen representatives who voted against the addition of the reservation to the ratification resolution and the legislators who voted against ratification despite the reservation permit insight into the two extremes on the question of emancipation. The fifteen who preferred an unqualified ratification were generally poorer members from north Alabama. Twelve were from the hill counties and only three from plantation areas. No large planters and only two small planters were in the group; seven of them had been nonslaveholders. Three were among the nine representatives who would become Republicans. Four were so opposed to the reservation that they proceeded to vote against the ratification resolution itself once the reservation had been added to it. Excluding these four produces a group of eighteen legislators (thirteen representatives and five senators) intransigent in their opposition to emancipation. This group was substantially more diverse than the opponents of the reservation. Seven of the eighteen were from plantation counties and eleven were not. Six had been planters, four of them large planters, but four had been nonslaveholders and an additional six had owned fewer than ten slaves. The group included future US Senator John H. Bankhead of Marion—only twenty-three and just out of the Confederate Army—and Greensboro attorney John G. Pierce, both of them from large slaveholding families. But it also included Dr. John G. Moore of Coffee, a future Republican, and Stockton merchant George W. Robinson, a nonslaveholding native of New York, who represented Baldwin. The group was small, but the considerable diversity of those utterly unwilling to accept the outcome of the Civil War constitutes an index to the surprises that the roll calls will hold as the legislature turned to consider the condition of the freedmen.

Although the opponents of the Thirteenth Amendment had worried that it might transfer authority over the freedmen to the federal government, it is clear that the members of the legislature regarded the status of the freedmen as a concern principally for the former planters in their body. The adjustment of the former slaves to free labor was a matter of desperate anxiety for large landowners, as it was for the freedmen themselves, of course. But for most of Alabama's whites, the war had left far more pressing matters in its wake. Substantial numbers were living on the food parcels given out by the US Army; even in late 1866, some 21,700 Alabamians—perhaps 10 percent of the state's families—were receiving federal relief supplies each month, with whites outnumbering blacks among them by two to one.[10] All of the state's banks had suspended specie payments, and only two had any prospect of resuming; their banknotes in circulation were nearly worthless, as a result.[11] Debtors were in dire straits, with virtually no way to meet their obligations; creditors consequently were in almost equally difficult circumstances. The state government had very little income, and its institutions were struggling to function; the schools had ceased to do so at all. Railroads lacked the credit to rebuild their tracks and turned to the state for endorsement of their corporate bonds. The legislature had before it proposals to try to meet each of these predicaments—a stay law to delay suits for debt; internal improvement schemes; bills to authorize specie suspension and to punish suspended banks; various suggestions for attempting to operate the schools, or closing them; ideas for how to recreate the state's revenue system, now that the principal source of antebellum taxes, the slaves, had been eliminated; radical proposals for retrenchment; and a proposal to issue state bonds to relieve the widespread destitution among the citizenry. All of these questions produced deep divisions among the legislators, and all of them seemed much more urgent to most poorer white Alabamians than did the labor system on the plantations. As a result, in the early months of the new legislature's first session, the freedmen seem to have been the focus of attention chiefly of better-to-do members.

The committees on the freedmen established in each house reflected this situation. The chairman of the House committee was the wealthy Montgomery planter Tristram B. Bethea, whose 221 slaves had made him the legislature's single largest slaveholder. Five of the committee's twelve members were substantial slaveholders, and seven were from plantation counties. Similarly, the chairman of the Senate committee was Aaron B. Cooper of Wilcox, who had owned ninety-one slaves. Five of its nine members had been extensive planters. Most of the bills reported from these committees—a ferocious bill to compel the freedmen to enter into labor contracts; a bill declaring any stubborn or refractory servant or any laborer who loitered away his time or refused to comply with a labor contract without just cause a vagrant, subject to being hired out to work on the county chain gang; an equally severe bill regulating black apprentices; a bill extending to every freedman all the highly discriminatory provisions of antebellum criminal law applying to free Negroes—passed with little discussion, by voice vote. The one bill that generated conflict—the one with general implications for poorer whites—opened the courts to freedmen on the same basis as all citizens and permitted black testimony in cases in which a freedman was a party.

Early efforts to get the legislators to take the rights of freedmen seriously were not hopeful. Senator Francis W. Sykes of Lawrence, though he had owned forty-seven slaves in 1860, was one of the legislature's most racially liberal members and would become a founder of the state's Republican Party. At the outset of the session he had introduced a bill to repeal all existing laws making a distinction of color. Senator Martin L. Stansel of Pickens, a Carrollton attorney, in an effort to convey his contempt for this proposal, moved to amend it to say "except the distinction which has existed since the days of Japhet and the curse of Ham." In the face of such scorn, Senator Sykes's bill was tabled, 16–11. Three of the eleven who opposed tabling were future Republicans, while none of the sixteen for tabling was.[12]

Although the chances initially looked bleak for an enlightened racial policy, then, the outcome would be very different. The reversal turned upon the intervention of Governor Robert M. Patton. Patton, a Florence merchant and planter, had strongly opposed secession, but he had owned 117 slaves in 1860, and he was certainly not moved by any sense of racial egalitarianism. In his inaugural address, he told Alabamians that "it must be understood that, politically and socially, ours is a white man's government. In the future, as has been the case in the past, the state affairs of Alabama must be guided and controlled by the superior intelligence of the white man." And in his annual message in November 1866, he had emphasized that the freedmen "should be especially taught the utter absurdity of expecting or aspiring to a condition of social equality with the white race. To do so would be to struggle against a palpable and inexorable decree of Providence."[13] Nevertheless, Patton was deeply committed to paternalist ideals. "We have a high moral duty to perform toward the freedmen," he said in the same annual message. "Let them be convinced that we are their friends and that we feel an interest in their prosperity and welfare. They should be assured of our firm purpose to give them all of their legal rights." And in his initial annual message he had lectured the legislators, "Surely no good, law-abiding citizen will desire laws for the government of the unintelligent negro which he himself is unwilling to abide by. No good to the country can result from having one code of laws for the whites and another for the blacks in their new relations, so far as concern the rights of persons and property."[14]

Against this background Governor Patton approached the mass of legislation regulating the former slaves that had passed the legislature with so little dissent. Patton was inaugurated on December 13, and two days later the legislature adjourned for its Christmas recess, leaving the bills on the new governor's desk. When the lawmakers returned just after the new year, Patton greeted them with a flurry of veto messages. The bill governing black apprentices was class legislation, he told the House; the general provisions of the code on apprenticeships were ample regulation for all persons of both races. No legislation governing the labor contracts of the freedmen was necessary, he said to the Senate; the state already had general laws governing contracts, and the freedmen should be able to look to the courts to protect their natural rights without any discriminating statutes. And the bill extending the antebellum laws governing free Negroes to the freedmen would create absurd or inoperable results; one of them, for instance, would require almost all freedmen to leave the state.[15]

The gubernatorial objections had an electric effect. The bills that had passed with essentially no dissent now suddenly provoked the deep divisions that questions surrounding banking, internal improvements, and social reform always had. The House sustained the governor's veto of the black apprenticeships bill, 42–51. Of the fifty-one voting to sustain the veto, twenty-three had been nonslaveholders and an additional fifteen had owned fewer than ten slaves. Just five had been planters. Eight came from plantation counties, while forty-three were from nonplantation counties. Of the forty-two voting to override the veto, fifteen had been planters. Only seven had been nonslaveholders, and an additional thirteen had owned fewer than ten slaves. Twenty-two came from plantation counties and twenty from nonplantation counties. The economic and geographical divisions in the voting thus are clear. In addition, eight of those voting to sustain the veto would become Republicans, while none of those voting to override would. The Senate sustained the governor's veto of the bill to compel freedmen to enter into and abide by labor contracts, 15–18. Here the divisions of wealth were less clear; six former planters voted to override the veto, and six to sustain it. But of the eighteen voting to sustain the veto, thirteen were from north Alabama and only five from south Alabama; while of the fifteen voting to override the veto, nine were from south Alabama and six from north Alabama. Only one senator—John Drake of Madison, who had led the fight against the Thirteenth Amendment—voted to override the veto of the bill extending antebellum laws governing free Negroes to all freedmen.[16]

Throughout the antebellum era, legislators from the small farm counties had been on their guard against the impositions the plantation sections threatened. Certain questions, such as taxation, had always aroused these conflicts. In the session of 1865–66, as legislators searched for some revenue source to replace the tax on slaves and thus to allow the real property tax to remain low, planter-legislators had hit upon the scheme of placing a high tax on the stills that throughout the hills turned the corn crop into liquor. The Revenue Act of 1866 placed a property tax on every still of two dollars for every gallon of its capacity and in addition a production tax of 50 cents for every gallon distilled. Representative James Williams from the Appalachian county of Jackson railed at this levy. Planters, he said, "have shaped the legislation of this session," and were half the membership of the Ways and Means Committee (an accurate allegation). Rather than tax the "great staple commodity, cotton," they had "shifted the burdens on other men's shoulders—on my constituents, and on North Alabama generally, by imposing an onerous capitation tax and by taxing their little distilleries. . . . If the poor pay the tax, fight the battles, hew the wood and draw the water, certain it is, a poor man in Alabama is not to be envied now." As Williams predicted, the tax on distilling created an uproar across the hills and the Wiregrass, and when the legislature reconvened the following fall, at the urging of Governor Patton, it repealed the Revenue Act altogether and substituted a new one, eliminating the property tax on stills completely and reducing the production tax from 50 cents a gallon to 5 cents.[17]

Struggles such as this one had formed Alabama's antebellum political culture, and the electorate fully understood their implications of culture and class. But these beliefs had not heretofore been extended across the barrier of race. In the days of slavery, black people, as property, were an element of wealth, to be envied or resented, perhaps, but merely a symbol in conflicts over political equality. And the persistence of such attitudes is apparent in the feeling widespread among less well-to-do legislators early in the session, as we have said, that the regulation of plantation labor was a concern of planters, but essentially irrelevant to the rest of the electorate. Governor Patton in his veto messages, however, had placed the matter in a different light. He had called the bills class legislation, because there were already general laws governing apprenticeships and contracts, and these bills sought to carve out a portion of the citizenry, at least as newly defined, to whom different, and harsher, regulations would apply. This was a logic that reached back to Jacksonian denunciations of special privileges for chartered corporations, and legislators from the small farming areas immediately grasped the threat. Planters who sought disparate regulations for their labor force were only too ready to seek disparate tax burdens, for instance, as their actions as to the revenue bill clearly showed. Suddenly the racial legislation became a matter of general concern.

An additional element at work perhaps was the number of novice lawmakers in the legislature. The substantial electoral repudiation of legislators from the 1850s and early 1860s had necessarily brought into the body many men who were new to it. Some 45 percent of the senators and 73 percent of the representatives had never served in the legislature before. Many of these men had understandably tended to be deferential to more experienced leaders early in the session. But the power of gubernatorial authority probably allowed some of them now to assume a more independent stance.

The one piece of legislation regulating the freedmen that Governor Patton had signed into law was the vagrancy bill, declaring all stubborn or refractory servants vagrants, subject to the county chain gang. But even this act was not long for the statute books. Later in the session the legislature passed a new state penal code, drafted by former and future state Supreme Court justice George W. Stone. The new penal code contained its own, nonracial vagrancy provisions, and it provided that all laws in conflict with it were repealed. The courts generally held therefore that the provisions of the new code had superseded the vagrancy statute, and to clarify the situation, the legislature at its second session formally repealed the vagrancy law.[18] The only piece of legislation then left with restrictions on the freedmen was the law opening the courts to them and permitting them to testify if a black person were a party to the case. But this act, which passed only after a considerable struggle and no less than two conference committees, had actually represented a victory by more progressive members over more racially conservative ones. Future Republicans had supported it overwhelmingly through all of its versions, against determined planter opposition; eleven of the twenty-eight representatives who voted against the bill on final passage were planters, and every future Republican voting favored it.[19] Governor Patton regarded the bill as such a success that he urged the legislature at its second session to eliminate all restrictions on black testimony, though the lawmakers were unwilling to reopen the question.[20] The legislature enacted one other statute with clear implications for the freedmen, a law making it a misdemeanor punishable by a fine up to $500 for one employer to lure away a worker under contract to another employer. But, though this act certainly limited the ability of freedmen to seek better pay, its criminal penalties were only directed at whites.[21]

The essential defeat of the Black Code in Alabama is too seldom emphasized. And the failure to emphasize it is especially regrettable because the circumstances that produced the defeat also formed the background to the rejection of the Fourteenth Amendment at the legislature's second session. Let us now turn to that half of the story.

As the first session of the legislature was coming to an end in February 1866, a joint committee cochaired by future Republican attorney general Joshua Morse of Choctaw submitted an angry report denouncing "the falsehoods propagated in the North and in Congress" about Southern racial conditions, which it said were "circulated only for the basest political purposes." It then submitted, and the legislature adopted unanimously, resolutions opposing the proposed Fourteenth Amendment; "Alabama will not voluntarily consent to change the adjustment of political power as fixed in the Constitution of the United States, and to constrain her to do so in her present prostrate and helpless condition, with no voice in the councils of the nation, would be an unjustifiable breach of faith."[22] By the time the legislature reconvened for its second session the following November, the Fourteenth Amendment had been formally submitted to the states for ratification. In his annual message, Governor Patton condemned it. Its provisions would vastly increase the power of the federal courts and submit state court decisions to the review of federal judges, he told the legislators, quite correctly. And unless the Southern states agreed to enfranchise the freedmen, they would lose half their representatives in Congress. For those and other reasons, Patton urged the legislature to refuse to ratify it.[23]

Two different lines of response to the amendment quickly emerged. In the Senate the racially liberal Lawrence County planter and physician Francis W. Sykes, seeking to save the amendment from Governor Patton's assault, proposed resolutions submitting the amendment to a popular referendum. A committee headed by future governor Robert B. Lindsay reported adversely to the resolutions, and they were tabled, 21–9. Three of the nine opponents of tabling filed a statement saying they had voted no merely to allow Senator Sykes to speak in support of his resolutions, but were opposed to them. Of the remaining six, four were among the five members of the Senate who would become Republicans.[24]

Early in December, just before the legislature was to take its Christmas recess, Governor Patton sent both houses a special message saying that it had now become apparent that the Congress considered ratification of the amendment a prerequisite to readmission of the Southern states to the union. Under these circumstances, Patton suggested that the legislature might ratify to regain membership in Congress, and then hope that the state's readmitted members could mitigate the amendment's effects in the future. In response the Senate formally voted to reject the amendment, 28–3, with only the three future Republicans, Middleton R. Bell, Adam C. Felder, and Francis W. Sykes, supporting ratification. Sykes once again sought a popular referendum on the amendment, but his proposal was tabled by voice vote.[25]

The Senate resolution refusing ratification then went to the House. The future Republican attorney general Joshua Morse took up Sykes's idea and proposed a popular referendum on the amendment. But the proposal was rejected, 49–24, and the resolutions refusing to ratify were then approved, 71–9. Only one of the nine supporters of ratification had been a significant slaveholder, Prattville attorney Charles S. G. Doster, who would become a Republican. Of the other eight, six had been nonslaveholders and the other two owners of ten and two slaves, respectively. The twenty-four representatives who had supported a popular referendum included only two owners of twenty or move slaves, Doster and Nathan L. Brooks of Lowndes, about whom we will have more to say shortly. Nine of the twenty-four had been nonslaveholders, and another nine had owned ten or fewer slaves. With these votes the idea of submitting the Fourteenth Amendment to a popular referendum died, as did any prospects for ratification.[26]

In the meantime, however, another line of response to Radical Republican demands was developing in the House. The leader of this effort was Nathan L. Brooks, a Lowndes County planter who had owned fifty-four slaves. Brooks's idea reached back to events at the state Constitutional Convention in September, 1865. Alabama's Constitution of 1819 had provided that membership in both houses of the state legislature would be apportioned among the counties on the basis solely of white population, and under this constitutional mandate the small farming counties had dominated the legislature throughout the antebellum period, to the great chagrin of the plantation counties. But with the emancipation of the slaves, delegates to the 1865 Constitutional Convention from the plantation counties had seen the prospect of changing this situation. Now that blacks were free, they argued, legislative representation should reflect their numbers. Plantation county delegates pushed hard for apportionment on the basis of total population. But the Constitutional Convention was itself apportioned on the white basis, and the Black Belt efforts had proven futile. The Constitution of 1865 repeated the apportionment provisions of the Constitution of 1819.[27]

The Fourteenth Amendment's section reducing the states' congressional representation by the proportion of their disfranchised male population offered Representative Brooks the chance to reopen this question, however. His initial proposal was to amend the state constitution to permit literate freedmen to vote. This change would have the immediate effect of blunting the reduction of congressional representation under the Fourteenth Amendment and in the longer term could provide the foundation for seeking increased legislative membership for the Black Belt counties. The House tabled this amendment, 72–16. Four of the sixteen filed statements saying that they had voted against tabling because they were so completely opposed to the amendment that they wanted to vote against it on the merits. Of the remaining twelve, six were from the Black Belt, all of whom had been large slaveholders, and five of the other six were from the hill counties, four nonslaveholders and two small slaveholders. Despite its overwhelming defeat, therefore, Brooks's proposal had begun to draw together the sort of coalition for which he clearly was aiming: Black Belters who sought greater legislative influence for their area and hill country progressives sympathetic to the ideas of the emerging Republican Party. Brooks and his allies therefore pressed on.[28]

Their next effort came after the legislature's return from its Christmas recess, when they pressed a proposal to submit to the voters the question of whether to call a new constitutional convention. A convention would allow the reconsideration of both the suffrage and the legislative apportionment provisions. The House tabled this resolution, 51–30.[29] Of the thirty members who supported Brooks's position, eleven were planters and fourteen were either nonslaveholders (four of them) or owners of ten or fewer slaves. Twelve came from plantation counties and eighteen from nonplantation counties. But in fact, Brooks's opponents represented the coalition that Brooks was attempting to build almost as well as his supporters did. Eight of the fifty-one members who voted to table were planters, seventeen were nonslaveholders, and eighteen more owned ten or fewer slaves. Nineteen were from plantation counties and thirty-two from nonplantation counties. It is clear that Brooks had failed to unify the plantation county representatives behind his strategy and especially had failed to draw many of the poorer members to his cause. Moreover, though three of the future Republicans in the House supported him, five voted with his opponents.

Brooks faced a twofold challenge. He had to convince the planters that they would be able to control a literate black vote in their counties, so that in gaining additional representation for their areas, they would not find themselves voted out of office. This evidently was Brooks's own belief, so that he could make this argument to his Black Belt challengers with sincerity. At the same time, however, quite probably in quieter conversations with representatives from the hill country and the Wiregrass, he had to make the case that enfranchised blacks would vote with poorer whites in defense of egalitarian policies and in opposition to planter hegemony. This for Brooks was a more disingenuous claim. But the fears many planters felt of the enmity of their former slaves was exceeded only by small farmers' general conviction that the planters would be able to manipulate the votes of their black dependents. Thus Brooks was placed in the position of having to advance to the different constituencies precisely contradictory predictions of blacks' possible behavior. Unless he could overcome both sets of white fears simultaneously, he had no hope of building the coalition he sought. And without such a coalition, he had no prospect of allaying the suspicions of the Radicals in Congress and forestalling their plans for draconian measures.

Brooks's third and final effort came at the end of the legislative session. By that time military reconstruction was pending in Congress, and Brooks clearly felt that the changed circumstances might lead enough legislators to reconsider their position that his ideas might now be accepted. And so in mid-February 1867, Brooks rose to seek a suspension of the rules to permit him again to propose a referendum on summoning a new state constitutional convention. He did do a bit better on this try, but the House again voted him down, 34–45.[30] The number of planters who supported Brooks's position fell from eleven to seven, while the number of nonslaveholders who voted with him rose from four to ten. Apparently the growing strength of Radical sentiment in the North had increased both planters' fears and at least some small farmers' confidence in the prospects for an independent black electorate. The support of nonplanter slaveholders remained about the same, fifteen on the earlier vote and seventeen on this one. Eleven of the thirty-four members supporting Brooks came from plantation counties and twenty-three from nonplantation counties. Only twelve of the thirty members who had voted with Brooks on the earlier roll call remained with him on this one. Eleven planters voted against Brooks now, along with fourteen nonslaveholders and an additional fourteen members who had owned ten or fewer slaves. Sixteen of his opponents came from plantation counties and twenty-nine from nonplantation counties. As on the earlier vote, three future Republicans supported Brooks and five opposed him. And so Brooks's last effort failed, and with it any prospect that the legislature might seek to accommodate Radical demands.

III

It is surely an irony of the darkest hue that the same social attitudes that had produced the legislature's rejection of a Black Code produced also its inability to compromise with the Radicals' suspicions. But that is the case. When Governor Patton warned that acts imposing disparate regulations on the freedmen constituted class legislation, poorer legislators joined overwhelmingly to sustain his vetoes. They fully understood the danger of creating special exceptions to general provisions of law to benefit the planters or other wealthy elements. It had been the central emphasis of Jacksonian politics, and the consequences of excessive planter influence had been starkly accentuated by the death and destruction of the war, which had produced the extensive repudiation of late antebellum leadership in the election of this very legislature. On the other hand, the dread of planter domination was equally at work in the prospect of eliminating the white basis for legislative apportionment and the resultant transfer of seats from the hill country and the Wiregrass to the Black Belt. Even an independent black electorate would have interests substantially different from those of white small farmers. But it was not independence that most hill country legislators actually expected; they foresaw—and the history of Alabama in the latter decades of the nineteenth century fully substantiated their fears—a black vote subject to planter manipulation, whether through economic pressures or physical force. The hostility to planter power underlay both small farmer legislators' rejection of the Fourteenth Amendment, with its provisions intended to push the Southern states into enfranchising the freedmen, and the repudiation of the possibility of such an enfranchisement itself, in the form of Nathan Brooks's efforts to summon a new constitutional convention or to amend the constitution to authorize it.

There can be no doubt that the Radicals in Congress had no real understanding of the subtleties of social conflict in the lower South. A great many of them were afflicted with a romantic faith in democracy that led them to believe that black enfranchisement would solve the region's problems at a single stroke. Virtually none of them appreciated that the addition of blacks to the electorate would represent for a state like Alabama a massive sectional shift in legislative and political influence from the small farming to the plantation counties. Indeed, almost all Radicals thought that planters controlled Southern politics already, and understood themselves to be attacking, rather than threatening to strengthen, planter influence. But legislators from Alabama's hills and Wiregrass were under no such illusions. We can certainly imagine measures that might have established an independent black electorate. But that would have required a permanent occupying army sufficient to protect black voters from reprisals, and an implacable refusal of amnesty for the planters' leadership. The number of Northerners prepared to maintain such measures on a long-term basis was vanishingly small. And given that the number of Southern whites who accepted the legitimacy of independent black electoral participation was almost equally minuscule, it was by no means unreasonable for small farmer legislators to regard the enfranchisement of the freedmen as a step toward planter rule of the state.

It is impossible today not to sympathize with those greathearted Americans who sought full citizenship for the freedmen. But however noble their goals, they reckoned without the force of history. A society that had assumed the naturalness of slavery for more than two centuries and that had experienced black freedom for only a matter of months could hardly have been expected to grasp the full possibilities of emancipation. And it is surely that chasm of white incredulity that, more than any other single factor, condemned radical Reconstruction to failure. The widespread violence and fraud that suppressed the black vote during radical Reconstruction itself and the electoral machinations of the Redeemers thereafter reflected the general white conviction that blacks were not—and were incapable of becoming—authentic partners in democratic decision making. Theirs was, as they said repeatedly, a white man's government.

Nevertheless, the voting in the Presidential Reconstruction legislature emphasizes another, equally significant truth. Although the legislators from the small farming counties were certainly not open to any recognizable notions of racial equality, their strong sense of class conflict and the threat their planter rivals posed could bring them to positions that had positive racial implications. This outcome was an especially important element of the Populist revolt.[31] But as the defeat of the Black Code demonstrated, this potential had been present from the beginning. Its sources stretch back to the battles of the Jacksonian era. The emergence of the one-party system after Reconstruction deprived it, except for the brief period of Populism, of the institutional structure that could otherwise have given it full scope for its expression. But it had always been there. A recognition of this fact is essential to a complete understanding of the patterns of Southern history.

Notes

This article appeared originally in Gary W. Gallagher and Rachel A. Shelden, eds., *A Political Nation: New Directions in Mid-Nineteenth-Century American Political History* (Charlottesville: University of Virginia Press, 2012), 167–87.

1. By far the most careful examination of the Southern state governments under Presidential Reconstruction is Dan T. Carter, *When the War Was Over: The Failure of Self-Reconstruction in the South, 1865–1867* (Baton Rouge: Louisiana State University Press, 1985). Also very useful is Michael Perman, *Reunion without Compromise: The South and Reconstruction, 1865–1868* (Cambridge: Cambridge University Press, 1973). On the period in general, the standard work is Eric Foner, *Reconstruction: America's Unfinished Revolution, 1863–1877* (New York: Harper and Row, 1988); see also W. E. B. Du Bois, *Black Reconstruction* (New York: Russel and Russel, 1935). On President Johnson, see Eric McKitrick, *Andrew Johnson and Reconstruction* (Chicago: University of Chicago Press, 1960); and LaWanda Cox and John H.

Cox, *Politics, Principle, and Prejudice, 1865–1866: Dilemma of Reconstruction America* (New York: Free Press of Glencoe, 1963). On the Black Codes, see Theodore B. Wilson, *The Black Codes of the South* (University: University of Alabama Press, 1965). On Alabama, see Sarah Woolfolk Wiggins, *The Scalawag in Alabama Politics, 1865–1881* (University: University of Alabama Press, 1977); Peter Kolchin, *First Freedom: The Response of Alabama's Blacks to Emancipation and Reconstruction* (Westport, CT: Greenwood Press, 1972); and Michael W. Fitzgerald, *Urban Emancipation: Popular Politics in Reconstruction Mobile, 1860–1890* (Baton Rouge: Louisiana State University Press, 2002).

2. See my *Politics and Power in a Slave Society: Alabama, 1800–1860* (Baton Rouge: Louisiana State University Press, 1978), 60–68, 296–99. The determination of class status is of course a very tricky business, and especially so before the census of 1850, when slaveholding is the only indication we have of an individual's wealth. In the work cited, I adopted the approximate relationships between class and slaveholding suggested by Ulrich B. Phillips in his *Life and Labor in the Old South* (Boston: Little, Brown, 1963; orig. pub. 1929), 339. Phillips calls twenty slaves "roughly a minimum for the plantation method" of agriculture. He ranks owners of five to nineteen slaves "as a middle class of large farmers and comfortable townsmen." Holders of four or fewer slaves, including the vast numbers of nonslaveholders, Phillips thus presumably places in a lower-middle and lower grouping. To these divisions I added a final boundary not suggested by Phillips, letting fifty slaves mark the division between small and large planters. With the census of 1850 we gain the value of the household head's real estate, and in 1860, both his real estate and his personal property. I formed scattergrams to relate legislators' slaveholdings with these figures and derived boundaries in dollars from them. In 1860, the upper limit for the poorest group was $3,000 in real estate and $10,000 in personal property; for the middling group, $10,000 in real estate and $27,500 in personal property; and for the small planters, $20,000 in real estate and $55,000 in personal property. I have carried all of these figures forward to the legislature elected in 1865. Of course all slaveholders were substantially poorer after emancipation, but my point here is how much poorer the legislators of 1865 were than those of 1859–60 even when judged by 1860 standards.

3. Thornton, *Politics and Power*, 61–64, 296–99.

4. Wiggins, *Scalawag in Alabama Politics*, 6–7.

5. President Johnson's policy had initially disfranchised persons who owned more than $20,000 in property, unless they received an individual pardon. But the president granted these pardons freely, and that the limitation barred very few former large slaveholders from political participation is demonstrated by the fact that so many of them were chosen to represent the plantation counties. It was not the presidential policy but the electorate that actually was responsible for the decline in legislative wealth.

6. In the case of young legislators who were residing with their parents at the time of the 1860 Census, I have used the property holdings of the head of the household in the summary statistics.

7. Thornton, *Politics and Power*, 64, 299, 426.

8. *SJ* 1865–66, pp. 83–84. The Congress had actually submitted the amendment to the states in February 1865, when the Civil War was still in bloody progress and slavery was intact in Confederate territory, so Senator Drake's argument was in fact anachronistic.

9. *HJ* 1865–66, pp. 85–88; *SJ* 1865–66, pp. 77, 79–80; *Acts of Alabama*, Sess. of 1865–66, pp. 597–98.

10. *HJ* 1866–67, pp. 26–27, 254–55.

11. *HJ* 1866–67, pp. 16–17.

12. *SJ* 1865–66, pp. 140–41.

13. *HJ* 1865–66, p. 159; *HJ* 1866–67, pp. 25–26.

14. *HJ* 1866–67, pp. 25–26; *HJ* 1865–66, p. 192.

15. *HJ* 1865–66, pp. 206–7; *SJ* 1865–66, pp. 162–64.

16. *HJ* 1865–66, pp. 236, 237; *SJ* 1865–66, pp. 188, 190. The initial recorded vote in the House was 40–51, but two additional members subsequently asked to be recorded as voting yea.

17. *HJ* 1865–66, pp. 424–25; *HJ* 1866–67, pp. 11–12; *Acts of Alabama*, Sess. of 1865–66, pp. 3–36, Sess. of 1866–67, pp. 259–96. On the general significance of tax policy in this period, see my "Fiscal Policy and the Failure of Radical Reconstruction in the Lower South," in *Region, Race, and Reconstruction: Essays in Honor of C. Vann Woodward*, ed. J. Morgan Kousser and James M. McPherson (New York: Oxford University Press, 1982), 349–94 (the preceding essay in this volume).

18. *Acts of Alabama*, Sess. of 1865–66, pp. 116, 119–24; Sess. of 1866–67, p. 504.

19. *HJ* 1865–66, pp.100–101, 106–7, 113, 116–17, 120, 127–28; *Acts of Alabama*, Sess. of 1865–66, p. 98.

20. *HJ* 1866–67, pp. 25–26; *Acts of Alabama*, Sess. of 1866–67, p. 435.

21. *Acts of Alabama*, Sess. of 1865–66, pp. 111–12.

22. *HJ* 1865–66, pp. 416–20; *Acts of Alabama*, Sess. of 1865–66, pp. 606–7.

23. *HJ* 1866–67, pp. 32–37.

24. *SJ* 1866–67, pp. 154–56. The four future Republicans were Dr. Sykes himself, Dr. Middleton R. Bell of Randolph, Montgomery attorney Adam C. Felder, and Dr. John T. Foster of Choctaw; three of the four were physicians. The one future Republican who consistently opposed the amendment was Tallapoosa farmer Alfred H. Slaughter, who shortly thereafter resigned from the legislature.

25. *SJ* 1866–67, pp. 176–77, 182–83.

26. *HJ* 1866–67, pp. 209–14.

27. Wiggins, *Scalawag in Alabama Politics*, 12–15. Professor Wiggins's account of these events, however, is marred by her apparent misunderstanding of the ante-

bellum constitutional provisions. See also Malcolm C. McMillan, *Constitutional Development in Alabama, 1798–1901: A Study in Politics, the Negro, and Sectionalism* (Chapel Hill: University of North Carolina Press, 1955), 90–109, esp. 104–5.

28. *HJ* 1866–67, pp. 160–62.

29. *HJ* 1866–67, pp. 395–96.

30. *HJ* 1866–67, pp. 476–77.

31. On this point see the work of C. Vann Woodward, especially *Tom Watson: Agrarian Rebel* (New York: Macmillan, 1938); *Origins of the New South, 1877–1913* (Baton Rouge: Louisiana State University Press, 1951); and *The Strange Career of Jim Crow* (New York: Oxford University Press, 1955).

4
Alabama Emancipation in the Courts

I

There could not have been much suspense about the action that Alabama's Constitutional Convention of 1865 would take on emancipation. Everyone who registered to vote in the August 31 election of the convention's delegates had been required to swear to "abide by and faithfully support all laws and proclamations which have been made during the existing rebellion with reference to the emancipation of slaves." And when the convention met on September 12, provisional governor Lewis E. Parsons came into the chamber, all the delegates rose and Parsons administered the same oath to all of them again.[1]

Moreover, the delegates overwhelmingly had been enemies of secession. In the election of the members of the Secession Convention in December 1860, only eighteen of the ninety-nine delegates had voted for the secessionist candidates. And in the presidential election the preceding month, just twenty-four of the ninety-nine had voted for John C. Breckinridge, though Breckinridge had received 54 percent of the state's vote; forty-five of the delegates had voted for John Bell and thirty for Stephen A. Douglas.[2]

On the other hand, the convention's members had been deeply involved with the institution of slavery. Just sixteen of the ninety-nine delegates had been nonslaveholders. Forty had been planters (owners of twenty or more slaves) and nineteen were large planters (owners of fifty or more slaves). Indeed, six of the delegates had owned more than one hundred slaves, including the convention's president, former governor and senator Benjamin Fitzpatrick of Autauga, who had held 118 slaves in 1860, and his almost equally prominent colleagues, former governor John A. Winston of Sumter, who had owned 112, and future governor Robert M. Patton of Lauderdale, who had owned 117. The majority of the delegates, however, had been smaller slaveholders. Fifty-nine of the ninety-nine were outside the planter class; twenty-nine had owned fewer than five slaves (including the sixteen nonslaveholders) and thirty had owned between five and nineteen. The median slaveholding among all the delegates was thirteen.[3] Given the delegates' extensive personal experience with slavery, it is hardly surprising that despite their oath, they approached emancipation with some ambivalence.

Convention President Fitzpatrick immediately appointed a committee on the restoration of Alabama to the Union, chaired by Circuit Judge William S. Mudd of Jefferson County, who was one of the twenty-one delegates who would become Republicans. The committee debated the question of emancipation for several days and issued majority and minority reports, revealing that the committee had been deeply divided over the legitimacy of the Emancipation Proclamation that the delegates had just sworn to "abide by and faithfully support." Judge Mudd for the majority proposed a resolution that attempted to finesse the question by acknowledging that "the institution of slavery had been destroyed in the state of Alabama," but without specifying how that destruction had happened. The resolution then went on, in a version of the words of the Thirteenth Amendment then pending for ratification before the states, to declare that "hereafter there shall be neither slavery nor involuntary servitude in the state, otherwise than for the punishment of crime whereof the party shall be duly convicted."

The minority report was offered by Alexander White of Talladega, a law partner and close friend of Provisional Governor Parsons. White, like Mudd, would become a leader of the state's Republican Party, and the Republicans would elect him to Congress in 1872. But now, in common with a great many attorneys, he remained convinced that the Emancipation Proclamation was in violation of the Fifth Amendment. For the committee's minority, he proposed a resolution that specifically attributed emancipation to the Proclamation and the acts of Congress flowing from it and pledged the state to obey them "unless and until the same shall have been declared invalid by the Supreme Court of the United States." White expected that the Supreme Court would eventually declare the Proclamation unconstitutional, and he did not want to write into the state constitution any provision that would then prevent Alabama from reestablishing slavery if it wished to do so.[4]

The question divided the convention just as it had the committee. The committee reported on September 16, and the convention voted to make its reports the special order for September 18. It then postponed consideration of the reports from day to day, each day from September 18 to September 22. During that time the delegates apparently argued the issue among themselves in private conversation. Finally, on September 22, the convention agreed to take the matter up. White made his case, in a speech filled with antebellum prejudice. "I wish to see the experiment of immediate emancipation tried," he assured the delegates, "and if it shall prove a failure, injurious to the North, ruinous to the South, and destructive to the negro race, I wish to keep open the only door by which we can escape such an accumulation of calamities." That it would prove a failure, however, White had no doubt.

> The man who was born a slave, and has arrived at years of maturity as a slave, cannot be made a freeman. . . . The negro's idea of freedom is exemption from labor, and being accustomed to compulsion to make him work, when that compulsion is withdrawn, he will not work. . . . Now, sir, contemplate the future of four millions of human beings, idle, improvident and thievish, suddenly thrown upon their own responsibilities and their own guidance, and tell me, if you can, the fate of that people? Misery and want and vice, degradation, prostitution, disease and death.

Eventually, "the calm, collected judgment of the Northern mind upon this great question, when it is enlightened by experience and can be guided by its teachings," would come to see "that it is the Anglo-Saxon who is suffering here, and that it is their own blood and race whom the radicals North would subordinate, or at least bring down to a level with the negro." At that point the majority of Northerners will accept reenslavement, or if not, "the political problem whether the negro and his confreres shall rule the United States will sharpen and intensify, until it will culminate in a war of races, and the extermination of the negro or the white man."

But this argument was overwhelmed by pragmatic considerations. As a practical matter, the freedmen could never now be reenslaved, proponents of the majority report maintained, and without a clear commitment to abolition, the Congress would certainly not permit Alabama's readmission to the Union. And as to the constitutionality of the Proclamation, they observed that emancipation had been in fact accomplished by military force, whatever might be the legal right involved. The minority report was rejected 79–17, and the majority report was the adopted.[5]

The identity of the seventeen delegates who voted for the minority report holds some surprises. Probably unsurprisingly, ten of the seventeen had been planters, a fourth of the planters in the convention. One might well expect that this group would have been especially reluctant to accept abolition. More portentously for the future of Reconstruction, four of the seventeen would become Republicans, or a fifth of the future Republicans in the convention. In addition to Alexander White himself, this group included future attorney general Joshua Morse of Choctaw, Dr. John G. Moore of Coffee, and Toliver Towles of Chambers. It is clear that for these men, as for a significant number of the state's native white Republicans, it was their commitment to unionism rather than their doubts about slavery that drew them to Republicanism.

And so, on September 22, 1865, slavery became unconstitutional in Alabama. But the delegates' acceptance of emancipation most certainly did not represent an acceptance of racial equality, or even of black citizenship. The state's antebellum Constitution of 1819 had proudly proclaimed "that all freemen, when they form a social compact, are equal in rights." But at the urging of David H. Thrasher, a Tallapoosa County farmer and schoolteacher, the delegates unanimously struck this statement from the new constitution, lest some court think it applied to the former slaves. And when a conference of freedmen meeting in Mobile petitioned the convention to consider granting black suffrage, the delegates tabled the memorial by voice vote, without debate.[6]

In the next stage of the stumbling efforts by Alabama's authorities to adjust their state to emancipation, the questions left unresolved by the Constitutional Convention almost immediately moved into the courts. One of the first actions of the legislature chosen under the new state constitution was the election of a new state Supreme Court. The incumbent chief justice Abram J. Walker sought reelection, and the legislature unanimously obliged. Walker, a native of Tennessee, had been a Jacksonian state representative and senator in the antebellum years, representing Calhoun County in the state's hill country. In 1853 the legislature had elected him a chancellor of the state's equity courts, and in 1856 had elevated him to the Supreme Court. He became chief justice in 1859. Incumbent justice George W. Stone also sought reelection, but he was not so fortunate. Stone was defeated by Selma attorney William M. Byrd. Byrd, an antebellum Whig, had practiced law in Linden and had been a state representative from Marengo County, in the western Black Belt. In 1863 the Confederate legislature had elected him a chancellor and he had moved to Selma to take up the post. The third justiceship was vacant and drew five candidates. But Thomas J. Judge, a former state representative and senator from the Black Belt county of Lowndes, was elected after three ballots. Judge, like Byrd, had been a Whig, but in the 1850s he, along with the humorist and newspaper editor Johnson J. Hooper, had become the leader of the extremist Southern Rights Opposition that demanded secession and denounced even Yanceyite Democrats as compromisers. During these years Judge practiced law in partnership with future Confederate attorney general and Civil War governor Thomas H. Watts. All three of the justices had been slaveholders. Walker and Byrd had each held eight slaves in 1860, but Judge owned an extensive plantation and sixty-seven slaves.[7]

The Constitutional Convention had, as we have seen, intentionally finessed the issue of precisely when and how emancipation had been accomplished. But the January Term of 1866 presented the new Supreme Court with a large number of criminal appeals that required a clearer answer. Ferdinand had for more than twenty years been a slave in Mobile, the property of a firm of cotton factors. On April 12, 1865, "the military and naval forces of the United States took" the city and Ferdinand "left their service on that day, without their consent, and never returned to them," though the cotton factors "never in any wise admitted his right to freedom" until the adoption of the emancipation ordinance by the Constitutional Convention on September 22. On September 16 Ferdinand was arrested for obtaining goods under false pretenses. Defended by one of Alabama's most distinguished attorneys, former chief justice Edmund S. Dargan, Ferdinand interposed the defense that on September 16 he was legally a slave and hence could not be tried under the statute under which he was indicted, which applied only to free persons. Justice Judge made short work of this contention.

> It is not denied that slavery has had no existence in this State since the . . . day the State convention . . . acted on the subject; but it is argued that it did exist in law, if not in fact, until that action was had. This position amounts to a denial of the legality of the destruction of slavery by the act of war, a question it would be utterly vain and useless to discuss. It is a historical fact that the consummation was effected by the act of war, anterior to the action of the State convention; and whether justly or unjustly, legally or illegally, are not now practical questions.

The Constitutional Convention, he added, "was not guilty of the absurdity of abolishing slavery which did not then exist; but it gave a high and solemn sanction to the truth of the fact, before well known, that the institution of slavery had 'been destroyed in the State of Alabama,' by expressly so declaring and prohibiting the existence of slavery in the State in the future."[8]

At the same term the court rejected the argument, offered in defense of a Tuscaloosa freedwoman by former congressman William Russell Smith, that trying a former slave under a statute that had applied only to free persons at the time of the offense violated the prohibition against ex post facto laws. But here, as in similar cases, Chief Justice Walker "dissents from any expression in the opinion which may be regarded as intimating that slavery was abolished in the State otherwise than by the action of the convention" on September 22.[9] Walker never filed an opinion making a legal argument for denying the existence of an earlier emancipation. But his practical reason for doing so is apparent in his decision in the case of *Burt v. State.*

Burt, alias Burton, was a Marengo County slave who had been indicted in 1863 for killing Christopher Toomey, a white man, which was a capital offense. Because of the dislocations of war, Burt was not brought to trial until September 27, 1865, by which time he was a freedman. Judge James Cobbs instructed the jury that if they found the defendant guilty of murder in the first degree, they had the option of sentencing him either to death or to life in prison, and the jury then ordered him hanged. But this was not the statute under which Burt had been indicted, the chief justice objected; this was rather the statute that had applied to free persons. When slaves killed white persons, under antebellum law they could only be executed because, as the chief justice explained, a sentence of life in prison constituted no deterrence for a slave; slaves were already bound to service for life, and therefore life in prison would have represented nothing more than a change in the location of their labor. Besides, the antebellum statute had required that in the trial of a slave, at least two-thirds of the jury had to be slaveholders. But since there were now no slaveholders in Alabama, no statutory jury could be impaneled. Clearly, then, the statute that Burt had been indicted for violating had been rendered void by emancipation. But since the general murder statute, under which Judge Cobbs had instructed the jury, had applied only to free persons, and Burt had been a slave at the time of the offense, it followed that in killing Christopher Toomey, Burt had violated no law. The Supreme Court ordered that Burt be released.

Justice Byrd filed a lengthy dissent arguing that when the statute that Burt had offended had become void, the effect had been to revive the common law offense of murder, for which the punishment also had been death. But to this contention the chief justice replied, "The punishment may be the same under the statute as at common law; but the offense, in this State, is not identical with murder at common law," because the common law "certainly knew nothing of the crime of murder by a slave, as distinct from all other homicides by all other persons, and subject to distinct punishment."

Under the *Burt* decision the Supreme Court proceeded to bar the prosecution of any freedman for an offense specific to a slave. But it is clear that this was an outcome with which neither Chief Justice Walker nor Justice Byrd was happy. In his dissent in *Burt*, Byrd had written, "If the prisoner is to be discharged, the anomaly will be presented that a white man may still be convicted and punished with death for the murder of a slave; and the slave for the same offense, on a white man or slave, be discharged; and even a white man and a slave may have participated in the crime, and the former be convicted while the latter is acquitted, although both are guilty. Against so singular a result I would labor hard before I would be instrumental in producing it." There can be little doubt that it was precisely in order to limit the effect of his *Burt* decision that Chief Justice Walker had wanted to delay the date of emancipation to the Constitutional Convention's action on September 22. Only Justice Judge was willing to accept the full implications of *Burt*. He had written the *Ferdinand* opinion in which Byrd had concurred. And now in concurring with Walker in the *Burt* decision, he wrote, "It is to be regretted that in cases like the present, offenders escape merited punishment. But if such be the law, courts cannot help it—they must expound the law as it is. The discharge of the prisoner is one of the evils resulting from the war, and is not by any means the greatest that has been brought about by that calamity."[10]

The precise dating of emancipation was no mere academic question, then. A series of three cases forced the court to confront the question more directly. The first of these was decided at the same term as *Ferdinand* and *Burt*. In October 1864, the Confederate legislature had adopted a statute imposing the death penalty for stealing a mule, and under it two Greene County freedmen, Washington and Lafayette Jeffries, were indicted for stealing two mules on August 28, 1865. Justice Byrd—joined by Justice Judge, but over the dissent of Chief Justice Walker—held that this and other Confederate statutes had been suspended by martial law during the summer of 1865, and so the indictment was void. Byrd noted that the federal War Department had issued General Order 100 on April 24, 1863, declaring that any district occupied by the Union Army was immediately under martial law, and no formal declaration of the Union commander was necessary. "Under the provisions of this order, the act of the 7th October, 1864, was suspended by the occupation of the State by the United States army, and the surrender of General [Richard] Taylor in May, 1865" following the Battle of Blakely. The occupation and surrender "thereby subjected the State and the citizens thereof to the status of a conquered country, in which the will of the conqueror becomes the law of the land, regulated and restrained by the principles and institutes of international law."[11]

This decision clearly accepted federal authority, but at the next term the court imposed a sharp limit on the recognition. In January 1865, in the western Black Belt county of Wilcox, John W. Leslie leased a slave named William from his owner, L. L. Langham, for the coming calendar year, and gave Langham a promissory note to cover the cost of the lease. When the note matured, Leslie refused to pay. He was represented by Selma attorney N. H. R. Dawson, Abraham Lincoln's brother-in-law, and Dawson interposed his brother-in-law's Emancipation Proclamation as a defense, arguing that the lease was void because under the terms of the Proclamation, William had ceased to be Langham's property on January 1, 1863. Justice Byrd, now writing for a unanimous court, would have none of this. "Whether the State was in or out of the Union at the issuance of the proclamation of President Lincoln in January, 1863, makes no distinction or difference. If in the Union, he had no constitutional authority, nor had congress any to confer on him, to issue and enforce it at that time; and if out of the Union, in either case, it could have no force or validity until the Federal government was enabled by conquest or the power of arms to enforce it." Therefore, "slavery in this State was destroyed [only] in May, 1865," when the state fell under martial law.[12]

At the June Term of 1868—the Presidential Reconstruction court's last session—the court again returned to this question, and again at the insistence of Lincoln's brother-in-law N. H. R. Dawson. On February 1, 1865, Leroy G. Weaver had purchased two slaves, Eliza and Caroline, from Selma attorney John W. Lapsley, and had given a promissory note for the purchase price. The note having matured, Lapsley sued Weaver to collect. Weaver's attorney, Dawson, again raised the question of the Emancipation Proclamation, arguing that the sale was void. But again writing for a unanimous court, Justice Judge replied, "As to the proclamation of President Lincoln, issued by him as 'President of the United States and Commander-in-chief of the Army and Navy thereof,' declaring the universal manumission of all persons held as slaves within any of the seceded States, we have to say that it was manifestly nought but a war-measure, and of no operative effect until carried into execution by force of arms. Such is believed to be the opinion of enlightened jurists and publicists in all sections of the Union. This proclamation, therefore, can bring no aid to appellant."[13]

Thus, despite the initial doubts of Chief Justice Walker, by the end of Presidential Reconstruction the state Supreme Court had come to a clear decision about the dating and means of emancipation. It did not proceed from the action of the state's Constitutional Convention, nor did it proceed from the Emancipation Proclamation. It was a product of martial law, and therefore dated from Confederate surrender—in Alabama, from the surrender of General Richard Taylor on May 4, 1865. The conclusion had important implications for both criminal and contract law, as we have seen. But it had equally significant implications in a third area. The state constitution, like the federal one, contained a prohibition against the taking of private property without just compensation, and the state's single most radical secessionist was eager to invoke the provision. George W. Gayle of Cahaba had just been released from jail, where he had been thrown following Abraham Lincoln's assassination because earlier that spring he had placed an advertisement in his local newspaper offering a reward to anyone who would murder the president. As soon as Gayle was released, he took up the cause of Mrs. Frances L. Logan, a Dallas County widow who sought to be paid by the state for her emancipated slaves. Gayle contended that the action of the Constitutional Convention in adopting the ordinance of emancipation had constituted a taking for which compensation was required. But Justice Judge replied that the *Ferdinand* decision had already held that the convention had not emancipated the slaves, but had merely recognized an emancipation that had already taken place. "The counsel for appellant earnestly and ably contends for a decision in this case which would be in direct hostility to the conclusion attained upon the same question" in *Ferdinand*. "We decline to disturb the decision in that case; and upon its authority, the judgment of the court below in this case must be affirmed."[14] And although it did not arise in this suit, the decisions of the court holding that the Emancipation Proclamation also was not the source of emancipation meant that there had been no violation of the federal Constitution's takings clause either. As Justice Byrd had said in *Jeffries and Jeffries*, martial law had "subjected the State and the citizens thereof to the status of a conquered country, in which the will of the conqueror becomes the law of the land, regulated and restrained [solely] by the principles and institutes of international law." Thus because emancipation had been a result exclusively of martial law, Mrs. Logan and her fellow slaveholders were out of luck. A contrary decision would have bankrupted the state and enraged the entire Northern populace; and it seems quite likely that the justices' knowledge of that fact may have shaped their decisions in all these cases from the outset.

II

The Constitution of 1867 and the new state Supreme Court that it created, however, allowed for a reexamination of these questions. The three justices who took office with the June Term of 1869 were all Republicans, and legal observers waited expectantly to see what the change portended.

Chief Justice E. Wolsey Peck of Tuscaloosa had been one of the state's most prominent attorneys in the antebellum period. The legislature had chosen him as one of Alabama's initial chancellors at the time of the creation of the separate equity courts in 1839, but he had soon returned to his successful private practice. A devoted Whig, he had nevertheless generally held aloof from party politics. But with secession Peck, a native of New York, became the leader of an anti-Confederate cabal in Tuscaloosa that actively supplied intelligence to the Union Army. And at the advent of Reconstruction he embraced the Republican Party and served as the president of the 1867 Constitutional Convention. Thomas M. Peters of Moulton had been a state senator from Lawrence County in the antebellum period. Initially a Whig, he had gone over to the Democrats because of his enthusiasm for manifest destiny; Henry Clay's "Alabama Letters" in the 1844 presidential campaign were addressed to him. He supported Stephen A. Douglas in

1860, bitterly opposed secession, and with the outbreak of fighting, crossed into Union lines. Benjamin F. Saffold of Selma, a son of antebellum Supreme Court justice Reuben Saffold, was a Democrat before the war. Like Peters, he supported Stephen A. Douglas in 1860 and crossed into Union lines with the commencement of fighting. On his return, he served as a circuit judge during Presidential Reconstruction. Both he and his brother, Milton, enthusiastically espoused the Republican Party as soon as it was created in Alabama.

All three of the new justices served as delegates to the 1867 Constitutional Convention. Professors Richard L. Hume and Jerry B. Gough, in their careful analysis of the convention's roll-call votes, rank both Peck and Saffold as moderate swing voters. But Peters they rate as one of the convention's most radical members. All three had been slaveholders in the antebellum years. Peters had owned seven slaves in 1860, Saffold twelve, and Peck nineteen.[15]

As soon as the Republican court took office, it was presented with the opportunity to reconsider its Presidential Reconstruction predecessors' dismissal of the significance of the Emancipation Proclamation, through the case of *Morgan v. Nelson*. Hamlin J. Smith of Dallas County had died in 1859, and his father-in-law, L. B. Vasser, was appointed administrator of his estate, including twenty-one slaves. Vasser himself died in 1867, with the administration of the Smith estate still open. Richard M. Nelson was then appointed administrator of Smith's estate as successor to Vasser, and future US senator John Tyler Morgan was appointed administrator of Vasser's own estate. Nelson thereupon sued Morgan, asserting that Vasser had wasted Smith's estate, especially by taking possession of Smith's slaves and working them for Vasser's own benefit. Morgan had been an ardent secessionist, but the policies of the Lincoln administration were now suddenly revealed to him in a more alluring light. The slaves had actually ceased to be a part of Smith's estate on January 1, 1863, with the issuance of the Emancipation Proclamation, Morgan argued, and so Vasser's estate should not be charged with any income from them after that date. Former Justice Byrd, now off the bench and back in Selma, represented Nelson, and Byrd relied on his own ruling in *Langham's Executors* to refute this contention. The Proclamation, if constitutional at all, had had no effect in Alabama until Union victory in May 1865, Byrd had held in that opinion. But Thomas M. Peters's understanding of recent history was very different from William M. Byrd's.

Slavery, Peters passionately observed,

> was an institution which depended upon force, and not right, for its preservation. No human being was ever created a slave. Slavery was the creature of force or fraud. . . . The great national decree which

> laid slavery prostrate in the dust forever upon this continent, was the proclamation of President Lincoln issued on the 1st day of January, 1863. . . . The nation fixed the day for its termination, and after that day, it was simply a struggle of the former masters of the slaves to prevent the decree of the nation from being carried into effect.

It was, he said, "an actual absurdity, as well as a legal impossibility, that the courts of our country cannot ascertain the precise day on and from which this great event, of such recent occurrence, should in legal contemplation be now deemed to have become operative. But no such day can be ascertained, if the first day of January, 1863, is not that day." And he added, "The Alabama convention of 1865 and its ordinance had as little to do with emancipation as they will have with the coming day of final wrath, when the grave will give up its dead. It would have been all the same had that convention never met."

If slavery had ended at the beginning of 1863, however, how would one describe the relationship of slaves and masters in the following years? Peters explained:

> If the freedmen remained on the farms and plantations or at the homes of their former masters, or elsewhere in the care and under the control of said former masters, and there was no actual force used to compel them to do so, it was a consent on their part still to acquiesce in the usages of the old system of servitude on the former terms, without pay except simply their support and lodgment, until the new relation was regulated by law and the rights and duties of each were properly defined. . . . But to the lasting honor of the new citizen, he has thus far shown himself worthy of his new estate. He has parted with his old master in peace and good will, and has shown himself too noble-hearted to quibble with him about pennies, when he has received in reward for his patience and his toil a boon that money could not buy.[16]

In this opinion Justice Peters spoke for a unanimous court, and it initially appeared that the conclusions of the Presidential Reconstruction jurists as to the legal origins of emancipation had been thoroughly repudiated. But only six months later, it became clear that Chief Justice Peck and Justice Saffold had not understood the matter in the same terms that Peters's soaring rhetoric had implied. The case of *McElvain v. Mudd* was the Alabama Supreme Court's final effort to deal with the question of emancipation, and it revealed that the Republican justices were quite as perplexed about it as the spokesmen of Presidential Reconstruction had been.

On February 1, 1864, Wallace S. McElvain had purchased three slaves from Judge William S. Mudd, the Jefferson county circuit judge and Republican who had been the sponsor of the emancipation ordinance that had been adopted by the Constitutional Convention of 1865. McElvain gave Mudd a promissory note for the purchase price, and when the note matured three years later, the judge sued to collect. McElvain was represented by Alexander White, the Republican leader who had opposed Mudd at the 1865 convention and had urged only a conditional emancipation, under the conviction that the Emancipation Proclamation would eventually be found unconstitutional. But now, relying on Justice Peters's decision in the *Morgan* case, White argued that the Proclamation, issued in 1863, rendered a contract for the sale of slaves concluded in 1864 void, and the promissory note with it. Chief Justice Peck, however, was not convinced.

The question, Peck wrote, was

> what influence and effect had the proclamation of the president on the institution of slavery in the rebel slaveholding States, and upon the contracts of the citizens of said States with each other, made in good faith, with reference to that sort of property, between the date of said proclamation and the final suppression of the rebellion, a period of nearly two years and six months? . . . At the time the said proclamation was dated, all the power of the United States could not enforce it within the territory of the rebel States; . . . and more, it was never, until the rebellion was suppressed, officially promulgated in said States, nor could it be. It would seem, therefore, if there were no other reasons, these people should not be permitted to resist a performance of their contracts made with each other in good faith, with a full and equal knowledge of all the facts relating to the subject-matter of their contracts, and each party assuming and taking upon himself all the risks attendant upon them.

Moreover, Peck continued, the text of the Proclamation itself ordered the armed forces of the Union not to repress the slaves "in any efforts they may make for their actual freedom," an explicit acknowledgment "that, notwithstanding said proclamation, the slaves, the subjects of it, were not then, by the mere force of the same, actually free." And the text was equally clear that it was issued as a war measure, to assist in winning the war, with the inescapable implication that it could have been revoked if subsequent military necessity had required the action. "Who can reasonably doubt but that, at the conference at Fortress Monroe, the president might not then have withdrawn the said proclamation if he had thought proper to do so, upon the rebel government and people stipulating to abandon their resistance to the government and authority of the Union and renewing their allegiance to the constitution and government of the United States? If this had been done, would not slavery have been continued under the same guarantees and protection that it had before the rebellion began?" And so he concluded, "We see, therefore that this proclamation, though positive in its language, depended upon a contingency—an uncertain event—the real end of which no one could then foresee, and no one could then know whether its purpose would ever be realized."

But if these were the chief justice's views, why had he concurred with Justice Peters in *Morgan v. Nelson*? "We remain satisfied with the decision in that case, and are persuaded, rightly understood, it was decided upon correct principles," the chief justice said, implying that Justice Peters did not correctly understand his own opinion. Peters in *Morgan* had concluded that, "notwithstanding the event of emancipation is fixed by the act of the nation at the first day of January, 1863; yet if an administrator used the slaves of his intestate for his own profits after that date, he should be charged with such profits up to the date of the discharge of the slaves from his control by the result of the war." "This," Peck said, "is unquestionably correct. It is common doctrine that a trustee is not permitted to profit by his use of trust property, but is bound to account for any profits he may make by such use to the beneficiaries. But in that case," Peck observed incisively, "if the proclamation by its own vigor so utterly and absolutely abolished slavery from its date that no interest or property remained in them whatever from that date, then it follows that from that date the slaves not only ceased to be trust property, but also ceased to be property at all; consequently, it would seem upon every principle of equity that the profits derived from the use of the slaves did not belong to the estate, but should have gone to those who earned them," the former slaves. But that had not been Peters's holding. "The plain inference from all this is that, notwithstanding the proclamation, there continued an uncertain, contingent interest and property in slaves until the proclamation became effectual by the suppression of the rebellion."

It is hardly surprising that Peters entirely disagreed, and he filed a lengthy dissent. The Emancipation Proclamation, he wrote, "proclaimed the absolute and unconditional emancipation of the slaves in certain portions of the United States, of which the State of Alabama was a part." After January 1, 1863, "it became the policy of the nation to enforce this proclamation; and it was persisted in until it was finally successful. . . . The nation achieved, in the end, what it had proclaimed. In such cases, it is a rule almost without exception that the effect of such measures must be referred to the beginning, or to the first proclamation of the purpose intended to be accomplished." Thus, for instance, treaties are held to take effect from the date of their signing, not the date of their ratification by the Senate. Moreover, the "proclamation was but the culmination of the policy of the several acts of congress which had preceded it, and which had the same tendency and purpose." Clearly, therefore, following the issuance of the Proclamation, the sale of slaves was "against the public policy of the nation, and for that reason also they were illegal and void." And finally, "Slaves were held in their unhappy condition by a regulation founded in force on the one hand and weakness on the other. . . . Slavery violated a great natural law, that is, that man is of necessity, for his own support, entitled to the proceeds of his own labor." To understand that the sale of slaves was a violation of natural law, we have only to imagine a contract "based upon the sale of our more favored fellow-citizens whose good fortune had colored their faces white instead of black." In that case, "very few would be found to stand up for the enforcement of the sales of the sons and daughters of the commonwealth, how long so ever they might have suffered in slavery. Yet this is the question now under discussion; and possibly an old, familiar and carefully cherished prejudice may interpose to prevent us from feeling its enormity." Peters explicitly added that former Justice Byrd's opinion in *Leslie v. Langham's Executors* "ought to be over ruled."

In addition, Peters continued, the principles of contract law also required voiding the contract at issue. The contract was founded upon a warranty deed for the sale of slaves for life. "If the consideration fails, the contract fails. Here the character of the person sold was of the very essence of the consideration of the contract. The sale was that of a slave for life. This was the main and sole condition of sale. It was the cause and purpose of the sale, and it constituted the entire consideration of the promise to pay the purchase-money by the vendee. . . . Emancipation was an assault by the law upon the consideration of the contract of sale which destroyed it." And yet the court's majority

> suffers the plaintiff to be released on his part, and then to turn round on the defendant and compel him to perform his part of the agreement of sale! There is, I apprehend, no admitted principle of law that sustains this result. It is radically wrong and unjust. . . . The seeming injustice of an affirmance of the judgment below appears from the fact that the appellant will be made to pay quite eight thousand dollars in legal funds to the appellee for property in persons now citizens of the State, who had been declared enfranchised by the nation and whose emancipation the nation was most solemnly pledged to make good; and yet, get comparatively nothing of any value for his money.[17]

The debate between Chief Justice Peck and Justice Peters in part turned upon this question of the sanctity of contract. Peters thought that McElvain was being forced to pay for nonexistent property, founded on a false warranty. Peck thought that both parties had entered the contract equally aware of the risk posed by Union victory, and so each party was obliged to live up to his undertaking. But the difference between them went much deeper, to the meaning of the Civil War. Peters understood the war as a crusade against slavery. The act of August 1, 1861, freeing any slaves used by the Confederate armed forces, the act of July 17, 1862, barring the return of fugitive slaves and President Lincoln's preliminary emancipation proclamation of September 22, 1862, all demonstrated the Union's hostility to slavery long before the Emancipation Proclamation itself, he said, and both Lincoln's amnesty proclamation of December 8, 1863, and Andrew Johnson's of May 29, 1865, made the acceptance of emancipation a condition of the restoration of citizenship. "This important system of measures from the year 1861 to the year 1865, shows that it was the purpose and policy of the government of the United States to abolish slavery in the insurgent States." For Peck, however, the war was about the preservation of the union. The Emancipation Proclamation "being a mere war measure, the president, if it failed to accomplish the object intended and desired, by the same powers and authority by which he had issued it, by his powers and authority as commander-in-chief, might . . . if he had believed it best, [have] withdrawn the proclamation altogether, and have issued any other proclamation or adopted any other war measure that he might have thought would better accomplish the end desired—that is, the suppression of the rebellion and the preservation of the Union and government of the United States," Peck wrote.

This distinction was a portentous one. It divided the scalawags from the very outset. There were fifty-seven native white Republicans among the delegates to the 1867 Constitutional Convention. Hume and Gough classify twenty-three of them (including Peters), or 40.4 percent, as Radicals, fifteen (including Peck and Saffold), or 26.3 percent, as moderate swing voters, and eighteen, or 31.6 percent, as conservatives. (One of the delegates cast too few votes to be classified.) The differences between Peck and Peters that the *McElvain* decision revealed reflect an important element in determining these insistent internal scalawag divisions, separating as they did those native whites who had been drawn to Republicanism primarily by their hostility to slavery from those who had been drawn to it primarily by unionism and patriotism.

To the thoughtful and arresting debate between Peck and Peters in their *McElvain* opinions was added a substantially less subtle contribution in

Justice Saffold's brief concurrence with the chief justice. Intent upon finding a definite point of time for emancipation, Saffold came up with yet another date, one that no other justice had suggested. "If it should ever become important to determine the precise time when the abolition of slavery was effected by law in this State," he wrote, "I am satisfied it will be referred to the date of the adoption of the 13th amendment to the Federal constitution." Thus Saffold joined with Abram J. Walker in believing that the legal end of slavery substantially postdated the end of the war, and went even further than Walker's date of the 1865 convention's emancipation ordinance on September 22, pushing the date back to December 18, the completion of the ratification of the Thirteenth Amendment. Apparently Saffold agreed with Peters in regarding emancipation as an act of the nation rather than of the states, but since he rejected Peters's belief that the Emancipation Proclamation was its source, he was left only with the Thirteenth Amendment as his authority. Saffold offered no rationale for his assertion, however, and so we are simply left to deduce what his argument might have been.

Thus the six justices who considered the question have bequeathed us a range of answers as to the date of emancipation. Chief Justice Walker and Justice Saffold placed it substantially after the end of the war, Walker on September 22 and Saffold on December 18—even though, as a practical matter, everyone knew that the slaves had actually been free for many months by then. And Justice Peters believed that it had occurred in the midst of the war, on January 1, 1863—even though, as a practical matter, everyone knew that slaves continued to be worked, and bought and sold, for years after that date. These three justices reached legal conclusions so at odds with common knowledge because each of them sought an official document on which to hang the event—for Peters the Emancipation Proclamation, for Walker the 1865 Constitutional Convention's ordinance of emancipation, for Saffold the Thirteenth Amendment. Chief Justice Peck and Justices Byrd and Judge all joined in attributing emancipation not to legal action but to military force. Byrd went so far as to call the Emancipation Proclamation unconstitutional. Peck clearly agreed with Peters in regarding it as a legitimate exercise of the president's war powers, inherent in his being commander in chief of the armed forces. But Peck agreed with Judge in considering it "a mere war measure," without effect until given it by military victory. Judge and Byrd, however, just as unconvincingly as Walker, Saffold, and Peters, fixed Union victory, and consequent martial law, at the surrender of General Richard Taylor to General E. R. S. Canby on May 4. Peck, more flexibly, seems to have thought of emancipation as a sort of rolling event, accompanying the progress of Union arms. This conclusion was truer to historical reality, for emancipation in fact came earlier to the Tennessee Valley counties, which fell to Union forces substantially before most of the state.

Peck, perhaps the best lawyer among the six, was also the most persuasive historian because, alone among them, he did not allow himself to be ensnared in the search for a "bright line," a specific date derived from a particular document or event. He understood that emancipation was not really a product of positive law, but of gathering historical contingencies. It was this fact that made the courts so manifestly ill suited to deal with emancipation's complexities—something that every one of the Alabama Supreme Court's decisions on the question makes quite clear.

Notes

This article originally appeared in a somewhat different form in Raymond Arsenault and Orville Vernon Burton, eds., *Dixie Redux: Essays in Honor of Sheldon Hackney* (Montgomery: NewSouth Books, 2013), 80–100, and is reprinted here with the kind permission of NewSouth Books.

1. *Journal of the Proceedings of the Constitutional Convention of the State of Alabama Held in the City of Montgomery September 12, 1865* (Montgomery: Gibson and Whitfield, 1865), 7, 12–13; Malcolm C. McMillan, *Constitutional Development in Alabama, 1798–1901: A Study in Politics, the Negro, and Sectionalism* (Chapel Hill: University of North Carolina Press, 1955), 90, 93.

2. McMillan, *Constitutional Development*, 92–93; J. Mills Thornton, *Politics and Power in a Slave Society: Alabama, 1800–1860* (Baton Rouge: Louisiana State University Press, 1978), 409–13.

3. I have developed these figures from the manuscript census returns of 1860.

4. *Journal of the Constitutional Convention of 1865*, 19–20, 29; McMillan, *Constitutional Development*, 94–95.

5. *Journal of the Constitutional Convention of 1865*, 48–49; McMillan, *Constitutional Development*, 95–97; Alexander White, "Speech to the Constitutional Convention of 1865," Pamphlet Collection, Alabama Department of Archives and History. The prohibition of slavery was an ordinance adopted by the convention, not a provision of the state constitution. The ordinance also amended the constitution of 1819 "by striking out all provisions in relation to slaves and slavery," and it ordered the legislature at its first session "to pass such laws as will protect the Freedmen of this State in the full enjoyment of all their rights of person and property, and to guard them and the State against any evils that may arise from their sudden emancipation."

6. *Journal of the Constitutional Convention of 1865*, 33–48, 79; McMillan, *Constitutional Development*, 103, 106.

7. *House Journal*, Session of 1865–66, pp. 76–79; Thomas M. Owen, *History of*

Alabama and Dictionary of Alabama Biography (Chicago: S. J. Clarke, 1921), 3: 277, 951; 4: 1714.

8. Ferdinand v. State, 39 Ala. 706. Ferdinand, who after his emancipation adopted the name Ferdinand Smith, was subsequently pardoned by Governor Robert M. Patton, who stated that Smith's arrest had arisen merely out of a squabble within Smith's church congregation. Following his pardon, Smith moved to Eufaula, and in 1871 he was elected Barbour County superintendent of education.

9. Eliza v. State, 39 Ala. 693.

10. Burt v. State, 39 Ala. 617, see also George v. State, 39 Ala. 675, Nelson v. State, 39 Ala. 667, Eitherby v. State, 39 Ala. 702.

11. Jeffries and Jeffries v. State, 39 Ala. 655; cf. Aaron and Ely v. State, 39 Ala. 684.

12. Leslie v. Langham's Executors, 40 Ala. 524.

13. Weaver v. Lapsley, 42 Ala. 601.

14. Logan v. State, 40 Ala. 733; on Gayle, see Thornton, *Politics and Power*, 190–94, 203, 243–45.

15. Owen, *History of Alabama and Dictionary of Alabama Biography*, 4: 1335, 1349, 1486; Glenda McWhirter Todd, *First Alabama Cavalry, USA: Homage to Patriotism* (Bowie, MD: Heritage Books, 1999), 238; Richard L. Hume and Jerry B. Gough, *Blacks, Carpetbaggers, and Scalawags: The Constitutional Conventions of Radical Reconstruction* (Baton Rouge: Louisiana State University Press, 2008), 282, 284, 312; Joel D. Kitchens, "E. W. Peck: Alabama's First Scalawag Chief Justice," *Alabama Review* (January 2001): 3–32; Paul Horton, "Lightning Rod Scalawag: The Unlikely Career of Thomas Minott Peters," *Alabama Review* (April 2011): 116–42. Benjamin Saffold had been a fire eater in 1850, but had moved in a more conservative direction over the coming decade (Thornton, *Politics and Power*, 241, 243, 455). The new constitution of 1867 had taken the election of Supreme Court justices from the legislature and given it to the people.

16. Morgan v. Nelson, 43 Ala. 586.

17. McElvain v. Mudd, 44 Ala. 48. The 1867 Constitutional Convention had adopted an ordinance voiding all debts contracted for the sale of slaves, and in this decision Peck and Saffold also joined to declare the ordinance in violation of the US Constitution's prohibition of laws impairing the obligation of the contract.

5
Redemption and the Jews in Montgomery

During the two hundred years of its history, Montgomery, Alabama, has had only two Jewish mayors. One was a Republican, Henry E. Faber, who served from 1870 to 1875, and the other was a Democrat, Mordecai L. Moses, who served from 1875 to 1881. The Jewish identity of the two men, their party affiliation, and the fact that one succeeded the other form a little noticed but very revealing aspect of the story of Reconstruction, and it is the subject of this article.

Henry Faber was born in Bavaria. He came to Alabama in the late 1850s, in his early twenties, and settled in Prattville, where he sought to establish himself as a merchant. At the outbreak of the Civil War, Faber was twenty-four and unmarried, and so was a prime candidate for Confederate conscription. But he was also a naturalized citizen, and he apparently took his oath of allegiance to the United States very seriously. He therefore moved across the river to Montgomery and joined one of the city's fire companies, a membership that exempted him from the draft. Shortly thereafter he married Ellnora, a native of New York, who was only seventeen. As the Confederate draft tightened, he enlisted as a private in the Montgomery Home Guard in August 1864, a position that virtually insured that he would see no action. Despite the fact that he thus became a Confederate veteran, it is clear that throughout the war, he was quietly but decidedly hostile to the Confederate cause. When the Alabama Republican Party was established in 1867, Faber at once embraced the movement and soon became a strong proponent of equal rights for the newly freed slaves.[1]

In the meantime, Faber had joined Montgomery's Jewish synagogue and become an active participant. The congregation was at this time in a period of transition that was creating significant strains within it. Chartered in the spring of 1852, the congregation initially was open only to German speakers. Its constitution required that all meetings be conducted in German and all minutes and records be kept in German. But in May 1863, just as Faber was joining, the membership adopted a new constitution. Debates and records were now to be in English, and membership was opened to any Jew age eighteen or over.[2] Faber apparently was enthusiastic about these reforms and soon sought to push them further. In April 1866, he was elected the congregation's treasurer and promptly offered a resolution calling the dues imposed on members "unjust and overbearing." That summer he successfully sponsored an amendment to the 1863 constitution placing the members in six income classifications and proportioning their temple assessments accordingly. And in the fall he obtained the adoption of a regulation giving members in arrears on their assessments six months to pay before they could be expelled. These actions apparently made Faber very popular, especially with the poorer members of the congregation, and he became a leader of its reform forces. In 1868 he was elected one of its trustees.[3]

However, the currents of reform that had been unleashed by the new temple constitution in 1863 encountered firm resistance from more conservative elements of the membership. After repeated clashes, the congregation voted to dismiss Rabbi M. H. Myers in June 1866, and the temple was without a rabbi until the summer of 1869. Faber championed the appointment of Dr. E. B. M. Brown as rabbi, and in August 1869, he succeeded in persuading the membership to appoint Dr. Brown to a one-year term. But Brown lasted only six months, and in February 1870, the congregation voted to fire him.[4] In October 1870, the leader of the conservative forces, dry goods merchant Leopold Waldman, obtained a one-year term for Rabbi Adolph Moses, but the bitter divisions within the membership continued. At the annual temple meeting the following April, Waldman defeated the leader of the liberals, commission merchant David Weil, for vice president by two votes on the third ballot, but only after president Albert Strassburger threw out as illegal two votes that had made the first two ballots ties. In July, Rabbi Moses was given a second one-year term by the margin of a single vote.[5]

In the meantime, Henry Faber had taken his reformist convictions into city politics. There had been a municipal election in December 1865, under the Presidential Reconstruction regime, and the still all-white electorate had returned to office the administration that had been elected in the midst of the Civil War, in December 1863, headed by Mayor Walter L. Coleman, a prominent attorney. The term of this administration was supposed to have expired in December 1867, but that spring the Congress had passed the Military Reconstruction Acts that had ordered a complete reregistration of voters, the enfranchisement of blacks, and the writing of a new state constitution, and this process made it impossible to hold a new municipal election. City attorney John Archer Elmore gave Mayor Coleman a legal opinion that the incumbent administration was still in power until its successors were chosen and qualified, and so they continued to sit. It was during this limbo period, in April 1868, that Coleman and his council took what would in future years become one of the most controversial acts in the municipal life of the era, issuing $500,000 in city bonds to help finance the building of the South and North Alabama Railroad, intended to run from Montgomery to Decatur and thus to close the one remaining link in the rail line from the Gulf to the Ohio River, and to open access to the mineral deposits that were known to exist around the isolated village of Elyton in Jefferson County.[6]

Meanwhile, the state Constitutional Convention had adopted an ordinance requiring the new governor, once he was elected, to dissolve such holdover city administrations as Montgomery's and to appoint a mayor and council to serve out the term to the next city election. Accordingly, the incoming Radical governor, William H. Smith of Wedowee, had replaced the Coleman administration in August 1868, with a new mayor and council. For mayor, Governor Smith chose Thomas O. Glasscock, who before the Civil War had been the register of Montgomery's federal land office and since the end of the war had become state president of the Union League, the backbone of the state's new Republican Party. To the city council he named ten whites and two blacks. These were the first black officeholders in Montgomery's history, and they did nothing to calm the apprehensions of many of the city's whites. At the council's first meeting, Councilman Holland Thompson, a grocer who was the most prominent leader of the city's freedmen and who served concurrently as one of Montgomery's state representatives, offered, and the council adopted, an ordinance requiring that half of the city's policemen be black. This directive was a virtual firebrand tossed into the midst of a white community feeling its way fearfully into the new racial order. It was in this context that the city approached the municipal elections of December 1869.[7]

The December 1869, elections would be the first to be contested by the Republicans and, of course, the first in which blacks could vote. The Republicans could count on essentially unanimous black support, but they were nervous that the conduct of the council appointed by Governor Smith might have similarly united much of the white electorate behind the Democrats. At this early stage of Reconstruction a significant number of former secessionists among the whites had been disfranchised, and others were reluctant to register to vote because the new state constitution required registrants to take an oath to "accept the civil and political equality of all men and agree not to attempt to deprive any person or persons on account of race, color or previous condition of any political or civil right."[8] This reluctance aided the Republicans in a city nearly equally divided between the races; in 1870, Montgomery had about 5,400 whites and a bit less than 5,200 blacks. But Republicans also saw that one element of the city's white population that might be lured to their support was the one hundred or so of its voters who were Jews, a group that during the antebellum period had never been courted by local politicians. On the Republican slate for the twelve council seats, therefore, in addition to two blacks, they selected three Jews. Thus it was that Henry Faber, now fairly well known as a leader of the reform forces within the synagogue, gained nomination to the city council. The Democrats quickly responded by nominating two Jews of their own, one of them future mayor Mordecai Moses. But the Republicans swept to victory, taking two-thirds of the vote and carrying all six of the city's wards.[9]

And then, only three months after the election, Mayor Glasscock fell gravely ill, and in September 1870, he died. Under the city charter, the council was to elect one of its members to serve the unexpired term, and on September 29, Faber was chosen by his colleagues. The thirty-three-year-old dry goods merchant, after only ten months in office, found himself mayor of the city. He would have to lead the Republican ticket in the upcoming December 1871, municipal election, which would be his very first citywide campaign.[10]

Despite their trouncing in 1869, the Democrats were enthusiastic about their prospects for 1871. In the first place, Democratic leaders had by this time persuaded almost all of even the most recalcitrant whites to take the registration oath, and so they were confident that they could now poll their full strength. And indeed, the total vote cast in the 1871 municipal election was more than double the total vote from 1869. In the second place, Faber was an untested candidate and was thought to be weak. Finally, the Democrats thought that the race question would help them. Faber and the elected council had reaffirmed the appointed council's requirement that half the police force be black, and Faber himself strongly supported it, both as a matter of simple justice given the racial composition of the city and also because he believed that black officers could gain access to information about criminal activity in the city that white officers would not know. The council had, moreover, agreed to pay the members of the city's street maintenance crew, almost all of whom were black, $1.25 a day, and Faber had actually voted for $1.50.[11]

The election of 1871 was the most closely contested city election in decades. Mayor Faber defeated the Democratic candidate, steamboat agent James P. Terry, by only 119 votes. But the Democrats captured seven of the council seats and the Republicans five—together with Mayor Faber making a seven to six division. In the council elections the total Democratic vote led the Republican vote by 144, so it was clear that Democrats had actually had a majority of the city's electorate. And yet Faber had won the mayoral race.

The Republicans could count on the essentially unanimous support of the city's blacks, and there was a significant group of whites—scalawags and carpetbaggers, the Democrats called them—who were committed to the Republican cause. The Democrats could win only if they succeeded in uniting every one of the other whites behind their campaign. But the outcome of the council elections indicated that they essentially had in fact succeeded in doing so. Therefore the only reasonable deduction was that Mayor Faber's popularity in the synagogue had allowed him to subtract many of the city's Jews from this white alliance and unite them with the blacks and the white Republicans to create a narrow rival majority. From this analysis the Democrats appear to have settled on a strategy. They made Mordecai Moses, one of the two Jews among the seven councilmen they had elected, the principal spokesman for their new council majority. And almost as soon as the new council had organized itself, they had Councilman Moses propose an amendment to the city charter requiring the payment of a poll tax to vote in city elections, a proposal intended to limit the number of poor black voters on whom the Republicans counted.[12]

Mordecai L. Moses was a native of Charleston, South Carolina, the son of Charleston merchant Levi Moses. He had come to Montgomery when he was eighteen, just before the outbreak of the Civil War, to clerk in the hardware store of a relative, A. J. Moses. With the beginning of the war, Moses had joined the Confederate secret service. He was sent to the Caribbean, where he apparently used his family's contacts among Jewish merchants in the islands to facilitate Confederate blockade running and the acquisition of strategic supplies. Toward the end of the war, he was shifted to Canada, where he presumably aided the Confederacy's ultimately unsuccessful effort to attack New England across the Canadian border. At the end of the war, he returned to Montgomery and formed an insurance and real estate agency with his brother, Alfred, who had served as an officer in the Confederate Army. Alfred had been a member of the Montgomery synagogue in 1862, before the introduction of English, but the reforms seem to have put both brothers off, and neither rejoined when they returned to the city. It appears that the sentiments of both of the two young Moses brothers were strongly conservative and Confederate.[13]

The divisions between the Democratic and Republican members of the council elected in 1871 were profound and bitter. At the council's inauguration, Mayor Faber swore in the five Republicans, three whites and two blacks. But the seven Democrats, all of them white, insisted on being sworn in by former mayor Walter Coleman instead. The Democrats' rancor, however, caused them to overplay their hand. Their proposal for a poll tax requirement to vote in the city election had never had any realistic chance of adoption because, as an amendment to the city charter, it would necessitate an act of the legislature, and everyone knew that the Republican-dominated state senate would never pass it. Its real point was to force the Republicans into a public defense of black voting. But Mayor Faber's alternative proposal to criminalize violations of the state registration oath that they all had taken, turned the tables on them. The result was a compromise act that required the reregistration of the voters in each ward before each city election and prescribed a sentence of a year in prison for anyone who either voted illegally or unlawfully obstructed a legal voter. Meanwhile, the Democrats' effort to reduce the number of black policemen by requiring all policemen to wear a prescribed new uniform and to pay for it personally out of their small salaries, only made the Democratic councilmen look petty.[14] Such actions alienated moderate whites, the so-called New Departurists, allied with the outgoing Democratic state administration of Governor Robert B. Lindsay, who wanted to accept the reality of black enfranchisement and seek to cooperate with amenable blacks to further community development. Under Mayor Faber, Montgomery had seen many municipal improvements: a street railway system, a waterworks and fire hydrants, a splendid new city hall and city market, the conversion of much of the sewer system to brick from its former wood, and more. Meanwhile, successive epidemics of meningitis, cholera, and yellow fever during which Faber had worked energetically to assist the afflicted families had earned him a great many friends.[15]

These developments all came together to produce the astonishing and overwhelming Democratic defeat in the city election of December 1873. The new registration law undoubtedly reduced the vote significantly, but the principal feature of the election was that moderate Democrats appear to have sat out the voting in large numbers. The total vote was a third less than it had been in 1871, and the Democratic candidate for mayor, wholesale grocer Milton P. LeGrand, received only a bit more than half the vote of Terry, the Democratic candidate two years earlier. Faber was reelected with 62 percent of the vote to LeGrand's 38 percent. And in the council elections, the Democrats took only three seats—one of them Mordecai Moses's—to the Republicans' nine. From their seven to six majority in 1871, the Democrats went to a ten to three minority.[16]

It was clear that the Democrats badly needed a new strategy, one that relied less exclusively on racial polarization. And just at this moment, the Panic of 1873 provided them one. The panic had begun on Wall Street with the failure of two large brokerage firms in September, but its effects had not yet really reached Montgomery at the time of the city election in December. Throughout 1874, however, economic conditions in the city grew steadily worse, and the Democrats quickly placed the blame on Mayor Faber and the Republican administration. The focus of their criticism became the special property tax necessary to pay the interest on the municipal bonds. The South and North Alabama Railroad, after a period in bankruptcy, had been absorbed into the Louisville and Nashville system and was completed in October 1872, and Montgomery was greatly benefiting from the rail connection while the railroad's investors were taking the lead in laying out the new city that the railroad had made possible, Birmingham. But despite these positive results, as the economic climate deteriorated, Democratic attorney Joseph S. Winter filed suit in state Chancery Court in May 1874, alleging that the bond issue that had supported the building of the railroad had been illegal, in particular because of the holdover status of Mayor Walter L. Coleman and his lame duck council. Winter received a temporary restraining order forbidding the collection of the property tax, and though the city then obtained dismissal of his suit on technical grounds, Winter appealed to the state Supreme Court and he and the Democratic Party leadership commenced a campaign to persuade the city's property owners to refuse to pay the tax until the city waived its technical objections and agreed to a decision on the merits. As the tax boycott took hold, the city soon was unable to meet its obligations. In addition to the $500,000 in railroad bonds, the city in 1870 had issued $100,000 in bonds to build the new city hall, championed by Mayor Faber, and then in 1873 had issued $40,000 in certificates of debt—authorized as another part of the compromise voter registration law—which it had used as collateral with the city's banks and insurance companies to obtain loans to see the construction of the city hall to completion. In addition, an antebellum bond issue of $18,000 to construct the city wharf on the Alabama River had just matured, and the city had no way to pay off the principal. The holders of the wharf bonds obtained an attachment on the new city hall and the holders of the city hall bonds countersued, saying their bonds gave them a first mortgage on the building. Meanwhile, holders of the railroad bonds sued in federal district court and received an injunction compelling the payment of their interest. The desperate city authorities issued $80,000 in tax anticipation warrants, but since the taxes that the warrants were anticipating were highly unlikely to be paid, the warrants could be sold only at ruinous interest rates, in one case 23 percent. The city began paying municipal employees with its warrants and made them receivable for city taxes. But the consequence was that very soon the city's revenue was comprised almost entirely of its own heavily discounted debt certificates, rather than cash. Democrats then began circulating false rumors that the Republicans had pocketed the city's funds. An outraged Mayor Faber replied in exasperation that the actual source of the problem was the Democrat-inspired tax boycott. But as the city approached the municipal elections of May 1875, the undeniable reality was that its finances were in shambles.[17]

While this fiscal crisis was developing, meanwhile, enmities within the Jewish congregation were increasing. The leader of the reform forces, David Weil—whose cousin, Councilman Henry Weil, was Mayor Faber's most important ally in dealing with the city's financial difficulties—pressed ahead with his liberal proposals, to which both Faber and Faber's business partner, Marcus Munter, gave virtually unwavering support. In January 1872, the congregation had voted some modernizing changes to the ritual, over conservative opposition, and in April, David Weil was elected the temple president. With that Rabbi Adolph Moses gave notice of his resignation. At the annual meeting in April 1873, the leader of the conservatives, Leopold Waldman, persuaded the congregation to employ Rabbi B. E. Jacobs for a one-year term to succeed Rabbi Moses. But at the same time David Weil offered a motion to adopt the American mode of worship in place of the German mode, and the proposal was referred to the congregation's ritual committee for study. That summer Mayor Faber was named chairman of a committee to remodel the synagogue, and his plans, which among other things eliminated the separate seating of women in the rear, were adopted a year later. In April 1874, Rabbi Jacobs was given a second term, but evidently reluctantly, because on motion of Henry Weil, the congregation voted that he could be dismissed at any time during the year if the members wished; David Weil was reelected as president.

It appears, however, that Rabbi Jacobs was working hard to bring the temple's factions together. At a meeting in July 1874, David Weil's earlier motion to adopt the American mode of worship was called up and the congregation approved using the reformed ritual of New York's Temple Emmanuel. But this was less the victory of the reformers that it might at first appear to have been, and more the first step in a factional compromise. In October the congregation accepted a new and more conservative constitution, increasing the minimum age for membership from eighteen to twenty-one and barring membership to anyone who had married a non-Jew. With the new year, Rabbi Jacobs was given a third term almost unanimously. David Weil then resigned as temple president in order to permit the election of a fusion leadership of the liberal Albert Strassburger as president and the conservative Leopold Waldman as vice president. This new willingness of the reformers and conservatives to try to reach an accommodation led Alfred Moses, the brother of Mordecai Moses, to rejoin the temple, for the first time since 1862, though Mordecai Moses himself never joined. And the more conservative direction of the congregation was confirmed that fall when the members soundly defeated an effort by the reformers to eliminate the requirement that men wear head coverings during services. In April 1876, despite the synagogue's adoption of the reform ritual less than two years earlier, the members overwhelmingly rejected a motion to affiliate with the reform Board of Delegates of American Israelites.[18]

The city election of May 1875, took place in the midst of these developments within the temple, just after David Weil's resignation as temple president and Alfred Moses's decision to rejoin, and just before the congregation's vote to continue requiring male head coverings during services. The city's Democratic leadership was certainly aware of the Jewish divisions and took them into account as the parties prepared for the electoral contest. As Democrats considered their prospects, they recognized that Faber's friendships in the synagogue appeared to have played a crucial role in his narrow victory in 1871, and they knew that their own assumption that the race issue could unite almost all of the white electorate had produced their disastrous defeat in 1873. Now they believed that they had the deepening economic depression and the disarray in the city's financial affairs going for them. But their past experiences made them eager to take advantage of the temple developments as well. And so, overcoming what may well have been misgivings about the implications of putting a Jew at the head of their municipal ticket, they turned to Councilman Mordecai Moses as their mayoral nominee, and put two other Jews, Albert Strassburger and Avon Levystein, on their council slate as well.

The results of the 1875 election demonstrated that the Democrats had actually had nothing to worry about, though their experiences in 1871 and 1873 could not have prepared them for the outcome. In 1874, after a violent and bitterly racial campaign, the Democrats had recaptured the state government. The newly Democratically controlled state legislature had enacted rigorous voting limitations that sharply diminished black participation. And the national and local economic dislocations, together with acrimonious internal factional squabbling, left the Republicans thoroughly dispirited. The total vote in 1875, as a result, returned almost to the level of 1869, when it had been artificially depressed by the registration restrictions; it was a fourth less than it had been in 1873 and barely half what it had been in 1871. And though Mordecai Moses received only 250 votes more than Milton LeGrand, the Democratic candidate in 1873, Henry Faber got less than half what he had received in that election. The Democrats carried every single council seat. And so it turned out that the Democrats need not have nominated Moses; they clearly would have won with virtually any candidate.[19]

Nevertheless, the election of Mordecai Moses had positive consequences that the Democratic leadership very probably had never anticipated. The new council, under the influence of young councilman and future governor Thomas G. Jones, quickly turned to restoring white supremacy, as the Republicans would have predicted. The police force again became all white and would remain so for the next eight decades. The council petitioned the legislature to de-annex several black sections of the city, even further reducing the black electorate. And it criminalized being on the property of another at night under suspicious circumstances and calling for the rescue of an arrested person.[20] In the meanwhile, however, Mayor Moses turned his principal attention to the city's bonded indebtedness.

The council had appointed a committee to seek the adjustment of the city's debt, consisting of three of Montgomery's most prominent citizens, railroad magnate Charles T. Pollard, planter-investor Tristram B. Bethea, and state Democratic Party chairman Walter L. Bragg. Acting for the committee, Pollard went to New York and, to the surprise of most observers, managed to obtain significant concessions from the city's principal bondholder, the Newark Trust and Savings Bank of Newark, New Jersey. But when Pollard returned to Montgomery, Mayor Moses announced that he was convinced that Montgomery could get an even better deal. He led the council in adopting an ordinance laying out the terms they wanted, and he dispatched Walter Bragg to New York to renegotiate Pollard's agreement on this basis. The source of Moses's confidence then became clear. When Bragg arrived in New York, Moses arranged for him to be joined in the discussions by two good friends of the mayor's, former Montgomery commission merchants Emanuel and Mayer Lehman. The Lehmans had only recently moved to New York to establish the brokerage firm of Lehman Brothers, and at the request of Moses, they plunged actively into bargaining with the creditors. In his report to the council, Bragg wrote that the Lehmans "were friends indeed, and our city is under everlasting obligations to them for their assistance in this matter. . . . Possessed of all the influence which flows from wealth, popularity, liberality and the highest order of business capacity, they threw it all into the scale to aid our settlement, at a time when the odds were fearfully against us and its friends were so few that their voices could scarcely be heard in the general din of opposition." The Lehmans' assistance was essential in identifying and tracking down the individual bondholders, and Emanuel Lehman personally went with Bragg to each of his meetings with the investors and urged the acceptance of the city's proposals. Bragg was convinced that his efforts would have been unsuccessful without the Lehmans' help, and there can be little doubt that the Lehmans gave that help in large part because of their warm personal relations with Mayor Moses. As a result, the bondholders agreed to accept new bonds for three-fourths of their debt, paying only 3 percent through 1881, 4 percent for the next five years, and 5 percent for the final twenty years; the remaining one-fourth of the debt was paid off by the distribution to the bondholders of the city's essentially worthless stock in the bankrupt South and North Alabama Railroad.[21]

The city's grateful Democrats nominated Moses for additional terms in 1877 and 1879. By the time he left office in 1881, there was for all practical purposes no Republican Party left in Montgomery; the entire Democratic slate in 1881 was elected unopposed.[22] When the two parties had been separated by a few hundred votes in the early 1870s, the city's Jews had constituted a crucial balance of power to whom Democrats had to pay close attention. By the end of Mordecai Moses's mayoralty, however, the Democrats no longer had anything to fear from their opponents, either electoral or racial. And so Montgomery would never have another Jewish mayor.

Ordinarily the central issues of Reconstruction in the South have been thought to be race and railroad bonds. And certainly those two questions do form the public face of Reconstruction politics in Montgomery. But the rivalry between Henry Faber and Mordecai Moses, and the social and spiritual divisions within the city's Jewish community that this rivalry represents, direct our attention to a deeper level. Reconstruction was a period during which the region sought—not always very successfully—to understand and adjust to change. The emancipation of the slaves and the building of the railroads transformed the life of the South in profound ways. The struggle within the synagogue was also about the adjustment to change: the deep desire to honor tradition and at the same time the need to adapt to the ways of a new land. It is likely the resonance between these encounters with change that for a time drew the temple's reformers toward Faber and its conservatives toward Moses, and as well drew Faber toward the Republicans, with their acceptance of the new age, and Moses toward the Democrats, with their reluctance fully to embrace it. The recognition of this resonance perhaps can clarify for us some of the emotional implications of Reconstruction that are not always so readily apparent at this distance.

Notes

1. This account is derived from the 1860 and 1870 manuscript census returns and the Alabama Civil War Service Database of the Alabama Department of Archives and History, Montgomery.

2. Nellie C. Weil, *150 Years of Kahl Montgomery, Temple Beth Or, 1852–2002* (Montgomery, 2002), 14–17; Kahl Montgomery Minute Book, May 3, 1863, Temple Beth Or Archives, Montgomery (hereafter cited as Temple Minutes, 5/3/63 [and

further particular dates]). I am grateful to Rabbi Elliot Stevens and the congregation of Temple Beth Or for allowing me access to these records.

3. Temple Minutes, 4/8/66, 7/8/66, 10/14/66, 4/12/68, 1/10/69.

4. Temple Minutes, 2/7/66, 3/18/66, 6/10/66, 7/11/69, 8/1/69, 2/6/70, 4/10/70.

5. Temple Minutes, 7/10/70, 7/24/70, 10/9/70, 10/16/70, 4/23/71, 7/23/71, 10/15/71. Rabbi Adolph Moses was not related to Mordecai L. Moses.

6. Minutes of the Montgomery City Council, February 3, 1868, April 9, 1868, Alabama Department of Archives and History, Montgomery (hereafter cited as MMCC, 2/3/68, 4/9/68 [and further particular dates]).

7. MMCC, 8/3/68, 8/15/68, 8/24/68, 11/2/68. On Holland Thompson, see Howard N. Rabinowitz, "Holland Thompson and Black Political Participation in Montgomery, Alabama," in *Southern Black Leaders of the Reconstruction Era*, edited by Howard Rabinowitz (Urbana: University of Illinois Press, 1982), 249–80.

8. Alabama Constitution of 1868, Article VII, section 3; Malcolm C. McMillan, *Constitutional Development in Alabama, 1798–1901: A Study in Politics, the Negro, and Sectionalism* (Chapel Hill: University of North Carolina Press, 1955), 124–33, esp. 126n.

9. MMCC, 12/20/69. It is difficult to determine exactly how many Jewish voters there were in Montgomery. The temple records report that there were seventy-three members in 1873 and eighty-two in 1874. But we know that there were Jews who were not temple members, whether because, like the Moses brothers, they had chosen not to join or because they had been suspended or expelled for nonpayment of assessments. It would seem reasonable, therefore, to put the total number of Jewish voters in this period at something over one hundred.

10. MMCC, 7/5/70, 9/23/70, 9/29/70.

11. MMCC, 11/2/68, 12/14/68, 12/21/69, 4/13/70, 12/18/71.

12. MMCC, 12/18/71, 1/22/72. The Minutes give the name of the Democratic mayoral candidate as Torry, but the Census and the City Directory spell it Terry.

13. Manuscript census returns of 1850, 1860; Thomas M. Owen, *History of Alabama and Dictionary of Alabama Biography* (Chicago: S. J. Clarke, 1921), 4: 1253; Weil, *150 Years*, 18; Temple Minutes, 2/23/62.

14. MMCC, 12/18/71, 1/16/72, 1/22/72, 2/12/72; Acts of Alabama, Sess. of 1871–72, pp. 275–90.

15. MMCC, 5/16/70, 8/2/70, 2/6/71, 4/30/72, 5/20/72, 8/6/72, 12/2/72, 12/9/72, 5/5/73, 7/15/73, 10/20/73, 12/15/73, 2/26/74.

16. MMCC, 12/15/73.

17. MMCC, 2/3/68,4/9/68, 7/1/68, 1/4/69, 5/3/69, 5/15/69, 12/18/71, 4/30/72, 10/20/73, 12/15/73, 2/23/74, 2/26/74, 5/4/74, 6/1/74, 6/22/74, 1/5/75, 1/18/75, 1/18/75, 1/25/75, 2/16/75, 5/17/75, 6/1/75, 10/4/75, 11/16/75, 12/18/75, 2/2/76, 8/21/76, 5/21/77; Acts of Alabama, Sess. of 1869–70, pp. 338–73, Sess. of 1871–72, pp. 275–90, Sess. of 1873, p. 151; Owen, *History of Alabama and Dictionary of Alabama Biography*, 2: 904.

18. Temple Minutes, 1/14/72, 4/14/72, 4/20/73, 6/22/73, 6/29/73, 4/12/74, 7/12/74, 7/26/74, 8/2/74, 9/5/74, 10/12/74, 1/10/75, 2/7/75, 2/12/75, 7/11/75, 9/19/75, 1/9/76, 4/16/76; Weil, *150 Years*, 21–22.

19. MMCC, 5/7/75; Acts of Alabama, Sess. of 1874–75, pp. 526–32. On the factional feuds within the Montgomery Republican Party, see Rabinowitz, "Holland Thompson," and Loren Schweninger, *James T. Rapier and Reconstruction* (Chicago: University of Chicago Press, 1978). Although Albert Strassburger was elected to the council as a Democrat, he had been close to David Weil and the reformers in temple affairs, and feeling disapproval from his constituency, he resigned only a week after taking office, leaving Avon Levystein as the only Jewish councilman (MMCC, 12/27/75). The new voter registration law repealed that of 1872, including the provision that had criminalized obstructing a legal voter. It increased the requirement to vote in the council elections from fifteen days' residence in the ward to three months. And it continued the provision for a reregistration of all voters before every city election but added a new requirement that the registrant be given a certificate of registration, which he had to retain and surrender to the poll workers at the election in order to vote. Poll workers were authorized to examine challenged voters and any witnesses, and then were empowered to make a final decision on the spot. It need hardly be said that the entire structure of the act, buttressed as it was with criminal penalties, worked to intimidate frightened and poorly educated blacks.

20. MMCC, 3/17/73, 1/10/76, 2/21/76, 7/3/76, 1/10/77, 5/21/77; Acts of Alabama, Sess. of 1876–77, pp. 254–77; Howard N. Rabinowitz, *Race Relations in the Urban South, 1865–1890* (New York: Oxford University Press, 1978), 273–75. Mayor Moses himself fully accepted the white supremacist sentiments of his fellow Democrats. In his inaugural address of December 1875, he hailed Alabama's newly adopted state constitution of 1875 as one "framed by our representatives—representatives of the intelligence, virtue, industry and property of the entire state." It marked, he said, a new era for "our down-trodden and suffering people," an era in which "virtue and intelligence no longer [are] forced to stand aside while vice and ignorance hold the reins." And similarly the Democratic victory in Montgomery had, he asserted, placed the city administration "in the hands of men elected by property holders and taxpayers from all classes of industrial and professional life" (MMCC, 12/20/75).

21. MMCC, 4/2/77; on the debt negotiations, see also MMCC, 1/3/76, 1/17/76, 1/20/76, 3/8/76, 3/22/76, 4/11/76, 4/17/76, 4/17/76, 6/5/76, 8/7/76, 8/21/76, 11/7/76, 12/2/76, 1/15/77, 1/22/77, 1/25/77, 2/5/77, 2/24/77, 3/5/77, 3/12/77, 4/3/77, 5/21/77, 6/18/77, 7/2/77, 8/20/77, 9/11/77, 9/17/77, 10/29/77, 2/4/78, 5/16/81; Acts of Alabama, Sess. of 1876–77, pp. 257–58.

22. MMCC, 5/5/81.

6

Senator J. Thomas Heflin and the Expulsion Movement of 1929

The fall of the Redeemers from power in Alabama after the turn of the century was more a voluntary than a forced abdication. Ever pragmatic in their approach to politics, the majority of the Redeemer elite took the lesson of the Populist period to heart. Without the black vote, they could not maintain themselves in power. But as long as blacks remained legal voters, there was always the danger that a dissident white group might capture the blacks' confidence, and with these allies go on to effect a complete revolution in state government. Clearly, the way to prevent such an eventuality was to admit to some degree of power the excluded white groups from whose ranks dissident movements had time and again arisen, while concurrently eliminating blacks from politics. Of course, such a program meant a considerable diminution of power for the Redeemers, but "half a loaf is better than none." The result was the Constitution of 1901. The Redeemers contented themselves with disproportionate power in the malapportioned legislature, while largely—through the institution of the direct Democratic primary—abandoning executive offices to the formerly excluded white groups. Blacks were removed as a possible bone of contention between the two segments of the white electorate by their effective disfranchisement.

By the time of the Henderson administration (1915–19), it was clear that the Redeemer ploy had been successful. The north Alabama hill counties and the Wiregrass counties in the southeast, the homes of the majority of the dissident whites, had accepted the degree of power that the Constitutional Convention had granted them and had made no further attempts to dislodge the Redeemers from their remaining strongholds. Redeemers continued to control Black Belt county governments (see map 6.1). The Black Belt bloc was unrivaled within the legislature for its coherence, consistency, and continuity. But very few of the ideological heirs of the old Redeemer elite would ever again achieve statewide eminence.[1]

By the end of the 1920s, the number of important officials who might fairly be called descendants of the old ruling group was small indeed. Henry De Lamar Clayton II, after a distinguished career in Congress cul-

6.1. Alabama's Black Belt

minating in the passage of the Clayton Antitrust Act, was now one of Alabama's federal district judges. Chief Justice John C. Anderson of Demopolis led a state Supreme Court made up largely of north Alabamians. William A. Gunter Jr., mayor of Montgomery, controlled with genial paternalism Alabama's most famous city machine, and his influence spread far beyond his city's boundaries. Edmund W. Pettus II of Selma, grandson of Alabama's longtime US senator and son of a former Speaker of the Alabama House and president of the Alabama Senate, served as chairman of the state Democratic Executive Committee. These men and others like them had just lived through a decade that had left them apprehensive for their positions—and with good reason.

The 1920s were hard times in Alabama. Like their forebears of the 1890s, north Alabamians and residents of the Wiregrass were growing restless under a Redeemer-engineered order. Although they might control the governorship, they seldom saw the legislature pass any laws regarded by the Black Belt as radical. If North Alabamians and their allies in the southeast were ever aroused and organized, there was danger that they might force the adoption of a program that would be anathema to the remnants of the Redeemers. The levees of power, however, had been carefully and lovingly constructed at the turn of the century. Only by breaking clear of, or taking over entirely, the Democratic Party and striking out as a self-consciously revolutionary force could the white small farmers and mill-workers of north Alabama and the Wiregrass hope to disturb the political status quo. The descendants of the Redeemers, aware of this fact, sought constantly to emphasize the necessity for white racial solidarity and party unity. It was particularly important to prevent the Republican Party from becoming a socially acceptable alternative to Democracy. But any organization that tended to give structure and purpose to north Alabama and Wiregrass frustrations was characterized by the Redeemers as dangerous.

At the dawn of the 1920s, the Republicans were still regarded as too radical to appeal to any but the most disenchanted voters.[2] Two other groups, however, were tending to weld north Alabamians and their sympathizers into an effective political bloc—the Anti-Saloon League and the Ku Klux Klan. The former had been a power in Alabama politics for some time, but the 1920s saw it reach such a position that no candidate dared incur its active opposition. The sectional character of the league, and of its ally the Women's Christian Temperance Union, was marked. Wet sentiment had always been strongest in the Black Belt. At the outset of the Prohibition crusade, however, there had been considerable sympathy for the effort in some urban centers. The Progressive movement had been particularly enamored of the cause. But once Prohibition had become a fact and the Progressive movement had largely been laid to rest, the experiment rapidly lost its urban support. By the 1920s, the backbone of the league's strength was in the rural hill counties.[3] Curiously, this narrowing of the league's base seems only to have strengthened it as a political instrument. As its membership took on a homogeneous character, it came to be regarded by its membership as a spokesman for their class. They were thus far more likely than before to support the candidates it endorsed. Therefore, despite growing repeal sentiment, no admitted wet ventured to offer himself for statewide office during the decade. It should be emphasized that this enforced conformity on the Prohibition question was largely abstracted from the nominal issue involved. The hill country and Wiregrass residents would have regarded a candidate advocating repeal as engaging in a calculated insult to their entire socioeconomic group, and would have repudiated him on this basis, quite apart from their sentiments on temperance. And it was to underscore that they did not hold small farmers in contempt that candidates no longer questioned the wisdom of Prohibition. The Anti-Saloon League might well have become the political voice of the hills and the Wiregrass had not its scope been so clearly limited to one issue. This fact forced those poorer white Alabamians who were seeking a vehicle for general protest to look elsewhere.

The vehicle to which they turned was the Ku Klux Klan. The rise of the Klan during the 1920s was phenomenal. Starting from almost nothing at the beginning of the decade, but building on the political awareness created among poor whites by the Anti-Saloon League, the Klan grew rapidly. It offered elaborate ceremonies to take the member's mind off his poverty. It offered specific villains who could be blamed for causing that poverty. And it promised vigorous, positive action to punish those villains and to undo their work. The hard-pressed farmers and millworkers were eager to support any organization that purported to identify their enemies and to take action to foil the antifarmer and antiworker conspiracy. Klaverns sprouted all over the state.

The height of the Klan's political success came in the elections of 1926. In the gubernatorial campaign, the incumbent administration of William W. "Plain Bill" Brandon gave its support to Lieutenant Governor Charles S. McDowell Jr., who also received the support of the conservative press, led by the *Montgomery Advertiser*. Also in the campaign was Archibald H. Carmichael, who was regarded as a candidate of the small business, education, and Prohibition forces. A. G. Patterson, president of the state Public Service Commission, canvassed as a "pay-as-you-go" highway construction advocate. The final candidate in the race, D. Bibb Graves, was distinct in the field for having no support among any important segment of the state press or party leadership. He proclaimed his support of heavier taxation of corporations, improved educational facilities, the end of the convict lease system, and extensive highway construction.[4] Graves's attitude toward corporations, the open hostility to him shown in Redeemer circles, and his self-proclaimed friendship for the "common man" attracted to his cause one major voting bloc: the Klan. Indeed, Graves had long been allied with the Klan and was a former Cyclops of the Montgomery klavern.

In the senatorial race, the Klan endorsed a young Birmingham attorney, Hugo L. Black. Black had served a term as solicitor of Jefferson County before fighting in World War I, but he was primarily known in the rest of the state for his efforts as a special prosecutor in the 1924 trial of a Mobile bootlegging ring led by future congressman Frank Boykin. Some three weeks after Black announced his candidacy, the aged and distinguished incumbent Oscar W. Underwood, a bitter enemy of the Klan, decided to retire without a fight.[5] This decision left John H. Bankhead Jr., a major corporate lawyer and the son of the former senator, as Black's principal opponent. Black took his campaign to every hill and hollow, lambasting the elements that Graves called the "Big Mules" and attacking the wet Roman Catholic Alfred E. Smith, a likely candidate for the Democratic presidential nomination in 1928.[6] The Klan's Imperial Wizard, Hiram Evans of Georgia, endorsed L. Breckinridge Musgrove, a millionaire industrialist who had given generously to the Klan cause.[7] But there was never any doubt as to whom the Alabama Klan was supporting for the Senate. State Klansmen simply could not resist Black's oft-repeated cry, "I am the candidate of the masses!"[8]

It should be noted also that in no race in 1926 was the Klan an open issue.[9] Here, as in the case of Prohibition, a direct attack upon the Klan would have been considered by a substantial part of the electorate to be an expression of upper-class contempt for "plain people." No candidate dared risk alienating this vote.

When the votes were counted, the extent of the Klan's victory became apparent. It had taken Graves, who had virtually no other organized support, and had made him governor over McDowell, who had a superior organization and great financial resources. It had made Black, who had never before even run for a statewide office, a US senator over three of the most famous names in the state. It had elected the attorney general, Charlie McCall, and according to the anti-Klan *Montgomery Advertiser*, "a large number of minor officials, a majority of county officials, a number of" congressmen, and about half of the membership of each house of the state legislature.[10] The mechanics of this achievement are extremely important for the understanding of later developments.

In 1915, the Anti-Saloon League had engineered the passage of the so-called double-choice primary law.[11] Prior to the passage of this act, Alabama primaries had been conducted under resolutions adopted by the party executive committee. These resolutions specified that when no candidate for an office received a majority of the votes cast, a runoff primary was to be held.[12] The new law, however, altered this procedure. It provided that the voter was to be permitted to indicate on the ballot a first and a second choice for each office. In the event that no candidate received a majority of all first-choice votes, the second-choice votes of the two leading candidates were to be added directly to their first-choice ones, and the one of these two candidates with the larger total was to be declared nominated. The Anti-Saloon League hoped that in a multicandidate race this complicated procedure would aid well-organized minority blocs, and indeed it did.

In the late 1920s, as the *Montgomery Advertiser* commented, "In Alabama it is hard to tell where the League ends and the Klan begins."[13] Certainly the two organizations spoke for very similar socioeconomic groups. As the best-organized pressure groups in the state, they had made the double-choice primary their road to political power. The arcane procedures for casting a double vote deterred many voters from attempting to indicate a second choice. But the Klan and the league were careful to instruct their members in the intricacies of the primary ballot. Moreover, when a voter through personal loyalty or family commitment was constrained to cast his first choice for a candidate other than the Klan or league favorite, he could nevertheless designate the organizations' favorite as a second choice. In 1926, according to a Black Belt newspaper, a model ballot, with the X's already marked in, was distributed "by the tens of thousands" from Klan headquarters in Birmingham, and many voters appeared to follow its recommendations absolutely.[14]

The operation of the double-choice law may be clearly seen in the 1926 gubernatorial results. In first-choice votes, Graves, McDowell, Carmichael, and Patterson received approximately 61,000, 60,000, 54,000, and 47,000 votes respectively. In second-choice votes, however, Graves with his Klan endorsement polled 21,978. McDowell received only 7,943. Graves was thus declared the winner by almost 16,000 votes. About two-thirds of those who participated in the primary, 141,770 voters, did not bother, or did not understand how, to indicate a second choice, while 40,054 second-choice ballots were voided because they were cast either for Carmichael or for Patterson.[15] It seems likely that a runoff would have resulted in a very different outcome. Graves would probably have fallen heir to the Prohibitionist and education elements among Carmichael's supporters, but the remainder of the corporate attorney's vote would likely have gone to McDowell, as would the bulk of the support for Patterson, given Patterson's strong doubts about what he regarded as Graves's extravagant highway proposals. Thus, under a runoff system, Charles S. McDowell would probably have been nominated by the Democrats and elected governor in 1926. As it was, Graves was generally understood to have been chosen on the basis of the Klan bloc—the one-third or more of the vote that the Klan and the league were said to control "in all weathers and under all circumstances."[16] An almost equally convincing case may be made for the nomination of Hugo Black for senator and Charlie McCall for attorney general, though each of them received a somewhat larger percentage of the first-choice vote than did Graves.

The conservatives were startled and disturbed by the Klan showing in 1926 and were determined to make a strong effort at the 1927 session of the legislature to break the back of the Klan movement by enacting antimasking legislation and a runoff primary bill.[17] At the same time, the Klan was determined to use its newly acquired legislative strength to enact incoming Governor Graves's legislative program and to pass the so-called press muzzling bill, designed to amend the libel statute in such a way as to suppress editorial criticism of the Klan. Klan legislators (whom the Redeemer press dubbed the "bedsheet bloc") held a slight majority in each house, but the conservatives possessed an advantage in their many years of legislative experience and their thorough knowledge of parliamentary rules and procedures.

The Goodwyn-Rogers runoff primary bill slipped through the House in the early days of the session, before the opposition to it had solidified. In the Senate, the bill was referred to the Privileges and Elections Committee, which was controlled by the forces inimical to it. Late in the session, Senator J. Miller Bonner of Wilcox, the leader of the Black Belt forces in the body, moved to recall the bill from Privileges and Elections and recommit it to the Judiciary Committee, which was prepared to report it favorably. The Klan and league senators, led by administration floor leader L. Handy Ellis of Shelby, vigorously contested this move. When the vote came, it resulted in a 15–15 tie, which was broken by Lieutenant Governor W. C. Davis of Jasper in favor of the administration.[18] The defeat of the runoff primary bill, as we shall see, played a crucial role in the development of the expulsion movement.

Meanwhile, clever tactics on the part of the conservatives killed the "press muzzling bill" also. While conservative leader R. Tyler Goodwyn of Montgomery, sponsor as well of the runoff primary bill, fought a valiant delaying effort in the House, where he was clearly outvoted, his allies in the Senate arranged for that body to adjourn early at its forty-eighth sitting. Administration forces were dismayed to learn later that, under the rules, the Senate was thus precluded from acting on the bill before the end of the session. The antimasking fight resulted in a compromise. The bill was defeated, but another was passed raising flogging from a misdemeanor to a felony. The rest of Graves's program was enacted. The convict lease system was abolished. A two and one-half percent gross business tax was placed on all public utilities, and the corporation franchise tax was doubled.

The *Montgomery Advertiser*, a principal Redeemer organ, decried the anticorporation spirit it alleged had characterized the legislature.[19] When the Revenue Bill was passed, it commented that "the most radical legislature since 1907 has fallen upon the industries and business of Alabama," and concluded bitterly that a good portion of the new money would go "to make the mothers of countless office-hungry politicians exclaim: 'I'm glad I raised my boy to be a Klansman!'"[20] Actually, the funds were put to good use. Expenditures for highways and public education were vastly increased.[21]

We cannot leave the legislature of 1927 without noting how archetypical its session was of all those held under the 1901 Compromise system. Even in their hour of greatest triumph, holding virtually every executive office and a majority in the legislature, the forces of the hill counties and the Wiregrass were compelled at every turn to negotiate with and often to yield to the Redeemers, still secure in the legislative fastnesses that remained of their once total power. Always the legislature placed a check on the reformist impulses of the more liberal governors. Always the governors goaded the legislature into more action than it would otherwise have taken. Inexorably but almost imperceptibly, Alabama government moved toward a more liberal position. If hill country leaders wished to effect any substantial reforms in a brief period of time, they would have to break out of and destroy this compromise system. They could not be content with primary victories, for control of the executive was not enough. And increasingly it seemed that in order to control the legislative branch, it might be necessary for the residents of the hills and the Wiregrass to leave the Democratic Party, as they had threatened to do in the Populist years.

While the progressive Klan-administration bloc spent its strength during the long summer months of 1927 battering against immovable Black Belt boulders, Alabama slipped closer to anarchy. In the 1926 election the Klan had captured a great many county offices. And, as Alabama Grand Dragon James Esdale boasted, though doubtless with some exaggeration, Governor Graves "made all of his appointments by and through the Klan."[22] As a result, something like a reign of terror gripped some rural sections of the state. For instance, in the Wiregrass county of Crenshaw law enforcement largely ceased to function.[23] Floggings and lawlessness over the state caused the Redeemer press more and more loudly to attack the Klan's hooliganism. As usual, the *Montgomery Advertiser* was in the vanguard of this movement.

In late June, Jeff Calloway, whom Redeemer papers were quick to describe as a young orphan, was severely flogged in the north Alabama hills of Blount County. On July 3, *Advertiser* editor Grover C. Hall wrote the first of a series of editorials for which he would win the Pulitzer Prize. Titled "The Glove of the Beast—Will the State Pick It Up?," it was typical of Hall's poetic style of writing and of the power of his imagery. Throughout the summer and fall Hall kept up his attacks. He was joined by editors of other newspapers, notably those of the *Selma Times-Journal*, the *Dothan Eagle* (whose editor was Grover Hall's nephew), the Birmingham *News*, and the Columbus *Enquirer-Sun*, which despite being a Georgia paper, had a substantial circulation in east Alabama. So much pressure was placed on the Klan that by the end of 1927, it had almost ceased the use of flogging as a tactic of intimidation.

The chief result of the vigorous attacks the conservative press launched was to convince many residents of the hills and the Wiregrass who were not Klan members that the Klan was a dangerous organization. The recruiting power of the Klan had so little to do with its ideology and so much to do with politics in this period that it was difficult for many hill country and Wiregrass residents to believe that the order was as evil as the Redeemers declared. The power of the Klan was concentrated in a limited area, and one does not usually suspect one's friends and neighbors of being vicious thugs. The farmers and millworkers had been told that Catholics, Jews, and other groups were responsible for the economic distress of, and the social threats to, the region. Violence represented primarily a protest against the distress and the threats. The floggings were abandoned chiefly because they did not appear to be ameliorating conditions in the section and because, thanks to the press campaign, they were alienating non-Klansmen who had formerly sympathized with the order's political efforts. The *Wiregrass Farmer* of Headland, a journal that sought to speak for the group in its title, warned, "If the Klan is to survive as a political organization in Alabama, it will have to . . . repudiate floggings and intimidation as a Klan principle."[24]

The abandonment of violent means of protest did not mean, however, that hill country and Wiregrass residents had abandoned their hopes of using the Klan in order to effect political and social reforms. Indeed, 1928 saw the Klan and its ally the Anti-Saloon League mount a major political effort, led by the state's senior US senator, J. Thomas Heflin, a dedicated Klansman, to defeat the Democratic Party's wet and Roman Catholic presidential nominee. J. Thomas Heflin came from a notable hill country family. Robert S. Heflin, his uncle, had been a prominent scalawag and had served a term in Congress from 1869 to 1871.[25] His father, Dr. Wilson L. Heflin, was a country doctor in Randolph County, and was the only doctor in that section of the state "equipped for performing surgical operations."[26] Dr. Heflin had eight sons. One of these, John, a farmer, represented Randolph County in the Constitutional Convention of 1901. Another son, Harrington, was for many years Jefferson County solicitor, but in 1914 was defeated for reelection by Hugo Black. After 1915, Harrington served as a circuit judge.[27] J. Thomas, generally known as "Tom," was elected mayor of LaFayette, the Chambers County seat, in 1893. He was state representative from his adopted county of Chambers from 1896 to 1900, and in 1901 he represented Chambers in the Constitutional Convention. From 1902 to 1904 he was Alabama's secretary of state, and for the next sixteen years was a congressman.[28] In 1920 he was elected to the Senate to replace the deceased senator John H. Bankhead Sr.

Tom Heflin was an extremely large man who was given to wearing wide-brimmed black hats, cream-colored frock-tailed coats, ornate vests, and string ties. His constituents greatly appreciated his theatrical qualities. A *New York Times* correspondent thus described him in debate with another senator: "Mr. Heflin raved. His face was a bright red and he swung his great body to and fro, coughing as he clinched his hands and swung one fist into the other. At times the two Senators shouted at the same time, waving their hands at each other." When Heflin said that the press gallery was filled with "squirrel headed" people, his opponent invited him to "compare their heads with his own."[29]

Heflin gained a reputation at the 1901 Constitutional Convention as a leader of the most racist forces, and his racism was of an extraordinarily virulent sort. During the 1930 campaign, he published a circular detailing his congressional record, in which he proudly wrote that "the failure to have separate street cars for whites and Negroes in Washington caused him to have to inflict severe punishment upon a drunken Negro who had insulted a white woman on the car." National notoriety had followed this incident of March 1908, in which Heflin, who apparently was himself the one who was drunk, had badly wounded a black man and wounded several other passengers as well. He was indicted for assault with a deadly weapon, but the case was eventually hushed up.[30]

Other than on racial policy, however, Heflin's record was far from consistent. His opponents often impugned his sincerity. The *Montgomery Advertiser* commented:

> If 51 per cent of the voters were Catholic, the Pope couldn't have alarmed Tom in a thousand years—on the contrary, Tom would have been the leader of the anti-Klan forces of the State and probably

> would have advocated the nomination of [Alfred E.] Smith. It is only in very recent years, when Tom found himself in need of an issue, that he discovered the Pope, in regard to whom he had been silent for 20 years before. When [William Jennings] Bryan was powerful in Alabama, Tom was a noisy Bryanite; in the days of [Oscar W.] Underwood's ascendancy, Tom was hot for him. He never turned on W. P. G. Harding until the chairman of the Federal Reserve Board became unpopular and seemed to have in himself the makings of a very good devil, in 1920 when economic distress in the South created the need for a devil. Tom never took any serious risks with prohibition. In 1909, when he, like a number of other politicians thought it would be ratified, Tom voted for the State prohibition amendment. It was beaten. Nine years later, when few thought it would be ratified, Tom voted and spoke against submission and ratification of the Eighteenth Amendment. It was ratified, and soon after Tom was so hot for National prohibition that many supposed he had been for it ever since [the Anti-Saloon League's] Bishop [James] Cannon was a boy. A few years ago Tom was in demand as a Fourth of July speaker under the auspices of the Knights of Columbus. Today Tom is teaching young Americans that the Knights of Columbus can have no possible interest in the Fourth of July.[31]

This summary of Heflin's intellectual odyssey is factually accurate, but we cannot assume that his frequent conversions were altogether self-serving. Heflin may merely have been acting as a son of the north Alabama hills, whose opinions followed, and were formed under the same pressures as, those of his constituents. His fervent embrace of Prohibition, for instance, coincides with the rise of the Anti-Saloon League as a political voice of hill country and Wiregrass residents. At any rate, by the end of the 1920s Heflin was firmly identified in the public mind with Prohibition, anti-Catholicism and, at least in intellectual circles, with political buffoonery.

During his early career in Congress, Heflin was ignored or granted minimal toleration by the Redeemer group. He talked a great deal, but not having the respect of his fellow legislators, he was rendered very nearly impotent in terms of actual accomplishment. Hence his enemies considered him harmless. Grover C. Hall, who strongly supported the Goodwyn-Rogers runoff bill, was merely amused when Heflin issued a statement opposing the legislation.[32] On another occasion Hall spoke of "the slender talents and negligible influence of this utterly commonplace man," and concluded patronizingly, "We do not know whether Tom is out of his head, or whether he is merely a simpleton. He is one or the other."[33]

Heflin's single significant legislative accomplishment was the passage of his bill creating the national holiday of Mother's Day, a proposal with which he had hoped to rally opposition to the then-pending Women's Suffrage Amendment by emphasizing what he took to be women's proper role. One suspects that very few who participate in this annual celebration today are aware of its actual origins.

A crisis in Heflin's senatorial career, however, was reached on January 19, 1928. After one of Heflin's frequent attacks on Catholicism, Senator Joseph T. Robinson of Arkansas, the minority leader, rose to reply. Robinson was a Prohibitionist and an opponent of Al Smith. Evidently he hoped that his reaffirmation of the virtues of religious toleration would free his forces from the taint of Heflinism. Rather than accepting Robinson's rather mild rebuke, though, Heflin shouted that if the Arkansan ever came to Alabama, he would be tarred and feathered. He demanded that Robinson resign as minority leader. Robinson accepted the challenge and called a caucus meeting for the following day to consider the matter.[34] The gathering of the caucus found Heflin utterly deserted by his brethren. The vote went against him by 33 to 1. Hugo Black, Heflin's junior colleague, abstained from voting.[35]

The encounter with Robinson marked something of a turning point in the conservative attitude toward Heflin. He no longer was a harmless nuisance. He was now a menace to party unity. Shocked at Heflin's attack on a fellow Democrat, a fellow southerner, and a man greatly admired throughout the region, the Alabama press was nearly unanimous in its condemnation of the Alabamian. Unlimbering the prose style for which he was famous, the *Advertiser*'s Hall commented: "What a callous and wretched demagogue Heflin is! What a disgrace to a proud State that its senior Senator should invite the Democratic leader of the Senate to come to Alabama to be 'tarred and feathered'! How humiliating and depressing a thing it is that such a man should be the keeper of Alabama's good name abroad! O, that the heart and soul of this people had a voice in the United States Senate!"[36] Meanwhile, Montgomery's Mayor Gunter invited Robinson to speak there as the city's guest, and the Mobile City Council adopted a resolution censuring Heflin.[37]

Alabamians were united in their opposition to Al Smith. The New Yorker received but one of the Alabama delegation's votes at the Houston convention.[38] But for the Redeemers, the maintenance of party regularity was of prime importance, regardless of the identity of the nominee. As we have seen, as long as the discontent of the small farmers and millworkers was confined within the bounds of the political status quo, the Redeemer position was secure. Only when protest spilled over the party levees and challenged the foundations of the system were the remnants of Redeemer power in danger. Senator Heflin's attack on the leader of Senate Democrats bespoke a dangerous tendency on his part to put principle above party. It was deeply disturbing that a Democratic caucus had chastened an Alabamian for lack of deference to party authority. And Heflin's course in succeeding months fulfilled the conservatives' worst fears. If Heflin were able to take his north Alabama and Wiregrass constituency out of the party, the Compromise of 1901 was in real danger.

Immediately after Al Smith's nomination, Heflin announced himself "shocked and dismayed" and predicted that Smith would lose.[39] This was not the sort of statement that a man contemplating acquiescence in the party's decision would be likely to make. On July 4, state chairman Edmund Pettus, attempting to forestall a bolt, warned that the Democratic Executive Committee had the power to bar the heterodox from the party's primaries.[40] In the weeks immediately following, Heflin remained silent—so silent, in fact, that by September 9 the *New York Times* predicted that Heflin might yet "slide into the Smith camp, or at least the Alabama end of it." On September 21, in an effort to force the issue, former governor William W. Brandon invited Heflin to speak on behalf of the Democratic ticket. He refused.[41]

On September 22, the state Democratic Executive Committee convened in Birmingham to organize for the coming campaign. Chairman Pettus read a telegram from the Lee County Committee stating that Heflin had met with Republican strategists in Opelika on September 20 and had announced that he would make an anti-Smith speech on September 25. The wire concluded, "He must not longer be tolerated."[42] Great consternation was generated by this revelation. A motion was carried to dismiss from the committee two of its members, Hugh Locke of Birmingham and Hamp Draper of Wetumpka, who were actively campaigning for the Republican candidate, Herbert Hoover.

The Democratic leadership was greatly disturbed by the fact that "white men and women" were "preaching the Republican doctrine," thus making the Republican Party appear to be a respectable opposition force in Alabama. With a US senator supporting a Republican, and any number of his followers thus having their habit of obedience to party decisions shattered, the status quo was in grave jeopardy. Chairman Pettus made it clear that opposition to Al Smith himself was not the sin involved. The sin was failing to recognize the outcome of an intraparty contest as binding on all concerned.[43] Appealing beyond the established institutional limits of the party directly to the voters was a threat to the entire system.

The committee invited the state's congressional delegation, including Heflin, to serve on the state campaign committee. This action finally induced Heflin to break his silence. On September 24, in an open letter to Chairman Pettus, he declined the offer and attacked Smith and John J. Raskob, the Democratic national campaign manager.[44] The campaign grew increasingly heated as frightened conservatives fought back. Montgomery's Mayor Gunter, whose powerful machine was an old and bitter enemy of Heflin, denied the senator the use of the city auditorium. When Heflin came to the capital anyway, Governor Graves had to dispatch a contingent of state police to protect him.[45] On October 26, the state campaign committee adopted a resolution denouncing him.[46] Finally, on October 30, Heflin took the step for which everyone had been waiting. Addressing a Dothan crowd, he declared, "I will vote against Al Smith, so help me God!"[47] The next week an Anniston audience pelted him with eggs.[48]

When the votes were counted, Smith won over Hoover by the tiny margin of 127,796 to 120,725.[49] Many observers felt that only manipulation of the returns in some Black Belt counties accounted for the Democratic victory. The sectional character of the vote was marked; the hill counties provided the backbone of Hoover's support, and the Black Belt went solidly for Smith.[50] The bolt was no longer an abstract fear, but a reality. It now seemed that only canny leadership and vigorous action could allow the Redeemers to save the 1901 Compromise system. Redeemer Democracy's one last hope was the expulsion movement. On November 25, it was launched.

The first public suggestion of the expulsion movement came from Geneva County attorney and businessman Edward C. "Bud" Boswell, who had recently headed the losing effort to keep his county in the Democratic column—and who, in future years, would become notorious as the author of the disfranchising Boswell Amendment. In a telegram to each member of the state Executive Committee, he lashed out at the bolters and urged that they be barred from the 1930 primary.[51] The Redeemer leadership, however, did not so quickly endorse this course of action.

If the Goodwyn-Rogers runoff bill could yet be passed, there would be little need to take such radical action as expulsion. Heflin and the Klan-backed gubernatorial candidate Hugh Locke would be defeated in a primary in which the Klan's endorsement would not be sufficient to ensure nomination through second-choice voting, the Redeemers believed. And without a public office, these officials would no longer be in a strong position to lead a political revolt. Hope for the runoff was stimulated by the likelihood that Governor Graves would be forced to call a special session of the legislature to obtain additional appropriations for his highway program. Graves was aware of the Redeemer plans, however, and was determined to confine any special session to the highway question. In order to control a rebellious House, he depended on its Speaker, J. Lee Long. Long had in the past been lukewarm at best in his support of the administration. But Graves hoped to effect a rapprochement with him. In late January the governor summoned Long to Montgomery to discuss the situation. There, on February 2, Long suffered a heart attack and died. Without Long's gavel in the House, a special session was too risky. The new Speaker was likely to be Alfred M. Tunstall of Hale, an old legislative warhorse but a man who in 1927 had been unable to control the House.[52] In addition, the number of vacancies that had occurred in the legislature, five in the Senate alone, would most likely be filled by nomination by the state Democratic Executive Committee. Were five senators hostile to the administration to be seated, it would break Graves's tenuous hold over that body. By February 14, Graves had decided against a special session.[53]

At this point a split developed within the conservative group as to the proper course to follow. One group, typified by Hugh S. D. Mallory Jr., of Selma, felt that the enactment of runoff legislation would be the only effective way to deal with bolters on a lasting basis. They desired to continue agitation for a special session. Mallory and other members of this group were closely identified with the industrial forces in the state.[54] Their position was best expressed by Birmingham congressman George Huddleston in his reaction to the Boswell telegram. "If we bar the anti-Smith Democrats from the next primary, it may easily transpire that we will raise up a respectable white opposition party that will plague the Democrats permanently," he said.[55] The other Redeemer group, led by Black Belters and typified by S. Hubert Dent of Eufaula, wanted to expel the bolters, feeling that expulsion, as an example of swift retribution for rebellion, would prevent future attempts to leave the party.

In mid-April, Mallory dispatched a telegram to Mrs. Mabel Jones West, president of both the Alabama Women's Democratic Club and the Alabama Women's League for White Supremacy, vigorously attacking the double-choice primary and demanding the institution of runoffs.[56] Some days later Dent replied in a letter to the *Advertiser*. He joined in deploring the double-choice primary but maintained that Graves would never allow a special session to consider its repeal, as Graves, while acting as a lobbyist for the Anti-Saloon League in 1915, "was largely responsible for the present primary law, if indeed he was not its author." With the legislature thus precluded from acting, the task of preserving the party devolved upon the Democratic Executive Committee. Expulsion was the only answer.[57]

Dent's letter also revealed that a movement was afoot to have all anti-Klan forces unite on a single candidate in both the senatorial and the gubernatorial contests. If such an alliance were achieved, of course, the disadvantages of the double-choice primary would be eliminated. But Dent disparaged the movement's chances for success, calling it "impractical." "There is no authority to enforce it and no machinery to execute it," he concluded.[58] The following week Mrs. West's Women's League for White Supremacy went on record as repudiating "Heflin as our representative in any sense" and deploring "his foolish and fanatical assaults upon those of our fellow citizens who are members of the Roman Catholic Church."[59]

While the discussions as to the best course to pursue continued, the Redeemer press set out to discredit Heflin in the eyes of the small farmer portion of his constituency. While Congress was in extraordinary session considering farm relief legislation in 1929, Senator Heflin occupied fully half of the Senate's time attempting to induce the body to adopt a resolution deploring a mob attack on him in Brockton, Massachusetts. Commented the *Advertiser*, "What does he care about the progress of the farm bill? His thoughts are occupied with something infinitely more important than the welfare of the farmers. He is thinking about himself. . . . For the simple fact is that Senator Heflin, Democrat, Alabama, considers himself far more important than any farmer, or all the farmers put together."[60]

On May 10, the *Advertiser* announced the decision of the first two state Democratic Executive Committee members to commit themselves publicly. They were for expulsion. But the Mallory faction was far from convinced. On July 7, Mallory, evidently still hoping to force a special session, released a statement flatly opposing expulsion. On July 10, Dent replied with a letter denouncing minority rule by organized blocs and demanding expulsion of all bolters. On July 12, the *Advertiser* broke its long silence on the issue with an editorial seeking to effect a compromise among its warring children. It suggested that all bolters be barred from becoming candidates in the party primary, but that anyone who pledged to support its choices be permitted to vote in it.[61]

The summer was also an active one for the antiexpulsion forces. Congressmen and county officeholders put substantial pressure on state Democratic Executive Committee members. Their position was a difficult one. Whereas over the state as a whole anti-Klan forces had a majority, in several congressional districts and many counties supporters of the bolters held dominance. If the Democrats expelled the bolters, their supporters might well wreak vengeance on the local party representatives at the general election.[62] Frightened by the prospect of alienating a group that was a majority in a number of counties and the largest single voting bloc in many more, county officeholders succeeded in convincing a group of committeemen of the rationality of their fears. By August 30 the *Advertiser*'s political columnist, Atticus Mullin, was forced to acknowledge the effectiveness of these efforts. Whereas in May thirty-one committeemen had been for expulsion, he wrote, at this time only twelve to fourteen could be counted on.[63]

This admission marked the low ebb of the expulsionists' fortunes. The *Advertiser* feared that the state, after all, was in for another Heflin campaign. "The serious public questions of the hour must be forgotten in the storm and fury that the Heflin jehad will raise. . . . The drill sergeants of organized hatred and fear are to march again in Alabama. Whispering couriers are to skulk from post to post by night and scatter their poison."[64] Mullin's revelation served to rally Redeemer leaders to action, and by September 10, Mullin reported hopefully that "supporters of the move [expulsion] say that there has been a noticeable stiffening of Democratic backs, so far as the state committee is concerned, in the last ten days." At the same time he suggested the compromise that was eventually to turn the tide. Admitting that "ninety-five per cent" of the state's county officials were opposed to expulsion, he suggested that the state Democratic Executive Committee's bar apply only to statewide races, and that the setting of qualifications for local races be left to the party's county committees.[65] During the coming days Mullin conducted a vigorous campaign in an attempt to alter party and public sentiment on the issue. Supporting him editorially, the *Advertiser* called the readmission of the bolters as candidates "unthinkable."[66]

Meanwhile, the effort received accidental support on September 4, when Governor Graves announced that there definitely would be no special session of the legislature. With the last hope of removing the electoral mechanics of Klan power through legislation thus eliminated, almost all of the conservatives began to accept the expulsion movement as the only avenue left open for dealing effectively with the bolters' challenge. In addition, Mullin's suggested compromise severely undercut the argument of county officials, for it would have the effect of placing the contest strictly on a pro-Heflin or anti-Heflin basis. Local personalities would not be drawn into the controversy, and local sentiment was consequently not so likely to be stirred up.

As a result of these factors, Mullin was able to report on September 15 that the crisis had passed. There had been, he said, "a big change of heart" within the state Democratic Executive Committee in "the last week."[67] The tide was now running in favor of the expulsionists. Even so, as a Heflin ally reported to him, the situation still remained fluid.[68]

On October 29 the *Selma Times-Journal*, which was close to Hugh Mallory, made one final effort to rally all of the anti-Klan forces behind the gubernatorial candidacy of W. C. Davis. But Davis's strong support from labor made him unacceptable in some Redeemer circles.[69] With the failure of this movement, the *Times-Journal* joined the expulsionist bandwagon and was soon saying that the existence of the double-choice primary in Alabama had compelled the crusade.[70]

By November the battle lines were clearly drawn. The conservatives had decided to risk everything on their belief that expulsion would crush the hill country–Wiregrass revolt. Once this commitment by the Redeemer forces had been made, Governor Graves could no longer hold aloof from the fray. He delegated his chief political lieutenant, Gaston Scott, to organize the antiexpulsionist forces, and he himself went to Washington to consult with Senators Heflin and Black.[71] While Scott traveled the state rounding up support for the administration position, Klan leaders from all of northeast Alabama gathered in Birmingham to plot strategy with Hugh Locke.[72] On November 12, Senator Black issued a statement pleading for party harmony and opposing expulsion. The *Advertiser* replied to what it called the "harmony boys" that they "know that with their minority-rule primary law, with numerous candidates for each office, they stand a good chance of electing their ticket in the next Democratic primary—provided the bars are kept down. . . . Klan politicians and Anti-Saloon League politicians . . . are now exerting themselves to 'keep the bars down' not because they love real party harmony, but because they love . . . the Klan and the Anti-Saloon League." The paper called the situation in Alabama an example "of what can be done by well-organized, shrewdly led minorities that know what they want. . . . Unless [the] majority finds some way to center on its own ticket in 1930, it is doubtful whether they can free themselves from this . . . minority gag rule."[73]

The leaders of the expulsionist forces within the state Democratic Executive Committee were Chairman Pettus; Cyrus Brown of Montgomery, the political boss of the powerful Gunter organization there; and Thomas J. Judge III, a Birmingham lawyer, former state legislator, and grandson of the prominent antebellum Whig politician and jurist.[74] One of the problems they faced was that many politicians who were up for election in 1930, fearing to anger any substantial voting bloc, remained neutral in the fight.[75] John Bankhead Jr., Heflin's only announced opponent, actively opposed expulsion, believing that Heflin would be easier to beat in a primary.[76] However, toward the end of November, Bankhead was induced to release those committeemen pledged to him, to vote as they chose on expulsion.[77]

Having achieved this major breakthrough, the expulsionists arranged a caucus in Birmingham for Thanksgiving Day, just before the football game between the University of Alabama and the University of Georgia. A count revealed that twenty-six of the fifty committee members were likely to vote for expulsion. Although a decision as to when to call the state Democratic Executive Committee together for a vote on expulsion could not be made at the Birmingham meeting, it was later decided that the committee would meet in Montgomery on December 16, 1929.[78]

It being now obvious that Pettus must have the votes, the opposition began frantic last-minute maneuvers. On November 22, Heflin had written an admirer that the "situation is fine in Alabama. The masses are for me."[79] After Pettus's announcement, however, Heflin's forces tried to cut loose from their erstwhile ally Hugh Locke. A movement was launched to have the committee bar Locke but not Heflin, since Locke had actually voted for Hoover, whereas Heflin said that he had merely refrained from voting.[80] On December 11, the *Montgomery Advertiser* carried an editorial condemning this plan. On the same day, Judge Harrington Heflin wrote his brother that the committee's action now seemed certain. It would endorse expulsion.[81]

The day before the committee was to meet, the antiexpulsionists played their last cards. Gaston Scott released a letter from W. L. Lee of Dothan, a bolter, promising to run for governor if the bars were not put up. Thus, Scott argued, the Klan vote would be split between Lee and Hugh Locke, and its power as a bloc would be destroyed. The argument was so clearly one of desperation that it was received with a laugh by the expulsionists.[82] A different reaction greeted a telegram from Democratic national chairman Jouett Shouse opposing expulsion.[83] His interference in local politics merely provoked resentment.

The committee meeting went as expected. Committeeman Seybourn A. Lynne of Decatur, significantly a close political ally of John Bankhead, introduced the resolution, which included both sections of the *Advertiser*'s compromise. It excluded from candidacy in statewide races all persons who had either voted for Hoover or campaigned actively against Smith. But it welcomed back as voters bolters of all stripes, provided that they pledged to support in November the nominees of the August primary. And it left to the discretion of the county Democratic committees the qualifications for local office.[84] Lynne told the committee, "Gentlemen, if we are to have a Democratic party, we must play the game. . . . If we are to have an organization, we must be willing to bow our heads when the majority is against our cause." John D. McQueen thundered, "Democrats must know that the rules of the Party mean something. They must know that when a primary election is legally called and legally held, that those men [nominated] of right are entitled to the support of Democrats." McQueen placed emphasis on observing the results of primaries, when in theory what was at issue was the outcome of a national presidential nominating convention. In this statement he revealed the true source of Redeemer fears.

Arthur F. Fite, speaking against expulsion, said that the bolt of 1928 "was not a revolt against the Democratic Party; it was a revolt against one man."[85] He pleaded with the committee not to turn its back on the bolters of 1928, some of whom had remained good and loyal Democrats in

1896, when other Alabamians—including as he implied, some of today's expulsionists—had bolted against William Jennings Bryan in order to follow the Goldbug standard of Palmer and Buckner.

The expulsion resolution was adopted 27 to 21. A correspondent for the *New York Times* analyzed the vote as follows: "When the roll-call came on the resolution . . . it became apparent that the central section of Alabama [the Black Belt] was opposing the bolters almost to a man. All five committee members from the Sixth [Congressional] District voted to bar the men who had supported Hoover. It was this district which was principally responsible for the 7000 majority given Smith in 1928. In the [hill country's] Eighth District, which was carried by the Hoover supporters, four of the five committee members voted not to read Heflin and Locke out of the party."[86] Indeed, only one Black Belter—Henry McDaniel of Marengo—voted against expulsion.

The campaign of 1930 is beyond the scope of the present inquiry. The postexpulsion situation was well summarized by the Thomasville *Times*: "If Alabama had not had its crazy election law, the bolters would never have been barred from becoming candidates. . . . The bolters are united. They have concentrated on one man for each office, knowing that the bolter vote would elect in a field of three or four. But their hopes have been shattered and now they must fight it out against one man, picked from the ranks of the loyal Democrats."[87] Heflin and Locke were barred from running in the Democratic primary. They ran as independents in the general election and received enough votes to indicate that they would have been nominated against a field of candidates under the double-choice primary law. In the general election, their opponents concentrated on the Democratic nominees, and both Klansmen went down to defeat. In the 1931 legislature, the now dominant conservatives succeeded in replacing the double-choice primary with the runoff system.

It is too much to maintain that the expulsion of their leaders from the primary crushed the Klan movement. The Klan had already been dead for some years in surrounding states.[88] Only the unique sociopolitical function that the Klan was serving in Alabama had kept it vital there. It had been losing members ever since its defeat in the presidential election of 1928, and to some extent even before that date.[89] In addition, the advent of the Great Depression in 1929 played a role in dissipating political protest within the state. There seems to be a point beyond which discontent, such as characterized Alabama in the 1920s, is converted into despair. And the plight of Alabama in the early 1930s was nothing if not desperate. Alabamians turned in greater numbers toward Washington and national politics for deliverance. The "New Deal" came with Franklin D. Roosevelt in 1933, opening new avenues of approach to some old problems.

Nevertheless, at least as important as these factors in suppressing the Democratic revolt was the nature of the political structure in Alabama, and the determination of the conservatives, as proven by the expulsion movement, to enforce the limits of that structure. Alabama had experienced hill country–Wiregrass political revolts before—the Greenbackers in the 1870s and the Populists in the 1890s. The Populist revolt was crushed by fraud and manipulation of the then-existing political structure. The Klan movement, which was in Alabama essentially a reflection of the same social conflicts that had underlain Populism, was dealt with far more effectively, thanks to the political structure that had grown out of the Constitution of 1901. Only by outright repudiation of this system could the hills and the Wiregrass have achieved their political goals. The demonstration that the Redeemers could still effectively discipline protesters who transgressed the borders of the status quo ended, for the present, all hill country and Wiregrass ambitions in that direction. It seemed to small farmers and millworkers, and to their political spokesmen, that revolt was unnecessary and inexpedient if the opposition to the Redeemers could win in the primary anyway. This was exactly the misconception that the Redeemers wanted to perpetuate. And it was to make sure that this myth was accepted in the future that Tom Heflin was expelled from the Democratic primary in 1930.

Thus in 1934 Bibb Graves, former Klansman and dedicated progressive who stayed within the party in 1928, became Alabama's first governor since the adoption of the Constitution of 1901 to be elected to a second term. And Hugo Black, who got overwhelming Klan support in 1926 but remained a loyal Democrat in the crisis of 1928, was reelected to the Senate in 1932.

The pattern remained fixed. A progressive under the system that had evolved out of the 1901 constitutional structure could win the governorship and other executive offices, but the conservatives prevented the reapportionment of the legislature. With their power in that body and in the party councils, they stood ready to discipline bolters who threatened their control.

Notes

This article appeared initially, in a slightly different form, in the *Alabama Review* (April 1968). It was a graduate seminar paper written for Professor C. Vann Woodward at Yale.

1. For a fuller account of the events surrounding the Constitutional Convention of 1901, see Malcolm C. McMillan, *Constitutional Development in Alabama: A Study in Politics, the Negro, and Sectionalism* (Chapel Hill: University of North Carolina Press, 1955), 233–59.

A word about the geography of Alabama is in order. The Black Belt is a band of thirteen counties across the south-central portion of the state. It is so named because its soil characteristically is rich in humus. Historically it has been a center of political and social conservatism. It is generally allied with four or five counties in the southwestern corner of the state whose social structures resemble those of the Black Belt. North Alabama is a mountainous region of small farms and, by the time of this study, mines and mills. It has historically harbored liberalism, and indeed radicalism, within its confines. It is allied politically with the Wiregrass region, a group of eleven counties in the southeastern part of the state. In the antebellum period the Tennessee River Valley in the far north constituted a distinct political region, but by the time with which we deal here, it differed from the rest of north Alabama in little except topography.

My use of the term *Redeemer* here also requires explanation. I do not mean that the leaders about whom I am writing in 1929 were the actual people who had ended Reconstruction in 1874 (though in a surprising number of cases, as I shall show, they were the sons or grandsons of the very men who had done so). I mean, rather, to characterize the political and social attitudes and convictions that these leaders were defending. I also use the term *conservative* to describe them, though no such broad term can capture their beliefs perfectly. Indeed, a principal point of this article is to clarify the structure of their commitments.

2. There were 30,000 to 40,000 Alabama Republicans able to vote in this period, out of a total registration (1930) of 356,627.

3. See the map contained in A. B. Moore, *History of Alabama* (Tuscaloosa: University Supply Store, 1934), 796.

4. Ibid., 769–70.

5. John P. Frank, *Mr. Justice Black: The Man and His Opinions* (New York: Knopf, 1949), 39. A rather naive account of the campaign is contained on pp. 39–43.

6. *New York Times*, August 9, 1926.

7. Ibid.; Frank, *Mr. Justice Black*, 42. This endorsement was made despite the fact that both Black and Evans had been born, five years apart, in the small Clay County seat of Ashland.

8. Frank, *Mr. Justice Black*, 42.

9. *Montgomery Advertiser*, August 21, 1929.

10. Ibid., May 29, 1929.

11. Ibid., November 12, 1929. For an extremely interesting account of how Prohibitionist forces had snatched control of the 1915 legislature from the Henderson administration, see ibid., January 28, 1915. "General Law 78," *General Laws of the Legislature of Alabama Passed at the Session of 1915* (Montgomery, 1915), 218–39.

12. E.g., "Resolution of the Alabama Democratic Executive Committee Adopted January 7, 1914," *Alabama Official and Statistical Register, 1915*, 396–98.

13. *Montgomery Advertiser*, November 13, 1929.

14. *Selma Times-Journal*, December 29, 1929.

15. Figures from *Alabama Official and Statistical Register, 1927*, 362–63.

16. *Montgomery Advertiser*, November 12, 1929. On the operation of the double-choice primary, see however Samuel L. Webb, "Hugo Black, Bibb Graves, and the Ku Klux Klan: A Revisionist View of the 1926 Alabama Democratic Primary," *Alabama Review* (October 2004): 243–73. Although Professor Webb's analysis casts doubt on the Klan's ability to manipulate the primary process, it remains true that political activists of every stripe at the time had no doubt of that ability, and proceeded accordingly. In a multicandidate race, the perceived ability of any organization to influence a significant bloc of votes inevitably made it significant in the eyes of the contestants. The point is not that Klansmen were a majority of Alabama's voters, but that under the double-choice primary system, the significance of an endorsement by an influential group was magnified. Professor Webb reports that the Klan endorsements appear to have determined the outcome in twenty of Alabama's sixty-seven counties, generally in the eastern hill country and the Wiregrass. See also Albert P. Brewer, "First- and Second-Choice Votes in Alabama," *Alabama Review* (April 1993): 83–94.

17. The Redeemers, out of touch with opinion among hill country farmers and millworkers, seem almost universally to have felt that McDowell and Carmichael were the frontrunners, and that Graves was lagging badly (*New York Times*, August 9, 1926; *Montgomery Advertiser*, August 21, 1929).

18. *Journal of the Senate of the State of Alabama, Session of 1927*, 1708; *Montgomery Advertiser*, August 22, 1929.

19. *Montgomery Advertiser*, July 13, 1927.

20. Ibid., July 15, 1927.

21. Summaries of the session are in the *Montgomery Advertiser*, September 5, 1927; the *New York Times*, September 11, 1927; and in Moore, *History of Alabama*, 771–76.

22. *Montgomery Advertiser*, May 28, 1929.

23. Moore, *History of Alabama*, 776.

24. Headland, *Wiregrass Farmer*, quoted in *Montgomery Advertiser*, September 4, 1927.

25. Thomas M. Owen, *History of Alabama and Dictionary of Alabama Biography* (Chicago: S. J. Clarke, 1921), 3: 783–84.

26. A. B. Moore, *History of Alabama and Her People* (Chicago: American Historical Society, 1927), 3: 443.

27. Ibid.

28. Owen, *History of Alabama and Dictionary of Alabama Biography*, 3: 783.

29. *New York Times*, February 21, 1929.

30. "By Their Fruits Ye Shall Know Them," 1930 campaign circular in private possession; *New York Times*, March 28, 29; April 3, 5, 7, 30; May 12, 1908, August 5, December 16, 1909.

31. *Montgomery Advertiser*, April 27, 1929.

32. Ibid., July 7, 1927.

33. Ibid., August 19, 1927.

34. *New York Times*, January 19, 1928.

35. Ibid., January 20, 1928. The lone dissenter was Park Trammell of Florida, a fellow Klansman.

36. *Montgomery Advertiser*, January 19, 1928. For other derogatory comments, see *Mobile Register*, *Decatur Daily*, *Selma Times-Journal*, and *Dothan Eagle* of same date.

37. *New York Times*, January, 21, 1928.

38. The one vote for Smith was that of W. S. Childers, chairman of the Walker County Democratic Committee. The bulk of the state's vote was divided about equally between Walter F. George of Georgia and Cordell Hull of Tennessee.

39. *New York Times*, June 29, 30, 1928.

40. Ibid., July 5, 1928.

41. Ibid., September 22, 1928.

42. Quoted in "Minutes of the Meeting of the Alabama Democratic Executive Committee, September 22, 1928," manuscript in Alabama Department of Archives and History, Montgomery.

43. Ibid.

44. *New York Times*, September 25, 1928.

45. Ibid., September 20, 1928.

46. Ibid., October 26, 1928.

47. Ibid., October 31, 1928.

48. Ibid., November 6, 1928.

49. *Alabama Official and Statistical Register, 1931*, 511–12.

50. See V. O. Key, *Southern Politics in State and Nation* (New York: Knopf, 1949), 324–25.

51. *New York Times*, November 26, 1928.

52. *Montgomery Advertiser*, February 9, 1929, and September 5, 1927.

53. Ibid., February 17, 1929; *Demopolis Times*, February 14, 1929. Under the Constitution of 1901, Alabama had only quadrennial legislative sessions. Without a special session, therefore, the 1927 session would be the last until 1931.

54. Moore, *History of Alabama and Her People*, 2: 8.

55. *New York Times*, November 26, 1928.

56. *Montgomery Advertiser*, April 15, 1929.

57. Ibid., April 19, 1929.

58. Ibid.

59. Ibid., April 27, 1929.

60. Ibid., May 4, 1929.

61. Ibid., July 7, 10, and 12, 1929.

62. Cf. speech of J. C. Inzer, "Minutes of the Meeting of the Alabama Democratic Executive Committee, December 16, 1929," manuscript in Alabama Archives.

63. *Montgomery Advertiser*, August 30, 1929.

64. Ibid., August 31, 1929.

65. Ibid., September 10, 1929.

66. Ibid., September 13, 1929.

67. Ibid., September 15, 1929.

68. Ben F. Ray to Heflin, September 16, 1929, J. Thomas Heflin Papers, University of Alabama Library, Tuscaloosa.

69. *Montgomery Advertiser*, August 21, 1929.

70. *Selma Times-Journal*, November 17, 1929.

71. *Montgomery Advertiser*, November 2, 1929.

72. Ibid., November 7, 1929.

73. Ibid., November 12, 13, 1929.

74. Ben F. Ray to Heflin, November 12, 1929, Heflin Papers. I discuss Thomas Judge Sr., in an earlier article in this volume.

75. *Montgomery Advertiser*, November 17, 1929.

76. Vincent J. Dooley, "United States Senator James Thomas Heflin and the Democratic Party Revolt in Alabama, 1930" (master's thesis, Auburn University, 1965), 34.

77. *Montgomery Advertiser*, November 27, 1929.

78. Ibid., December 4, 1929; Ben F. Ray to Heflin, November 30, 1929, Heflin Papers. Alabama lost the game, 12–0.

79. Heflin to L. Fitzpatrick, November 22, 1929, Heflin Papers.

80. Emmett P. Smith to Heflin, December 4, 1929; J. Johnston Moore to Heflin, December 4, 1929, both in Heflin Papers.

81. Harrington P. Heflin to Heflin, December 11, 1929, Heflin Papers.

82. *Montgomery Advertiser*, December 16, 1929.

83. Ibid.

84. "Minutes of the Democratic Executive Committee, December 16, 1929." Dooley reports (p. 47) that thirty-three counties barred bolters from running for local office, twenty-eight did not, and that the action of six is unknown.

85. Ibid.

86. *New York Times*, December 17, 1929.

87. Quoted in *Selma Times-Journal*, December 21, 1929.

88. Cf. Charles C. Alexander, *The Ku Klux Klan in the Southwest* (Lexington: University of Kentucky Press, 1965), passim, esp. 209.

89. *Montgomery Advertiser*, May 28, July 22, 1929.

7
Hugo Black and the Golden Age

The sheer variety of twentieth-century southern political figures who at one time or another have been called Populists must give the historian pause. Jimmy Carter, George Wallace, James Folsom, Eugene Talmadge, Strom Thurmond, Theodore Bilbo, Huey Long, Orval Faubus, Ross Barnett, Sam Ervin, Jesse Helms, even the anti-Semitic propagandist Gerald L. K. Smith—commentators have identified all of them as standing in the Populist tradition. It is also worth noting that southern black politicians essentially never are called Populists, though no mass political movement occurred in all of southern history, with the exception of the Reconstruction Republicans, in which black participation was a more significant element. These two observations alone should be sufficient to make the student suspicious when he finds Hugo L. Black's judicial philosophy attributed to a Populist intellectual heritage. The careful scholar would wish to see that heritage defined quite specifically, and he would want to know precisely how and when it exerted its influence on Black.

The looseness with which the term *Populist* is bandied about is not, however, the only warning signal. Investigation reveals Hugo Black's background in Clay County in the years of the Populist revolt to have been one exceedingly unlikely to have sensitized him to the Populist perspective.[1] Black's father, LaFayette Black, was politically unsympathetic not only to Populism proper but even to its watered-down Bryanite free silver version; in 1896 LaFayette Black voted for the Goldbug ticket of Palmer and Buckner. Furthermore, the elder Black was just the sort of man who would have seemed the apotheosis of evil from the perspective of Populist true believers: the proprietor of a general store in the county seat of Ashland, LaFayette Black earned a substantial part of his income from advancing to area farmers credit secured by crop liens.[2]

Hugo Black grew up in a relatively bustling county seat, in a family atmosphere fashioned by an economically conservative father, and by the examples of ambitious and upwardly mobile siblings, among them a doctor, a lawyer, and a merchant.[3] That young Hugo internalized many of the attitudes that surrounded him is evidenced sufficiently by his refusal to be satisfied with the limited education afforded by Ashland College, from which he received his initial diploma; by his determination—against some financial odds—to attend the University of Alabama; by his selection of law as a career, after a brief flirtation with medicine; and by his decision, shortly after his admission to the bar, to settle and practice in Alabama's booming metropolis, Birmingham.

The likelihood appears to be small that a young man from such a background would have rooted his developing personal and political ideology in a sympathy for the doctrines of the isolated farmers who were attracted to the banner of Populism, doctrines that reflected deep fears of and hostility toward the expanding market economy that threatened to overwhelm and marginalize them. Such an explanation for the origins of Black's outlook would need the clearest evidence, given its inherent implausibility. But in fact, no contemporary evidence indicates that Black felt any enthusiasm for Populism; we have only nonspecific assertions of such a sympathy by later commentators.

If, therefore, the roots of Black's judicial philosophy are not likely to be found in Populism, do other, more credible sources explain his emerging attitudes? Three influences on Black in his early manhood suggest a positive response to the question: his membership in the Ku Klux Klan, his passionate attachment to Prohibition, and the strong orientation of his law practice toward personal injury suits against corporations. An additional source may have been another ideological tradition profoundly influential in Alabama, a tradition that by Black's time was more generalized than Populism and of which Populism is, in a sense, a subset: Jacksonianism.

The Ku Klux Klan of the 1920s too seldom is recognized as a fountainhead for liberalism in later decades, and Hugo Black's involvement with the Klan very often is understated. Both are grave errors, whose sources, however, are entirely understandable. To be sure, thinking of the Klan as a breeding ground for liberals is quite difficult. Its highly unpleasant tactics in the 1920s included intimidation, masked floggings, and strident rhetorical condemnations of Catholics and Jews. Senator Black himself, during his struggle for confirmation to the Supreme Court, first attempted to minimize his earlier role in the Klan, and later admirers' attempts to prove that the senator's account of his activities was an accurate one are hardly surprising.[4] But however easily one may explain the origins of these misinterpretations, they nevertheless have served to obscure an important element in the formation of Black's judicial philosophy and hence have contributed to the acceptance of the false notion that his philosophy's roots lie in Populism.

To take the second misconception first, careful investigation makes it clear that Black's involvement in Klan activities was extensive and ardent.[5] One of his law partners, Crampton Harris, was Cyclops of Birmingham's largest klavern. Two of his closest friends and associates, Ben Ray and Hugh Locke, were among the Klan's most vocal public spokesmen. In the battle over the expulsion of the Klansman, demagogue and anti-Catholic bigot Senator J. Thomas Heflin from the Democratic Party in 1929, Ben Ray was the leader of the pro-Heflin forces on the state Democratic Executive Committee, and Hugh Locke was Heflin's gubernatorial running mate on the Bolters' ticket in the general election of 1930.[6]

Black first gained statewide attention as the attorney who successfully defended a fundamentalist Protestant preacher who had murdered a Catholic priest in Birmingham in 1921—a defense that featured explicit appeals to racial and religious prejudice. In 1922 Black defended the Birmingham City Commission in impeachment proceedings founded on its refusal to prosecute masked floggers. In 1923 he officially joined the Klan at a public ceremony attended by some 25,000 spectators. Alabama's Grand Dragon, James Esdale, actively managed Black's senatorial campaign in 1926, and there is little doubt that the Klan's support supplied him with the margin of victory in that election. Black himself did not doubt it at the time. At a great Klan celebration shortly after the order's triumphs in the 1926 Democratic primary, Black told the audience: "I do not feel that it would be out of place to state to you here on this occasion that I know that without the support of the members of this organization I would not have been called, even by my enemies, the 'Junior Senator from Alabama.'"[7] He went on to praise the Klan for "loving the pride of Anglo-Saxon spirit" and for remaining "true to the heaven-born principles of liberty which were written in the Constitution of this country, and in the great historical documents, straight from the heart of Anglo-Saxon patriots."[8]

Black's intimate association with the Klan hardly can be denied. The role of the Klan in contributing a group of distinguished leaders to Alabama liberalism is noted less often. Yet the development is a fascinating and an important one. Black is certainly the most prominent of these men at the national level. But in the history of Alabama, quite a number of others join him. After Black, the best known is Bibb Graves, the Yale graduate and Cyclops of the Montgomery klavern who was elected governor, also with Klan support, in the same primary in which Black was elected to the Senate and who was chosen for a second term in 1934. Graves's terms were marked by numerous important progressive measures, including the abolition of the convict leasing system and substantial increases in expenditures for public education and highway construction.

Perhaps Black's closest parallel is Judge Richard T. Rives. An active member of the Montgomery klavern, Rives was a law partner of two close relatives of congressman and senator J. Lister Hill, and served for many years as a general steward of Hill's political affairs at home. In the late 1930s and early 1940s, Rives met the early stirrings of efforts by blacks to obtain voting rights by acting as the attorney for several Black Belt Boards of Voting Registrars. He successfully defended the Montgomery County board and the Macon County board in separate test cases brought by blacks during and just after World War II. In Montgomery city politics in the 1920s and 1930s, Rives was a leading opponent of Montgomery's staunchly anti-Klan mayor, William A. Gunter. Yet despite these rather unpromising credentials, once appointed to the US Fifth Circuit Court of Appeals by President Truman, on Senator Hill's recommendation, Rives promptly revealed a judicial philosophy almost identical to that of Hugo Black. That these two former Klansmen came to espouse from the bench attitudes so markedly sympathetic to civil liberties and civil rights is no coincidence. Lister Hill, a third Montgomerian, also may be added to this list. Although Hill apparently was not active in the Montgomery klavern as were Graves and Rives, the family of which he was the most prominent spokesman was allied closely with the Klan in its wars with Mayor Gunter and the *Montgomery Advertiser*'s Grover C. Hall. Hill himself launched his political career, as chairman of Montgomery's Board of Education, by conducting a successful crusade to drive from office the city's widely respected superintendent of schools, William F. Feagin, primarily on the basis of dubious hearsay charges that Feagin had engaged in sexual relations with black teachers, or as Hill called them, Feagin's "negro wenches." Yet Hill in Congress pursued an unswervingly liberal course on all questions other than those involving race.[9]

A third example from the ranks of the judiciary is Justice J. Bascom Brown of the Alabama Supreme Court. Actively sympathetic to the Klan, whose support elected him to the court over the incumbent, future governor B. Meek Miller, Justice Brown was the sole member of the court to support Senator Heflin's position in the suit seeking to prevent Heflin's expulsion from the Democratic Party. In the 1940s, however, Brown became known for his willingness to insist upon the rights of blacks in criminal proceedings. Perhaps his most famous dissent appeared in *Ex parte Taylor*, a capital conviction of a black Mobile teenager for the rape of a white girl.[10]

A particularly striking example of the tendency of former Klansmen to embrace liberal causes in later decades arose during the battles of the Dixiecrat years. In 1929 anti-Klan elements in command of Democratic Party machinery set out to crush the Klan's power in state politics by barring from the Democratic primary any candidate who had failed to support the party's presidential nominee in 1928, the Roman Catholic wet Alfred Smith. Because of the Klan's vitriolic hostility to Smith's Catholicism, those expelled under this rule included a great many of the Klan's leading politicians. Pro-Klan forces under the leadership of Ben Ray vigorously, though unsuccessfully, fought this proposal in the Democratic Executive Committee. The anti-Klan forces insisted that all Democrats were under an obligation to support the party ticket, and the Klansmen denounced such enforced support for an obnoxious candidate as a violation of fundamental freedoms. In 1948, at the time of the Dixiecrat revolt, in many cases the same cast of characters played out the same drama, but the roles were exactly reversed. The leaders of the Loyalist faction, who insisted on a rule barring from subsequent primaries any candidate who had opposed Harry Truman in 1948, were in large part the Klan sympathizers who had denounced expulsion for failure to support Al Smith in 1928. When the Loyalists captured control of the Democratic Executive Committee in 1950, Ben Ray became state party chairman. The anti-Klan forces of 1929 and 1930 were now the backbone of the Dixiecrat states' rights leadership and insisted on obedience to the dictates of conscience. Like the stripes on the Confederate battle flag, the two factions had crossed each other and had ended up in opposite corners.[11]

The reasons for this peculiar migration are complicated. The enforcement of party loyalty in 1929 meant holding the surging popular revolt represented by the Klan candidates' victories in 1926 within the bounds of the balanced power-sharing arrangements between poor whites and wealthy planters and industrialists that had been erected at the Constitutional Convention of 1901. The enforcement of party loyalty in 1949 strengthened the hand of the forces who, under the leadership of Governor James E. Folsom, had managed to place the 1901 system on the defensive and who, even at that moment, were attacking its very heart, the malapportionment of the Alabama legislature. That pair of observations, however, forces us to recognize the Klan of the 1920s for what it was: a mass protest movement of poorer and more marginalized whites, whether urban, small town, or rural.[12] The politicians affiliated with it were led to associate with, and thereby increasingly were sensitized to the viewpoints and the circumstances of, the poor whites who constituted the bulk of its membership. That experience explains in part the number of Alabama's leading liberals of the 1930s, 1940s, and 1950s who came from the Klan's ranks.

But if the Klan is to be seen as a mass protest movement, seeking a definition of its ideological orientation becomes necessary. What attitudes did the Klan communicate to its members? A part of the answer to that question is all too obvious. An important element in its appeal relied upon the manipulation of religious and racial prejudice to create scapegoats upon whom its less well-to-do members could blame their hard lot. However, the Klan had more appeal than this merely negative aspect. Hugo Black praised it for being "true to the heaven-born principles of liberty which were written in the Constitution of this country." Are we to take this accolade as simply empty oratory? I think not. I believe that Black saw something in the Klan difficult to discern at this distance. To understand this perspective, a brief look at the other cause with which Black was most enamored in the 1920s, Prohibition, becomes important.

The step from the Klan to Prohibition is a very short one. The *Montgomery Advertiser* commented in the fall of 1929: "In Alabama it is hard to tell where the [Anti-Saloon] League ends and the Klan begins."[13] The two organizations worked closely together in their political and lobbying efforts. The Klansmen embarked on many of their nocturnal flogging expeditions to enforce Prohibition. Hugo Black was most definitely not alone in coupling the two enthusiasms. While Black's defense of the murderer of the Catholic priest in 1921 first gained him statewide notice, his real fame before his election to the Senate resulted from his appointment in 1924 as a special US attorney to handle the prosecution of more than one hundred public officials and prominent citizens in Mobile, including future congressman Frank Boykin, who had been indicted for participation in a bootlegging conspiracy. His vigorous conduct of the trial unquestionably proceeded from his own deeply felt Prohibitionist convictions. In 1916 he had served as a special state prosecutor in a similar bootlegging case in Phenix City and had done his duty with equal zeal on that earlier occasion.

What drew together, in the minds of Black and a great many far humbler Alabamians, admiration for the Klan and for Prohibition? In the booming 1920s, with suddenly shortened women's skirts, rapidly rising divorce rates, and flaming youth, the feeling was abroad in the land—and especially among more poorly educated Americans from fundamentalist and less cosmopolitan backgrounds—that a falling off from the standards of conduct of earlier years had occurred. The Klan attempted the public enforcement of morality through the pressure of community vigilantism upon deviants, and the Prohibition movement sought to compel the universal adoption of its principles of private moral conduct through legal and constitutional mechanisms. Both drew much of their emotional appeal from this sense of the necessity to restore America to an earlier, happier time. The belief that American morality was in a marked decline, that the republic itself was threatened by that decline and by the alien forces that played upon it, and that the preservation of all that the United States had come to mean in the world depended upon the restoration of the faith, attitudes, and modes of behavior that had distinguished the nation's founding years, characterized the outlooks both of Klansmen and of Prohibitionists. Of course, their outlooks were characterized too by a certain intellectual rigidity, by a historical absolutism that refused to recognize that the age of America's founding fathers, like all ages, was filled with complexities and crosscurrents. Rather, the period of our national youth easily came to seem to them a golden age.

All these attitudes influenced Hugo Black. Black was appealing to them when, at the great Klan gathering, or Klorero, of 1926, and quite sincerely, he breathed his "undying prayer that this [Klan] will carry on, sacredly true to the real principles of American manhood and womanhood, revering [the] virtue of the mother of the race, loving the pride of Anglo-Saxon spirit—and I love it—true to the heaven-born principles of liberty which were written in the Constitution of this country, and in the great historical documents, straight from the heart of Anglo-Saxon patriots."[14] The genius of the restorationist faith fairly sings beneath these sentiments.

One more element added to the compound of influences on the early manhood of Hugo Black: the nature of his law practice. From the time that Black first entered private practice in Birmingham in 1907, he had taken on many personal injury lawsuits against the region's corporations. When he returned to private practice in 1919, after service in World War I, he devoted himself almost exclusively to these cases. A practice of this kind necessarily emphasized to him the least admirable traits of corporate America. Day after day, in his office and in the courtrooms of Jefferson County, he saw unfold before him stories of incompetence or, worse, insouciance on the part of the managers of the area's mines and mills in discharging their responsibility to protect the health and safety of their employees. When workers became the victims of these managerial attitudes, he saw corporations respond by employing every device of bureaucratic and legal delay to avoid compensating the often financially desperate injured. Unsurprisingly, the conviction began to grow in his mind that capitalist enterprise was guided primarily by motives of heartless greed. This perspective obscured or slighted many far more positive contributions of corporations to the life of the community. Black's sample of employer-worker relations was by its very nature an unrepresentative one. It is hardly a source of wonder that Black's professional experience should have engendered in him a growing hostility toward the wealthy industrialists of Birmingham, men he easily came to see as supercilious, self-satisfied, and blind to the social costs of their exploitative conduct.

These three sources of influences—the restorationist ideology of Prohibition; the sensitivity to the fears and aspirations of marginalized whites formed in the Klan, and the Klan's own powerful restorationism; and the image of a pitiless capitalism devoid of any public spirit not wrung from it by law, gained from his legal practice in Birmingham—accounted for the genesis of the principal components of Hugo Black's later judicial philosophy. Black's absolutist devotion to the Bill of Rights, his antipathy toward all exploitative or manipulative concentrations of power (expressed, toward government, both in his generous conception of constitutional limitations upon it when he understood it to be defending the powerless or American freedoms, and in his indignant strict construction when he understood it to have become itself despotic), and his peculiarly romantic notions of the republic's early history and of the motives of the Constitution's framers, all are adumbrated in the ideological orientation derived from these early experiences.[15] Black's idiosyncratic reading of American history, so much commented upon, particularly can be seen hiding within the restorationist fervor of his youth. To think of the Constitution as an institutional arrangement crafted by practical and conservative men of affairs who sought to deal with specific political, economic, social, and moral problems was emotionally foreign to him. Rather, he perceived the Constitution to be the written emanation of a democratic faith, summoning later generations to defend in their own time the shining vision which, he believed, had informed the republic's birth, standing as a judgment against the unworthy deviations of subsequent lesser ages. Professor Gordon S. Wood has taught historians to think of the intellectual movement from the Revolution to the Constitution as characterized by a hesitant empiricism, motivated by the necessity to chasten rampant democracy while also preserving popular discipline upon government. One suspects that Justice Black would have approached such an account of the origins of the Constitution from precisely the same perspective as that of a Creationist encountering the evolutionary theories of Charles Darwin.[16] So necessary was the Bill of Rights for Black, so much an embodiment of fixed and fundamental principle rather than a product of historical circumstance, that he even convinced himself that every provision of it, every jot and tittle, inevitably was implied by the Fourteenth Amendment's simple phrase: "the privileges and immunities of citizens of the United States." This religion—for such it was—reflects the inflexible absolutist fundamentalism and the condemnation of the delinquencies and the mistaken accretions of our latter days that had typified the Klan-Prohibitionist culture in which the young Black had moved.

These attitudes are apparent in almost all of Black's constitutional writings, but perhaps in none more clearly than in his 1964 opinion for the court in the case of *Wesberry v. Sanders*. This landmark decision requires that all of a state's congressional districts must be substantially equal to each other in population. In appealing to the Supreme Court, attorneys for Wesberry, a resident of Atlanta, Georgia, whose congressman represented double the population in an average Georgia district and treble the population in its smallest one, had relied primarily on the equal protection clause of the Fourteenth Amendment. But Black in his opinion never reached the Fourteenth Amendment claim. He had disposed of the question at hand far earlier—in fact, at the very birth of the republic. He held that congressional districts were required to be equal in population by the terms of the first article of the original Constitution, when it says, "The House of Representatives shall be composed of members chosen every second year by the people of the several states."

In his opinion, Black recited the story of the "Connecticut compromise" at the Constitutional Convention, noting correctly that under the terms of this agreement, the states were to have equal representation in the Senate, but representatives were to be allotted to the states in proportion to their population. He cited the arguments of the delegates from the large states that justice required that a greater number of people have a greater number of representatives. And because the House of Representatives reflected in its structure the views of the large states' delegations, he deduced that their arguments in favor of proportional representation in Congress necessarily implied also a desire to have the congressional districts within the states equal to each other in size. He thus reached the conclusion that the unadorned words "by the people of the several states," required in and of themselves that congressional districts must be of equal population. This view of the matter, he wrote, vindicated "our Constitution's plain objective of making equal representation for equal numbers of people the fundamental goal for the House of Representatives. That is the high standard of justice and common sense which the Founders set for us."

For the dissenters in this six-to-three decision, Justice John Marshall Harlan II called Black's reasoning "whimsical." The historian can only agree. In the first place, the very text of the first article itself is against Black's reading of it. The Constitution allots additional representatives to states for three-fifths of their slaves, inhabitants who not only could not vote but were not even citizens. It requires that every state have at least one representative, no matter how small its population. And in exactly the same sentence that contains the phrase upon which Black focused, it incorporates all the disfranchising sex, age, and property tests of the various state constitutions of the time, by requiring that no one could vote for a member of the federal House of Representatives who was not eligible to vote for a member of his state legislature's House of Representatives. The "high standard of justice" to which Black appealed, demanding that every person's vote be equal to every other person's, was to say the least of it, not very evident in these companion provisions.

The textual objections to Black's position, which are advanced in Harlan's dissent, would appear conclusive by themselves. But the consideration of the rationale for popular election actually put forward at the Constitutional Convention by the proponents of that mode of choosing representatives, renders Black's account of their intentions simply untenable. As Gordon S. Wood and other careful students of the making of the Constitution point out, the principal goal of the framers was to develop some institutional mechanism that, without abandoning the principles of popular self-government, would still channel the votes of the electorate toward the selection as its officials of men the framers would regard as sufficiently honorable, experienced, and well educated to be able to see what was actually in the voters' long-term best interests, rather than demagogues who would pander to what the framers considered the voters' own narrow and ill-informed notions of what would be good for them. At the convention, two possible strategies for achieving this goal emerged. The first rested on what James Madison called "refining appointments through successive filtrations"—that is, for instance, having the voters elect state legislators, the state legislators elect the federal Congress, and the Congress elect the president. The reasoning behind this strategy was that if the electorate were small enough, the persons doing the electing could know the candidates personally, and thus could distinguish the demagogues from the honest statesmen. But this strategy had been tried in a number of the state constitutions and had not proven entirely successful.

The second, and newer, strategy found its chief exponents in James Wilson of Pennsylvania and James Madison of Virginia. It rested on the direct election of the official from a very large district. The theory behind this approach was that if the district were large enough geographically, it would be physically impossible for a demagogic candidate to meet the majority of the voters and make personal pledges to them. The electorate, in the absence of such personal contact, would be obliged to rely on what today is called "name recognition," that is, the voters could only know and would be left to vote for the candidate whose background, career, and social prominence had prepared him for the office, the candidate who therefore had a "district-wide name." The Constitutional Convention ended up using elements of both strategies in the document it drafted. But the House of Representatives was based essentially entirely on the latter strategy, the large-district method. In designing the House, the delegates considered the most crucial provision one that we today almost never notice: the requirement that no district contain fewer than 30,000 people. The Constitution provides no maximum population; a district could never be too large for the framers' purposes. But they believed that no district could be formed embracing as many as 30,000 people that would not be so vast geographically as to preclude the pernicious practice of making campaign promises to the voters, or as they would have put it, demagogy. Of course, developments the founding fathers could not have foreseen—enormous increases in population density, the creation of political parties, and the increasing perfection of mass-marketing techniques—rather rapidly rendered the insights that underlay the large-district scheme irrelevant to its operation in practice. But once we understand those insights, and the goals they were designed to effect, we must recognize Black's portrait of the framers' motives for what it is: arrant sentimentalism.

Were we able to present this analysis to Black himself, there can be no doubt at all that his reaction to it would be the same as his reaction actually was to Justice Harlan's critique in his trenchant dissent: Black would reject it. No matter how massive may be the evidence for the elitist presumptions and aims of the framers—and it is quite massive, indeed—Black would not, could not, accept its validity, because if he were to do so, he would thereby in effect abandon the restorationist vision that gave meaning to his life and work. He was unwilling to follow the far more hard-minded, but far less judicially acceptable, example of his colleague William O. Douglas in frankly seeking to shape constitutional requirements to reflect his own concept of what was just. For Black, the ideals that had formed the Constitution, the ideals of the men who had written and ratified it, were themselves already truly just. The evil of later and lesser eras had obscured the luster of those ideals. But to achieve the just society for which the republic ought to stand, there was no need to impose new constitutional requirements; they had only to be recovered and restored to their rightful place.

The attribution of Black's emerging attitudes to his experiences with the Klan, Prohibition, and an apparently unfeeling big business has the virtue of finding their origins in influences whose importance to him, unlike that of Populism, is fully demonstrable. We can prove that these forces really existed in and shaped his early life. But our task is not yet done. A critic might reasonably object that restorationism, the belief that the republic's natal years were a golden age, and a deep and bitter hostility to the monopolistic power of corporate America were central to the doctrines of the Populist revolt also. Even if Black absorbed these notions through intermediate movements and circumstances, the critic might ask, are not their ultimate origins to be discovered in Populism? Let me attempt to answer that objection.

The home environment of Black's boyhood was virtually the antithesis of a Populist one. Many enthusiasts of the Klan and Prohibition movements were like Black in this regard. The Klan and Prohibitionism were mass movements of protest against the social and moral climate of modern America, as was Populism, yet the constituencies to which the Klan and Prohibitionism appealed were different from that of Populism. Indeed, the Klan-Prohibitionist constituency was more nearly comparable to that of Progressivism than to that of Populism.[17] The Klan and to a lesser extent Prohibition appear to have drawn many of their adherents from Alabama's small towns and cities, and from the lower-middle as well as the working classes. Membership in an organized religious denomination, Protestant and usually fundamentalist, also seems to have been normal among them.[18] Populism, on the other hand, found its most enthusiastic support in the most rural and isolated areas; any frequent contact with the wider world—even the presence of a village nearby, or regular attendance at an organized church—militated against allegiance to the Populist crusade.[19]

What, then, accounts for Populism's sharing with the Klan and Prohibition movements of thirty years later such powerful and ruling concerns? My own notion is that the mass protests of the 1890s and 1920s drew upon attitudes general, though appearing in a variety of guises, in the political culture of Black's Alabama, and inherited from the ideology that had dominated the state in the antebellum period—Jacksonianism.

The source of antebellum political divisions, and the fears on which they were founded, is to be sought in the same phenomenon that later generated Populism: the expansion of the market economy in rural America in the years between the War of 1812 and World War I. Resistance to the marketplace implied a conception of the meaning of freedom widely held in the Jacksonian generation and undergirding the program of Jackson's party, the Democrats, a party dedicated to defending the ethic of subsistence agriculture. For Democrats, freedom was something that the citizenry had gained in the American Revolution and that it now held by right, but that evil, antidemocratic forces were attempting to take away. A man was free when he was dependent on no one else for his livelihood and welfare. Movements and institutions whose success would diminish the autonomy of the individual were, thus, by definition aristocratic and inimical to the American experiment. Jacksonians saw themselves as fighting to preserve in its purity the revolutionary ideology of Thomas Jefferson, an ideology they believed to be threatened with subversion by urban, commercial, broad constructionists. Democrats campaigned for the abolition of property qualifications for voting and officeholding because they hoped that a broadened electorate would be able to use the government to restrict the growth of corporations and, ultimately, to destroy them. They conceived of their political party as a sort of trade union of the electorate, through which ordinary citizens, individually weak, could band together and use their numbers to counterbalance the power of the wealthy. The Democracy's enthusiasts usually were concentrated in those areas most insulated from market agriculture. Alabama was one of the party's chief strongholds, and within Alabama, its bastions were the hill counties of the northern part of the state and the Wiregrass counties of the southeast.

In the years between the Mexican-American War and the Civil War, as America entered upon a period of unexampled economic prosperity, the Jacksonian movement gradually lost its social and ideological coherence. A group of ambitious younger Democratic politicians, who generally accepted the label "Young America," began to use aspects of Jacksonianism, especially its devotion to laissez-faire and strict constructionist doctrines, in ways that defended commercial and industrial interests, instead of attacking them. The ideas that originated with Young America often have been called, though anachronistically and quite misleadingly, "Social Darwinism." Adopted in most instances as well by the leaders of the Republican Party during the 1850s, these ideas became the ideology of America's dominant culture after the Civil War. The Populist revolt stood squarely against them. For that reason, Populism appears on the surface to repudiate so many articles of the Jacksonian creed: Jacksonianism favored a hard money, wholly specie circulation, but Populism liked a soft money, inflationary policy; Jacksonianism favored a small and inactive government, but Populism supported an expansive, highly active one; Jacksonians would have been horrified by any suggestion of federal intervention in the agricultural economy, but the Populists' subtreasury scheme sought just that; Jacksonians stood for individual autonomy, but Populists, like the antebellum Whigs, stood for the cooperative commonwealth. In all these respects, the doctrines the Redeemer Democrats preached in the South in the 1880s and 1890s remained truer to the precedents of Jacksonianism than did the remedies proposed by the Farmers' Alliance and the People's Party. Yet clearly the Populists had their own strong claim on the Jacksonian legacy. The Populists' agrarianism, their suspicion of the ethic of market capitalism, their hostility toward great corporations and other manipulative power centers, and their defense of the isolated and the marginalized all had precise counterparts in Jacksonianism. In short, Jacksonian ideology, having bifurcated at midcentury, had become by the end of the century so generalized a part of the social faith that aspects of it were to be found across the entire southern ideological spectrum.[20]

One element of the Jacksonian creed descended to all its heirs: its restorationist analysis of American history. An essential component of Jacksonianism was the sense that powerful forces in American life were betraying the Revolution and that the Democratic Party was engaged in a crusade to defeat their machinations and to restore the republic to the virtues of its founding years.[21] An identical viewpoint is to be found in Populism. But although seldom noted, an analogous position marked the Redeemers' outlook as well. After the Civil War, Redeemer politicians began to claim that the essence of the Confederate cause had been not the defense of slavery but the defense of the purity of the Constitution. They depicted their own Democracy's states' rights, laissez-faire, low tariff platform as an extension of this sacred movement. The belief that the United States following the Civil War had deserted its founding Jeffersonian doctrines permeated all white social and economic classes in the late nineteenth- and early twentieth-century South. Thus Klansmen and Prohibitionists in the 1920s did not have to rely on Populism to teach them restorationist attitudes. At least a mild restorationism was almost a characteristic of being a white southerner in the period. The Klan and Prohibition merely were intensifying and playing upon sentiments widespread in the culture and present in it since antebellum times.

If Hugo Black were here today, we cannot doubt the principal source that he himself would cite for his philosophy. He would tell us that its roots lay primarily in the thought of Thomas Jefferson. We know that he spent much time throughout his life studying and reflecting upon Jefferson's writings. Black's Jefferson, however, was a romanticized, I may even say a modernized Jefferson—Jefferson the democrat and civil libertarian, not Jefferson the believer in a natural aristocracy. Black's understanding of Jefferson was, in other words, a Jacksonian understanding of him. Black's belief that he was a disciple of Jefferson, as powerful as it was, was no stronger than Andrew Jackson's own. But it is not the spirit of the eighteenth-century Age of Reason, implicit in all of Jefferson's ideas, that one encounters in Hugo Black; it is the spirit of egalitarian democracy; it is the spirit of the Jacksonians.

Far too much southern historiography has failed to challenge the rank perversion of the region's history that depicts the South as having been dominated thoroughly by conservatism. Populism seems to be the one liberal movement whose importance in shaping the southern past all concede. Consequently, when they encounter a southern liberal like Hugo Black, too many scholars are puzzled by his liberal manifestations and rush to label the challenge to their preconceptions a recrudescence of the Populist crusade. The time has come to outgrow that tendency. We now must recognize the many and diverse sources of liberalism in the South's intellectual heritage. The careful study of the experiences and the thought of Hugo Black, and of the many other southern political leaders like him, is certainly the first step toward the general acceptance of such a position.

Notes

This article appeared initially, in a slightly different form, in *Alabama Law Review* (Spring 1985), and in Tony Freyer, ed., *Justice Hugo Black and Modern America* (Tuscaloosa: University of Alabama Press, 1990), 139–55.

1. On Black's family background and youth, see Virginia Van der Veer Hamilton, *Hugo Black: The Alabama Years* (Baton Rouge: Louisiana State University Press, 1972), 3–28.

2. On southern Populists' ideology in general, and their hostility to merchants and crop liens in particular, see Bruce Palmer, *"Man over Money": The Southern Populist Critique of American Capitalism* (Chapel Hill: University of North Carolina Press, 1980).

3. On the importance of rural isolation in forming the Populist outlook, see James Turner, "Understanding the Populists," *Journal of American History* 67 (1980): 354–73.

4. Particularly guilty of such extenuation is John P. Frank, *Mr. Justice Black: The Man and His Opinions* (New York: Knopf, 1949), 38–45, 95–108.

5. Hamilton, *Black: The Alabama Years*, 46–170.

6. The preceding article in this volume contains a more detailed account of this episode.

7. Hamilton, *Black: The Alabama Years*, 137 (quoting the stenographic transcript reprinted in *New York Times*, September 15, 1937).

8. Ibid., 138.

9. On Graves, see William E. Gilbert, "Bibb Graves as a Progressive, 1927–1930," *Alabama Review* (January 1957): 15–30. On Hill, see Virginia Van der Veer Hamilton, *Lister Hill: Statesman from the South* (Chapel Hill: University of North Carolina Press, 1987), esp. 34–38. Judge Rives has not received the attention he deserves, but see Jack Bass, *Unlikely Heroes* (New York: Simon and Schuster, 1981).

10. Ex parte Taylor, 249 Ala. 667, at 671.

11. On the Dixiecrat struggle, see William D. Barnard, *Dixiecrats and Democrats: Alabama Politics, 1942–1950* (Tuscaloosa: University of Alabama Press, 1974), 95–124.

12. See the preceding article in this volume.

13. *Montgomery Advertiser*, November 13, 1929.

14. Hamilton, *Black: The Alabama Years*, 138.

15. The most thorough study to date of Black's tenure on the Supreme Court is Gerald T. Dunne, *Hugo Black and the Judicial Revolution* (New York: Simon and Schuster, 1977). Dunne's acceptance of the notion that Black's views had their roots in Populism, however, mars this work's careful scholarship.

16. Compare, for instance, the portrait of the motives of the Framers in Gordon S. Wood, *The Creation of the American Republic, 1776–1787* (Chapel Hill: University of North Carolina Press, 1969) with Black's in Wesberry v. Sanders, 376 U.S. 1.

17. Sheldon Hackney carefully distinguishes these two constituencies in Alabama in his *Populism to Progressivism in Alabama* (Princeton, NJ: Princeton, University Press, 1969).

18. I venture these generalizations with some confidence, yet they are based entirely upon impressionistic evidence. Samuel L. Webb, "Hugo Black, Bibb Graves, and the Ku Klux Klan: A Revisionist View of the 1926 Alabama Democratic Primary," *Alabama Review* (October 2004): 243–73, emphasizes the difficulties of using electoral returns to determine Klan identity. But the voting in the county option referenda of 1906 and 1907 and the repeal referendum of 1935 might well provide a good basis for a quantitative investigation of the identity of the Prohibitionists, and it would be a welcome addition to our knowledge.

19. My conception of Populism is much influenced by James Turner (note 3, above), though I believe that his notion of the temporal specificity of the social developments he cites is erroneous. I should emphasize, however, that no matter how isolated the Populist communities were, they were still very much communities, bound together by reciprocal exchange of produce and labor, and knit by evangelical assumptions and attitudes. On the Populist movement, see especially Robert C. McMath Jr., *American Populism: A Social History, 1877–1898* (New York: Hill and Wang, 1993).

20. Not all the developments discussed in these paragraphs have been studied as thoroughly as they ought to be. For more detailed discussions of at least some of them, see Steven Hahn, *The Roots of Southern Populism: Yeoman Farmers and the Transformation of the Georgia Upcountry, 1850–1890* (New York: Oxford University Press, 1983); Michael Holt, *The Political Crisis of the 1850s* (New York: Wiley, 1978); and Harry L. Watson, *Jacksonian Politics and Community Conflict: The Emergence of the Second American Party System in Cumberland County, North Carolina* (Baton Rouge: Louisiana State University Press, 1981); and see as well the first article in this volume and the various works cited there.

The loss of coherence in Jacksonianism in the 1850s produced a similar disintegration of orthodoxy within the Whiggery. As Michael Holt correctly emphasizes, the economic positions of the parties converged in the final antebellum years. Consequently, elements of the Whig faith are to be found mixed with elements of Jacksonianism in the doctrines of both Redeemers and Populists at the end of the century.

21. Marvin Meyers, *The Jacksonian Persuasion: Politics and Belief* (Stanford, CA: Stanford University Press, 1957) properly emphasizes the restorationist theme in Democratic doctrine, though I believe that he concedes a greater enthusiasm for upward mobility among Democrats than was actually usual among the true believers.

8

The Structure of White Supremacy in Alabama in the Era of World War II

On September 6, 1944, Walton H. Craft, a sixty-five-year-old white resident of Mobile, dispatched a letter of complaint to Alabama's governor, Chauncey Sparks. Craft had come to Mobile in early 1942 to take a job at the city's booming Brookley Air Force Base, and each day he rode a city bus from his home to the field. He had become increasingly concerned about the pattern of racial segregation on the Mobile buses, under which there was no fixed racial dividing line. Whites filled from the front and blacks from the back, and the dividing line was wherever they met. On this particular morning, as often happened, the driver "allowed the Negroes to fill [the] rear and continue up the aisle two thirds of the way . . . hanging over the white women and girls. Frankly, it is not pleasant, not to mention the fact you have paid your fare to be transported to work, only to have some Negro hanging over you or his body touching you from time to time, the 'Negro Odor' sometimes almost more than a person can stand." That morning Craft had left the bus in disgust before reaching his destination. "I would suggest that a start be made in our own state to correct these practices that have grown to the extent they have, and I am of the opinion there is a State Law which requires the segregation of races, which is *not being followed by the present bus company.* The excuse some drivers give is, 'The orders are to bring a full load.' That may be an instruction; however, it does not give the Bus Company or the driver the right to disregard a State Law that is on the State's Book, as to the separation of the races. I called the Driver's attention to this matter as I left the Bus," but he seemed wholly uninterested.

The obviously deeply agitated Mr. Craft must have been astonished at the reply he received from Governor Sparks, to whom he had so confidently appealed. "If you will investigate the matter you will find, I think, that there is no law requiring the segregation of races in busses. . . . Our segregation laws are few, and apply to such matters as schools, asylums, penitentiaries and things directly under the control of the state. Of course," the governor added, "we have what is known as the Jim Crow, or segregation law on railroads. This has been in existence for many years." But he concluded, "You can readily see, therefore, there are few segregation laws to be enforced."[1]

Many accounts of the Jim Crow South share Mr. Craft's misconceptions, unthinkingly depicting segregation in the region as a universal and uniform system. This error has distorted explanations of segregation's origins and of the course of events by which it eventually was overcome. But Governor Sparks, an attorney who practiced law in the small Black Belt county seat of Eufaula, knew what he was talking about. In fact, in the summer of 1942, assistant Alabama attorney general Walter W. Flowers had undertaken a thorough survey of all state statutes and regulations bearing on racial segregation. State law required racial segregation in most institutions directly funded by the state, though not in all of them; the segregation of the state universities and of the state mental hospitals was merely a policy of their administrations, for instance. But beyond the state's own institutions, state statutes required racial segregation only in county jails (where sexual segregation was also required), railroad passenger cars and stations (a regulation that specifically exempted municipal trolley lines), and poor houses and tuberculosis sanitariums. State law criminalized miscegenation and interracial sexual relations and forbade white female nurses to nurse black men. The voter qualification provisions of the state constitution, though they did not mention race, had of course been adopted with conscious discriminatory intent, and the law did require that poll tax receipts be recorded separately by race. But that was the extent of state legislation on the subject of segregation.[2] The laws were exactly as Governor Sparks had said: few indeed.

Other facially nonracial provisions of the state constitution also had important implications for the structure of race relations, as did disfranchisement. White hostility to the substantial black influence on the county commissions of the plantation counties during Reconstruction had induced delegates to the Constitutional Convention of 1875 to place thoroughgoing restrictions on county authority, and these restrictions had largely been carried forward into the Constitution of 1901. As a result, the activities of county commissions in twentieth-century Alabama were essentially limited to rural road construction and the maintenance of county property. Commissions did not have the power to adopt such social regulations as ordinances requiring racial segregation. If the legislature had not enacted such a requirement by statute—and generally it had not—then segregation existed in rural Alabama only as a result of the private actions of individual property owners. Rural taverns and roadhouses, for instance, certainly had racial identities, but only because their proprietors chose to serve only a white or a black clientele. Legal enforcement, when it was necessary, was available not as a result of a segregation ordinance, but through prosecutions for trespassing or disorderly conduct.

This observation leads to an important distinction between the worlds of urban and rural Alabamians. Race relations in rural Alabama were characterized not by segregation, but by white supremacy. Segregation, the statutory requirement of racially separate institutions, is only one manifestation of white supremacy, and by no means the most widespread one. In northern states, where legal segregation was very rare in the early twentieth century, racial discrimination was common. Stores, theaters, and restaurants frequently refused to serve blacks, and businesses quite generally refused to hire them. The Congress of Racial Equality (CORE) had its origins in an effort by University of Chicago students in 1942 to induce downtown Chicago restaurants to accept black customers. And the hiring of black bus drivers in Philadelphia, as a result of wartime labor shortages, provoked a transit strike there in August 1944, which eventually required the intervention of the US Army. In the North, as in rural Alabama, trespassing and disorderly conduct prosecutions could lend legal force to the discrimination.[3]

But the pattern of white supremacy in rural Alabama was actually of a third sort. The discriminatory practices of rural stores and businesses were not its essential feature. Rather, it rested on the fact that the overwhelming majority of rural black Alabamians, especially in the Black Belt, were tenant farmers or sharecroppers on the property of white landowners. The direct, personal control by white landlords of each individual black tenant family rendered the compulsion of the state merely ancillary, and the discrimination of rural shopkeepers and restaurateurs simply supplemental. Other than in the public schools, white supremacy in rural Alabama did not express itself in the form of separate institutions, nor was it usually embodied in law. Rather, it was nongovernmental and peremptory, dependent not on political but on economic authority. If it became necessary, the county sheriff could be called in, and here again trespass and disorderly conduct, mounting quickly to far more serious charges, could be deployed to reinforce the landlord's dominion. But intervention by the agencies of the state was not often needed. And when it was, courts, especially in the Black Belt, tended to defer to the landlord's authority. If the landlord appeared at a hearing for one of his tenants and assured the judge that he could handle the matter, the formal charges were very often dismissed.

Because the exercise of this control was by definition personal and private, it did not usually come to public attention. But in the first stages of the civil rights movement, practices that in earlier times would have obtained no official notice could sometimes make it into the records upon which the historian depends. Such is the case of Lonnie Brown. Lonnie Brown was a black man in the rural western Black Belt county of Wilcox, who made his living by selling burial and life insurance policies to black tenant farmers, which the tenant farmers paid for with small amounts that Brown collected in weekly visits to their homes. When a young field secretary for the Student Nonviolent Coordinating Committee (SNCC), Frank Holloway, came to Wilcox in February 1963, Brown embraced SNCC's message, and in his rounds among the tenant families, began trying to enlist them to attempt to register to vote. At this time there was not a single black person registered in the county, and none had tried to register in a generation. Indeed, the county's Board of Registrars had used this fact in responding to the Justice Department's complaint against it, charging it with racial discrimination; the board could not possibly have discriminated against black applicants, the members argued, because there had been none. Brown hoped to assist SNCC in testing the validity of this defense. When the *Selma Times-Journal* in neighboring Dallas County learned of Brown's efforts and reported them in a news article, white Wilcox County landowners immediately took action. Banding together at an emergency meeting, they resolved to bar Brown from coming onto their property to collect their tenants' weekly premiums. Thus cut off from his source of income, Brown was driven out of business and as a result was forced to move from the county. Even a decade earlier, these actions would have ended the affair, and information about it would never have seen the light of day. Because of trespass laws, the landlords had essentially absolute control over their tenants' contacts with the outside world, and they were accustomed to using it. We know about this particular episode only because Justice Department attorneys got wind of it and brought Brown back to Selma to testify about it in federal court, in their suit against the Wilcox Board of Registrars.[4]

White supremacy thus found many social expressions and took diverse institutional forms. It was only in the South's towns that circumstances compelled white supremacy to express itself in the form of legal requirements of segregation. And even here, as the situations of towns varied, so the structures of segregation that city authorities imposed were correspondingly manifold. The one thing that towns all shared, to a greater or lesser degree, depending on their size, was anonymity. And it is anonymity that most commended legal segregation to white supremacists in the cities. In urban areas, the direct personal control possible in the countryside was attenuated. The compulsion available to rural landowners to maintain social discipline was in the towns vested in the police, and police officers sought to use it aggressively, freely administering extralegal punishment or arresting persons they thought troublemakers whenever it seemed to them necessary, whether or not any law had actually been violated. But the social dominance of the police in the cities either rested on force and fear or was mediated through the courts and thus lacked the personalized pervasive quality and the economic component that made the rural landowners' power so inescapable. The diverse occupations and varied sources of economic and social consequence characteristic of urban life afforded black town dwellers a level of independence and self-determination, however limited it may seem to us today, that was seldom available in rural areas. And so, as the relations of blacks and whites became increasingly impersonal in the urban setting, so white supremacy inevitably came to seem to its advocates most effectively expressed in the same impersonal terms of statute and ordinance.

In addition, urban areas had a far greater range and variety of institutions and services that were subject to being segregated than did the countryside. Because the institutions involved were so various and the towns numbered in the many thousands, it is hardly surprising that the structure of segregation differed greatly from subject to subject and from place to place. A municipal government often used an existing ordinance in another municipality as its model, and that practice lent some measure of uniformity to requirements across the region. But the uniformity was not in fact very great. Even very detailed ordinances left much to the decision of individual businessmen or local managers. A restaurant segregation ordinance, for instance, would often provide that if the restaurant served both races, they had to be separated by a wall or barrier of specified dimensions and each race be provided a separate entrance. But very few restaurants actually complied and served both races. Almost all avoided the question by restricting their clientele to one race, though some officially served only whites but permitted blacks to come to the rear door and purchase food on a take-out basis, or sometimes to eat it in the kitchen. The particular practice was a matter of local knowledge, but could often create incidents for travelers. Similarly, whether or not a city had an elevator segregation ordinance, some buildings maintained separate elevators, some permitted blacks only to use the freight elevator, while others relegated them to the stairs. In some cities, usually smaller ones, theater segregation took the form of seating blacks in the balcony and whites on the main floor. In other, usually larger cities, there were separate black and white theaters. White hospitals often had separate, all-black wards, frequently in the basement. But larger cities often also had separate, all-black hospitals—something particularly important for black doctors, because otherwise they could not obtain admitting privileges. And so it was across the entire range of institutions; the permutations were almost as many as the number of towns and the objects of the municipal regulations.

Recognizing the great variety and radical localism of segregation as a manifestation of white supremacy goes far toward clarifying the persistent historiographical controversy over its origins. Howard N. Rabinowitz noted that the initial expressions of segregation in southern towns stretched far back into Reconstruction, immediately after emancipation, and often were adopted on the initiative of blacks themselves, as they pressed municipalities, for instance, to create a park to serve the new black citizens, as a parallel to an existing one for whites. C. Vann Woodward noted that through the 1870s and 1880s, most institutions in most southern towns still lacked any legal requirement of racial segregation, and that such ordinances became general only in the decade from 1895 to 1905, as municipal politicians, responding to the political events of the Populist and Progressive eras, rushed to emphasize their devotion to white supremacy by emulating segregation ordinances being adopted in neighboring towns across the region.[5] Each of these contentions is correct. They have appeared to be at odds only because scholars have so often confused the absence of legally mandated segregation with the absence of white supremacy. Segregation as a manifestation of white supremacy, outside the schools and churches, ordinarily came quite late to the region, and when it came, it came as a requirement of law, with the exception of the railroad trains, only to the region's towns and cities. Moreover, its particular expressions evolved throughout the twentieth century, as municipal authorities tinkered with their ordinances and as individual business owners and managers quietly altered its patterns in their own establishments. It was never a uniform system, though by about 1910, some form of it was to be found in virtually every institution in every town in the South. But the white supremacist attitudes of which the segregation ordinances were a manifestation long preexisted segregation and, in fact, persisted almost as vigorously after segregation's elimination; the end of segregation as a specific expression of white supremacy by no means represented the extinction of white supremacist beliefs, nor foreclosed their appearance in other institutional forms.[6]

The diversity in practice and the radical localism of segregation also form the key to understanding another point too seldom emphasized: that politics and policies at the state level during the twentieth century had very little influence upon the actual experience of race relations in the South. A succession of vitriolic racist demagogues—James Vardaman and Theodore Bilbo in Mississippi, Thomas Watson and Eugene Talmadge in Georgia, Thomas Heflin in Alabama, Benjamin Tillman and Cole Blease in South Carolina, and too many like them elsewhere—manipulated racial animosities and exploited prejudice to attain political power. It is very easy to think of such men as the embodiment of segregation and to conceive the ebb and flow of their influence as indicating harsher or more hopeful periods in the lives of black southerners under the regime of Jim Crow. Nor was the violent rhetoric of such leaders without power to exacerbate tension and provoke violence. But the daily life of black people was shaped by local circumstance, ordinance, and practice. It could, and often did, vary greatly from town to town, even within a single county. Local authorities and employers, not state or national figures, were the true powers in the lives of ordinary black people, in both town and country. The impact upon black southerners of state figures, like that of national figures, was episodic, fleeting, and primarily symbolic. This point is crucial because it permits us to understand why the mobilization to disestablish segregation came, once it did, from local demonstrations growing out of particular situations in individual cities and towns.

Alabama's three governors of the era of World War II—Frank M. Dixon, elected in 1938; Chauncey Sparks, elected in 1942; and James E. Folsom, first elected in 1946—held views on race relations as divergent as the mainstream white South had to offer at this time. The fact that, with their very different racial attitudes, they followed each other immediately and served within so short a chronological period—a mere dozen years—makes an examination of their racial policies particularly instructive. It not only clarifies the practical limits that the political culture of the early twentieth-century state imposed upon the range of views that successful politicians of the era might hold; it also reveals how very small was the significance of these differing attitudes for the actual lives of black Alabamians. The three governors came and went without altering the structure of white supremacy in Alabama in any but the most incremental ways.

Frank Dixon attended Phillips Exeter Academy in New Hampshire, received his undergraduate degree from Columbia University, and took a law degree from the University of Virginia. A war hero, he lost a leg in air combat over France in World War I. The principal influence on the young man's developing views was his uncle, Thomas Dixon, the former Baptist minister and graduate school friend of Woodrow Wilson, whose racist novels *The Clansman* and *The Leopard's Spots* were best sellers during Frank's childhood. Dixon spent much of his youth on his uncle's tidewater Virginia estate, and he thoroughly imbibed Thomas Dixon's deeply antagonistic beliefs about both blacks and Reconstruction. Following World War I, Frank Dixon commenced a law practice in Birmingham, firmly associating himself with the city's great corporations and wealthy industrialists. With their financial backing, he ran unsuccessfully for governor against Bibb Graves in 1934, and then successfully in 1938, defeating Chauncey Sparks.

The archetypal business progressive, Dixon sought efficiency and economy in government and was a fierce opponent of Franklin Roosevelt's New Deal. Dixon's pro-labor, anti-industrialist predecessor, Graves, had built a powerful political organization on the dispensation of state patronage, and Dixon was determined to eliminate this source of liberal influence in the state. In the principal achievement of his administration, Dixon succeeded in driving through the legislature the state's first civil service law, the "Merit System," as he called it. He also oversaw a thorough reorganization of the state bureaucracy.

In race relations, Dixon was an aggressive and inflexible segregationist. He vigorously opposed federal antilynching and anti-poll-tax legislation. Within Alabama, he did support, though unsuccessfully, a state constitutional amendment to limit the accumulation of unpaid back poll taxes to two years, but he insisted on the preservation of the poll tax itself. And though he claimed that state authorities could suppress lynching on their own, when the antilynching crusader Jessie Daniel Ames asked him to investigate one such incident, he simply denied that any lynching properly so called had occurred, and told her that he feared violence was always likely when the citizenry lost confidence in the willingness of the courts to punish rapists. When a white woman wrote him to complain about overhearing black men on a Birmingham bus ask white girls on dates, he replied that the situation "is one which is being brought on you by the activities of certain elements within the Federal Government. It is extremely serious and we are doing all that we can, but so long as those elements in Washington keep fomenting the disturbance, there is very little that we can do." And indeed, it was the Roosevelt administration that Dixon regarded as the root of the problem. "How far certain elements of the national administration are willing to go to try to force a change in the social structure of the South, I do not know," he wrote a member of Marengo County's governing body. "But I do know that every white man in Alabama has to be on one side in that particular matter: there aren't any two sides."[7]

It is hardly surprising, therefore, that President Roosevelt's executive order of June 1941, forbidding employment discrimination in war industries and establishing the Fair Employment Practices Committee (FEPC) seemed to Dixon to pose the direst threat, and especially so when, a year later, the FEPC came to Birmingham to hold investigatory hearings. Dixon responded to these hearings with an executive order of his own, creating the Alabama War Manpower Committee with the explicit charge to see that war mobilization did not in any way weaken the barriers of racial separation. Chaired by the segregationist circuit judge Walter B. Jones of Montgomery, and with the equally segregationist Greensboro newspaper editor Hamner Cobbs as its executive director, the committee actively sought to forestall the federal challenge to white supremacy. As Dixon explained to a prominent railroad executive: "As a result of the continued pressure of a small group of Northern fanatics at present connected with the national administration, the entire social and economic structure of the South is in danger. It is my sincere belief that the danger is real. Conditions make it impossible for the Southern white people to surrender their control without resistance, and the fact that we are engaged in war is being used by unscrupulous fanatics to put over a program of social revolution. I sincerely hope that we can cause them to see the error of their ways."

With the assistance of his legal advisor, the archracist J. Miller Bonner of Camden, Dixon forbade all state agencies from accepting contracts that contained nondiscrimination clauses; constantly pressured the War Department to keep a tight rein on black troops; and strongly opposed efforts to expand the training of black soldiers and airmen in the state. In 1948, Dixon would deliver an impassioned keynote address to the Dixiecrat convention that nominated Strom Thurmond for president.[8]

Dixon's 1938 challenger and his successor, Chauncey Sparks, worked his way through Mercer University and its law school, and commenced a law practice in his native Eufaula in 1910. He was elected to the state House of Representatives in 1918 and became a legislative floor leader for the Progressive governor Thomas E. Kilby. In that capacity he played a significant role in the passage of Kilby's important educational program, which more than doubled state expenditures for the public schools, expanded the authority of the state board of education, and placed new emphasis on vocational education programs. Sparks's deep devotion to the cause of education dates from this time. In 1930, Sparks was elected to the state Senate as an opponent of the Ku Klux Klan and its Montgomery Cyclops, outgoing governor Bibb Graves. Over the next eight years, in response to the devastating national depression, he became a principal legislative advocate of retrenchment and an opponent of tax increases. Although he lost the 1938 gubernatorial election, the campaign allowed him to develop a statewide following. Nevertheless, he entered the 1942 race as an underdog behind his old nemesis Graves, who was seeking a third term. When Graves suddenly died shortly before the election, however, Sparks unexpectedly became the best known candidate in the field, and won handily.

Sparks's advocacy of governmental parsimony during his time in the state Senate led many observers to expect that he would obstruct progressive efforts, but the booming wartime economy and the resulting rapidly increasing tax receipts allowed him to return to his earlier enthusiasm for education. He obtained a doubling of support for public schools, which funded an extension of the school year from seven to eight months. He sponsored the establishment of a full-scale medical school in Birmingham for the University of Alabama, the creation of a forestry school at Auburn University, and a doubling of state support for Auburn's agricultural extension programs. But most importantly for our present focus, his racial attitudes, he championed very large increases in the appropriations for the state's two black universities, Alabama State College at Montgomery and Alabama A&M at Huntsville, which permitted each of them to obtain Class A accreditation for the first time. And he sponsored an equally significant increase in state assistance to the semiprivate Tuskegee Institute and the creation of a school of veterinary medicine there.

Commentators outside Alabama often thought Sparks's racial views essentially identical to those of Dixon, but the differences were quite clear to Alabamians of both races. Sparks was a classic paternalist. Following his election as governor but before his inauguration, Sparks received a letter from J. J. Green, the president of the Birmingham branch of the NAACP, asking him to meet with a black delegation. Although the letter took what for the time was a rather aggressive tone, insisting that the membership of any such delegation be chosen by blacks themselves rather than by Sparks, the governor-elect responded immediately and warmly. The result was his meeting with the Birmingham and Montgomery NAACP leadership on October 9, 1942, which produced proposals for expanding vocational training to qualify black workers for positions in war industries. Such a meeting with Dixon—whose War Manpower Committee was fighting just such efforts at the same time—would have been simply inconceivable and moved a delighted Green to acknowledge Sparks's "friendly and enlightened point of view." In early 1945, a black reporter for the *Pittsburgh Courier*, John H. Young, visited Montgomery to assess the state of race relations there. Although he found the racism that he doubtless expected from many white leaders, his interview in the governor's office was of a very different order. Sparks greeted him cordially, explained in detail his extensive efforts to improve black higher education, spoke enthusiastically of the decline in black farm tenantry, and in response to the US Supreme Court's recent decision forbidding white party primary rules, welcomed the participation of qualified black voters in the state's Democratic primaries. "He is prejudiced," Young concluded. "At the same time he is no race-baiter or demagogue. I found him a gentleman who respected me." If Young had been the president of the United States, he said, Sparks could not have received him more honorably.[9]

Sparks' commitment to segregation was uncompromising. In his inaugural address in January 1943, he said: "The Negro and the white can live in peace in Alabama if they recognize and lay down as fundamentals two principles which are inviolable: first, complete racial segregation; second, independent racial development. With these fundamentals there can be built in the South a relationship which carries with it justice, fair dealing, [and] equal opportunity on the part of each race to acquire rights to which it is entitled, and which the laws will grant to it when achieved."

But the object of segregation was not, as he saw it, subordination. The acceptance of the inviolability of segregation would permit a society "relieved of the boogey and fear of inter-racial marriages, of amalgamation of any kind, of social equality," he told a convention of the black CME church in Birmingham in May 1944; it would thus allow the races to recognize their mutual interests and cooperate to achieve them. "The friendship between the two races in the South has been one of mutual benefit," he said in an address at Tuskegee Institute in April 1943. "I know there have been exploitation of the colored man and a considerable measure of economic cheating that today should be over. And it will be when we place our relationships upon fixed bases and strive for the bigger and better things of life." He continued, "Do you want economic justice? You are entitled to it. It should be guaranteed upon a basis of complete equality. Do you want a fair deal and all the protections of a civilized government? You are entitled to these and they should be guaranteed and will [be]."

He told the CME delegates, "White Supremacy does not mean injustice, exploitation, unfair discrimination; but means the preservation of that influence and that guiding hand which has enabled both the white race and the Negro race to advance thus far."

Sparks emphasized in his thinking the extraordinary material and educational progress among black Alabamians that he had witnessed since entering public life in 1919, and he conceived of white supremacy as the paternal mechanism through which that progress could be brought to ever greater heights. He defined the three pillars of his program for black racial uplift as education, economic improvement, and civil rights. It will seem odd today that a leader fully committed to segregation could understand himself as an advocate of civil rights, but he was explicit about the claim. "The Negro should be given his civil rights, which includes the right to vote, when he is qualified, on the same basis as the white man." He had, he said,

> urged, and will continue to urge, Boards of Registrars to reappraise their situation and to place upon the voting lists those of all races qualified by education, by training, by intelligence and by character to vote. . . . There can be no trouble here. The interests of the two races are identical. We have our homes side by side. We have our separate schools and churches, our communities. We have those things which tie us to a country and instill that loyalty which is essential.

> Why should we feel that the Negro, any more than the white man, will stray away from those things that are for the best interests of his community, of his State, and of his section?

It is clear that Sparks understood civil rights in exactly the same terms as he understood educational and economic progress, not as something inherent but as something into which people grew.[10] Sparks, like Dixon, bristled at the interference of northern reformers and the federal government. He denounced the FEPC as a foolish gesture. "To say that employment must be on a race percentage basis, denies the right to reward ability, fitness, experience and character. . . . We [might] just as well try to make individuals go to a certain church, dress according to a given style and pray thus." He strongly supported the poll tax. When the *Montgomery Advertiser* reported in August 1944, that the War Department had opened recreational facilities at Maxwell Air Force Base to airmen of both races, he dispatched an outraged telegram of protest to President Roosevelt, and indeed his complaint caused base authorities quietly to suspend black access. This telegram brought a letter of hearty congratulation from former Governor Dixon himself. But neither man would ever have thought they saw eye to eye on such questions. In 1948, while Dixon was taking an active role in organizing the Dixiecrat revolt, Sparks denounced it and supported the reelection of Harry Truman. This action damaged Sparks's reputation with many of his Black Belt admirers, and when he sought a second term in 1950, at the conclusion of James Folsom's first term, he was easily defeated by Gordon Persons. Such was the extent of the polarization in racial attitudes that had overtaken the state by the time of Sparks's death in 1968 that, as one historian observes, obituaries were hard-pressed to determine whether he was best described as a conservative liberal or a liberal conservative. But the commentator was probably closest to the truth who called him a Whig.[11]

James E. Folsom was both the son and the son-in-law of powerful political leaders in his native Coffee County, in Alabama's southeastern Wiregrass region. He dropped out of college after his sophomore year at the University of Alabama, served for a time as a local functionary of the New Deal's Civil Works Administration, and eventually became an insurance salesman. Following unsuccessful campaigns for Congress in 1936 and 1938, he moved to Cullman, in the state's hill country, and in the gubernatorial election of 1942, he finished second to Chauncey Sparks, taking a fourth of the vote. This showing positioned him for his successful run for the governorship in 1946, when he defeated Lieutenant Governor Handy Ellis, an ally of the late governor, Bibb Graves. He would be elected to a second term by an overwhelming margin in 1954.

Folsom was an egalitarian Populist, committed to the cause of the state's small farmers and aggressively hostile to the alliance of Black Belt planters and Birmingham industrial and commercial forces who in great measure controlled the legislature. But he was also an alcoholic who readily gave his confidence to a group of venal associates who exploited his personal weaknesses in order to line their pockets at the public expense. Despite his idealism, therefore, his time in office achieved far less than his admirers had hoped. The principal achievement of his first term was an extensive farm-to-market road-paving program. His conservative opponents defeated his strenuous efforts to hold a new state constitutional convention, to reapportion legislative seats to break the power of the Black Belt in the body, to repeal the poll tax, and to liberalize Alabama's highly restrictive voter registration laws.

Folsom's sincere desire for these reforms has often misled scholars about his racial views. They were reforms for which black leaders also very much wished, and that would have significantly strengthened the position of blacks in the state's political life. But Folsom's enthusiasm for them primarily proceeded not from a concern for blacks but from his eagerness to elevate the fortunes of the white small farmer Wiregrass and hill country regions and to diminish the influence of Black Belt planters. Prominent blacks greeted Folsom's inauguration with great hope and at once presented him with an extensive list of proposals to advance their race. As the months passed, it gradually became apparent to them that their proposals had simply disappeared into Folsom's files. In a letter to a white constituent in February 1949, Folsom stated flatly that he was opposed to the admission of blacks to white schools or universities under any circumstances. His legal advisor, Ira B. Thompson, informed a correspondent from Chicago, "As you are aware, the South will always insist on segregation as the best means of preventing race disturbances. In reality there is no race problem in the South. The Governor is very strong for each state settling all such problems by enactment of laws by its own legislature, or in other words the great principle set forth in the foundation of this government of states' rights."

In part, Folsom's refusal to embrace the cause of civil rights derived from such principles, but in even greater part it derived from an essential indifference. As a resident of the white sections of Alabama, he simply did not have a sufficiently strong understanding of the plight of blacks in the plantation and urban areas to see the elements of uniqueness in these areas' social and racial problems. He tended to conflate blacks' plight with the disproportionate political influence of the planter-industrialist alliance, and therefore to think it essentially an aspect of the predicament of white small farmers in the hills and the Wiregrass. His approach to the problem of legislative reapportionment is an example of his fixation on this dimension of the state's larger dilemma. He wanted to redistribute seats in the state House of Representatives on a population basis, but he wanted to abolish the population basis altogether in the state Senate and instead to give each of the state's sixty-seven counties one senator. This plan would have eliminated Black Belt control of the legislature but would have done very little to address the specific and pressing social problems of either the cities or the plantation counties. Instead, it would have delivered permanent power to the rural white regions and their small farmer majorities. From Folsom's perspective, this represented the essential transformation necessary to set the state on the road to social justice.

A third factor that limited the extension of Folsom's egalitarianism to civil rights was that his own poor white electoral base was deeply divided on racial questions. The Ku Klux Klan's imperial wizard, Dr. Elihu P. Pruitt, an elderly Birmingham physician, wrote Folsom in the summer of 1949, amid rising racial violence in that city, to emphasize, "Your enemies are my enemies, my friends are your friends." Folsom himself had absolutely no sympathy for the Klan; indeed, he sought unsuccessfully to persuade the state's liberal attorney general, Albert A. Carmichael, to sue to have the Klan's corporate charter revoked, and he led successful efforts to induce the legislature in 1949 to adopt an antimasking law. But he relied on the support of many strong segregationists. For instance, though Folsom campaigned against the disfranchising Boswell Amendment to the state constitution, its author, attorney E. C. "Bud" Boswell of Geneva, was a powerful Folsom ally, and would become Folsom's legal advisor during the second term.

Against this background it is perhaps less surprising to learn that, though the social philosophies of Folsom and Chauncey Sparks differed vastly, the actual racial policies Folsom pursued built upon those of the Sparks years. Folsom obtained further large increases in appropriations for the state's black colleges, and in 1949 he appointed a commission whose report urged even more aggressive efforts to expand the colleges' programs. Like Sparks, Folsom urged the county Boards of Voting Registrars to display less hostility to applicants to register, though placing his pleas primarily on the ground that returning veterans should have the right to participate in the government of their state. Several of Folsom's appointees to the boards were indeed open to the registration of blacks. But these appointments had less to do with a concerted policy on Folsom's part than with rewarding Folsom's supporters in the gubernatorial election, for at least as many of the governor's appointees showed no particular willingness to accept black applicants. And even when the governor's own appointee was favorable, he was restrained by the appointees of the other two appointing officials, the state auditor and the commissioner of agriculture, each of whom was independently elected. Folsom summoned the auditor and the commissioner to public hearings at which rejected applicants told of their experiences before the boards; he hoped that this evidence would lead the other two officials to place pressure on their appointees to reform the various boards' practices, but the tactic was not successful. As complaints continued to pour in, the administration essentially threw up its hands. Folsom's executive secretary, O. H. Finney, wrote a black applicant rejected by the Jefferson County board that Folsom "has made every effort to force the Boards of Registrars of this State to register the people of Alabama according to the law. If the boards fail in their duty to the State and the Federal Government, they cannot blame this office." Folsom did repeatedly, if fruitlessly, urge the legislature to propose a constitutional amendment abolishing the poll tax, something Sparks had flatly opposed. But in truth, Folsom's small farmer Populism proved able to bring no more genuine changes to the lives of the state's black citizens than had Sparks's plantation county paternalism.[12]

Like characters from Central Casting, Dixon the segregationist urban Progressive, Sparks the Black Belt paternalist, and Folsom the egalitarian hill country Populist each played his role to type. They represented in successive gubernatorial terms virtually the entire spectrum of racial attitudes that white Alabama politics had to offer. The hopes of Alabama's blacks rose and fell with the changes in administration. However great were the differences in the racial attitudes of the three governors—and within the constraints of Alabama's political culture in the era of disfranchisement, they were very great—the gubernatorial succession nevertheless made virtually no genuinely lasting impact on the daily lives of black Alabamians.

The reason for the continuity is that the structures of white supremacy did not proceed downward from the state government that the governors headed. Changes in gubernatorial administrations or philosophies—or for that matter, changes in federal administrations or national or global attitudes toward race—therefore had few real implications for blacks in Alabama. The structures of white supremacy, rather, were intensely, radically local, with the forms of legal segregation differing significantly from town to town and from institution to institution, and with white supremacy in the countryside largely a matter of personal power relationships, and hence even more various. State government was far removed from the realities of segregation, and state policies, in practical terms, in large measure irrelevant to them. The life of each town actually determined the shape of segregation within it, and when resistance to segregation arose, it invariably arose because of considerations and events as local as was the segregation itself. Events at the level of the state or the nation might contribute to a general mood, whether among whites or blacks. But because such a mood was general, it cannot account for the rise of resistance in one place rather than another. If we are to distinguish those towns that produced direct action against segregation from those quite comparable ones that did not, we must attend to the localism of segregation, the peculiarities of its forms, and the fabric of the particular political relations that created and sustained it.

These are the dynamics that underlie the exchange of letters between Governor Sparks and Walton H. Craft about racial segregation on the buses of Mobile in 1944. Craft had assumed that Mobile bus segregation was, or should have been, merely an extension of a statewide pattern. The governor informed him that no such pattern existed. But the specific shape of the segregation on the Mobile buses that Craft noted would in fact have profound significance for the future history of the United States, and is worth further explication.

Segregation had first come to Mobile's streetcars at the beginning of November 1902, when the city council adopted an ordinance mandating it that was modeled on one adopted in Montgomery in August 1900. As had happened in Montgomery, the blacks of Mobile responded to the new ordinance with a boycott of the trolley lines, but in Mobile, unlike Montgomery, the ordinance also produced protests from whites. The ordinance required the streetcar conductors to order the reseating of passengers to preserve racial separation, and passengers of both races resented the inconvenience involved in being moved. Only a month after the ordinance had taken effect, the trolley company announced that the complaints had been so numerous that it had instructed its employees no longer to reseat customers. Blacks then resumed riding. The city at first arrested several conductors for dereliction of duty, but the company held firm and eventually the city quietly yielded. In April 1917, after more than fourteen years during which the streetcars had operated in practical defiance of the ordinance's terms, the city commission finally repealed it and substituted one that codified the actual practice. Under the new law, blacks seated from the back and whites from the front, and the dividing line was wherever they met. No passengers were unseated; the racial division was readjusted only by riders leaving the streetcar as they reached their destinations. When the trolleys were replaced by buses in the mid-1930s, the same arrangement was transferred to them. It was this pattern of segregation that Walton Craft found so unsettling.

Meanwhile, in Montgomery the unseating of black passengers remained the norm. In a pattern that Montgomery streetcars adopted from those in Lynchburg, Virginia, in January 1907, several front seats were kept reserved for whites, an equal number of rear seats for blacks, and the racial designation of the middle seats was readjusted by the conductor to accord with the changing composition of the ridership as the trolley moved along its route. This arrangement too was transferred to buses when they replaced the trolleys in 1936. Because it required the frequent reseating of black riders, and when the bus was full, often forced them to stand, in violation of the actual terms of the city ordinance, it became a particular focus of black resentment in the crowded conditions on the buses during and just after World War II, when gas rationing greatly increased bus ridership. Beginning with an appearance before the city commission in October 1952, black leaders began to press the commission and the bus company to adopt the pattern of segregation in use in Mobile. The Mobile arrangement was actually used in a number of other cities, but its use in Mobile seemed especially salient to Montgomery blacks because both cities' bus companies were divisions of the same corporation, National City Lines of Chicago.

Black leaders continued to raise the Mobile plan of bus segregation in a series of meetings with city and transit officials throughout the early 1950s. It headed the list of proposals that black spokesmen presented to candidates for the city commission in the municipal election of March 1955. And during the campaign it became an even more emotional question when a black teenager, Claudette Colvin, was arrested and convicted for refusing a bus driver's order to vacate her seat. After the candidate endorsed by blacks for commissioner of public safety was defeated by a strident white supremacist, black leaders began searching for some way to compel city officials to take their various concerns, and especially their concerns about bus seating patterns, more seriously. These events came to a head on the evening of December 1, 1955, when Mrs. Rosa L. Parks, the secretary of the Montgomery branch of the NAACP and a woman fully acquainted with the series of negotiations over the adoption of the Mobile seating plan, was ordered to yield her seat and was arrested for refusing the order. The black leadership at once rallied to her cause and initiated a boycott of the bus lines on the day of her trial, December 5. In negotiations during December 1955, and January 1956, the black organization created to run the boycott, the Montgomery Improvement Association, made the adoption of the Mobile pattern of segregation a prerequisite for ending the boycott. Only when these negotiations reached a stalemate at the end of January did the MIA's executive board finally—and quite reluctantly—authorize their attorney to file suit in federal court to seek to have the city bus segregation ordinance declared unconstitutional.[13]

Thus the differences in the particular patterns of bus segregation that had so angered Walton Craft in 1944 were precisely the same differences that lay at the heart of the Montgomery Bus Boycott in 1955. The fact that the leaders of the Bus Boycott initially sought simply the adoption of the

Mobile pattern of seating segregation, and only very slowly came to embrace an attack on segregation itself, has sometimes caused students of these events to regard them as distinctly conservative. The NAACP refused to assist the boycott in its first months expressly because the Montgomerians were not seeking integration. A version of these attitudes is to be found also in some accounts of the civil rights struggles in the South during the Depression and World War II. Because those black and liberal white activists in the region who were outside the orbit of the Communist Party generally sought reforms to ameliorate the injustices of white supremacy, rather than genuine racial equality, they are often dismissed as little more than timid ratifiers of the status quo. But such analyses ignore the profound effects that the diverse municipal expressions of segregation had upon regional conceptions of social reality.[14]

Since the patterns of segregation in any one town could differ substantially from those in neighboring ones, and might often impose rather less onerous burdens on its black residents, the result was that reformers of both races conceived of the social reality that surrounded them, though suffused with racism, as malleable. Only after segregation came under sustained assault as the civil rights movement developed, and white supremacist true believers roused themselves to defend the racial status quo, were most blacks, and later whites, able to discover the pervasive inflexibility of the system. This discovery was the greatest contribution of the civil rights movement's direct action phase, because it produced a willingness to embrace far more radical solutions than most racial liberals had theretofore contemplated. Earlier, the gradual amelioration of racial discrimination within the confines of separate development had seemed manifestly possible, because reformers could look to the existence of less burdensome arrangements in other cities and there seemed to be nothing institutional that inhibited their adoption. The solution appeared merely to be the mobilization of sufficient community goodwill. Therefore the absolutist demands of the far left for immediate transformations in race relations seemed foolishly utopian; to the extent that they were ideally desirable, they would be achieved over time through the example of more progressive municipalities acting on more recalcitrant ones.

In the light of massive resistance and the violence that surrounded too many of the direct action demonstrations, of course, the true rigidity of white supremacy became undeniable. The region did not possess within itself the capacity to save itself, in large part exactly because of the variety and complexity of its racial structures, since any fundamental reform of them would affect an almost infinite assortment of social interests. Only internal pressure sufficient to compel intervention from outside the South on the broadest possible scale could transform all of these structures at once. From that new perspective it becomes clear that the hopeful reformers of the Depression and wartime South were the genuine utopians. But to denigrate their moderation and optimism is to fail to recognize fully how diverse were the structures of segregation in the region's cities, and how apparently malleable they were in the requirements and the specific application of the various municipal ordinances.

Those who are not attentive to the emphatic localism of segregation and its manifold peculiarities of place, then, will fail to understand how it came into being in the first place and also the process by which it was finally disestablished. Each is a story that is entirely told only through a careful consideration of the level of the individual municipality.

Notes

This article originally appeared, in a somewhat different form, in Kevin M. Kruse and Stephen Tuck, eds., *Fog of War: The Second World War and the Civil Rights Movement* (New York: Oxford University Press, 2012), 51–69, and is reprinted here by permission of Oxford University Press, USA.

1. Walton H. Craft to Chauncey Sparks, September 6, 1944; Chauncey Sparks to Walton H. Craft, September 7, 1944, Governor's Correspondence, SG 12491, folder 8, Alabama Department of Archives and History, Montgomery (hereafter cited as ADAH).

2. Walter W. Flowers to Thomas S. Lawson, memorandum, June 29, 1942, in Governor's Correspondence, SG 12491, folder 9, ADAH; see also Bernard F. Sykes to William McQueen, memorandum, August 28, 1944, ibid.

3. August Meier and Elliott Rudwick, *CORE: A Study in the Civil Rights Movement, 1942–1968* (Urbana: University of Illinois Press, 1975), 3–17; *New York Times*, August 2, 4, 5, 6, 7, 9, 11, 14, 15, 16, 17; October 5; December 9, 1944.

4. U.S. v. Bruce, 353 F.2d 474; *Selma Times-Journal*, May 15, 1963; July 10, 1964; Frank Holloway, SNCC field reports, February 15, March 19, 1963, Student Nonviolent Coordinating Committee Papers, microfilm edition.

5. Howard N. Rabinowitz, *Race Relations in the Urban South, 1865–1890* (New York: Oxford University Press, 1978); C. Vann Woodward, *The Strange Career of Jim Crow*, 3rd ed., rev. (New York: Oxford University Press, 1974), and his *Origins of the New South, 1877–1913* (Baton Rouge: Louisiana State University Press, 1951). See also Joel Williamson, ed., *The Origins of Segregation* (Lexington, MA: D. C. Heath, 1968), and his *After Slavery: The Negro in South Carolina during Reconstruction, 1861–1877* (Chapel Hill: University of North Carolina Press, 1965), and his *The Crucible of Race: Black-White Relations in the American South since Emancipation* (New York: Oxford University Press, 1984); John W. Cell, *The Highest Stage of White Supremacy:*

The Origins of Segregation in South Africa and the American South (Cambridge: Cambridge University Press, 1982); C. Vann Woodward, *American Counterpoint: Slavery and Racism in the North-South Dialogue* (Boston: Little, Brown, 1971), 234–60, and his *Thinking Back: The Perils of Writing History* (Baton Rouge: Louisiana State University Press, 1986), 81–99.

6. I develop these points in J. Mills Thornton III, *Dividing Lines: Municipal Politics and the Struggle for Civil Rights in Montgomery, Birmingham, and Selma* (Tuscaloosa: University of Alabama Press, 2002), 1–3, 78, 87–88, 354–56, 405, 500–502, 562–64.

7. Frank M. Dixon to Jessie Daniel Ames, June 5, 1942, Dixon to Editors of *Encyclopedia Britannica*, July 9, 1941, both in SG 12278, folder 13; Dixon to Kenneth McKellar, March 4, 1940, SG 12248, folder 8; Mrs. Estelle Cassimus to Dixon, November 13, 1942, Dixon to Mrs. Cassimus, November 24, 1942, Dixon to E. A. Barley, September 17, 1942, all in SG 12277, folder 29, Governor's Correspondence, ADAH. On Bibb Graves, see the preceding article in this volume.

8. Richard H. Powell to Frank M. Dixon, November 30, 1942; Dixon to Powell December 1, 1942; Dixon to Lister Hill, May 12, 1942; Dixon to Gen. John P. Smith, March 4, 1942; Dr. R. B. McCann to Dixon, May 11, 1942; Dixon to McCann, May 13, 1942, all in SG 12275, folder 5; Dixon to Pete Jarman, November 25, 1942; Dixon to Paul B. Johnson, November 25, 1942, both in SG 12277, folder 25; Dixon to R. M. Jefferies, September 11, 1942; Dixon, undated memorandum to file [summer 1942], both in SG 12277, folder 26; Minutes, War Manpower Committee meeting, September 3, 1942; Dixon to Horace Hall, August 21, 1942, SG 12277, folder 28; Dixon to Donch Hanks Jr., October 26, 1942; Dixon to Fitzgerald Hall, September 18, 1942 (quotation), SG 12277, folder 29; Dixon to Ralph D. Williams, July 22, 1942; Henry T. DeBardeleben to Joe Starnes, July 29, 1942; Wallace D. Malone to Dixon, July 31, 1942; Joe Starnes to Dixon, July 24, 1942; Dixon to Frank Bone, August 24, 1942, all in SG 12277, folder 30; Major Thomas H. Vaden to Chief of Labor Relations Branch, Civilian Personnel Division, Services of Supply, September 15, 1942, and attachments, all in SG 12277, folder 31; Dixon to Richard H. Powell, October 13, 1942; Dixon to W. Logan Martin, October 22, 1942; Harry M. Ayers to Dixon, October 17, 1942, and attachments, all in SG 12278, folder 1; Walter B. Jones to Dixon, September 3, 1942, and attachment; Dixon to John Temple Graves, September 1, 1942, SG 12278, folder 11, all in Governor's Correspondence, ADAH. On Dixon, see the sketch by Glenn A. Feldman in Samuel L. Webb and Margaret E. Armbrester, eds., *Alabama Governors: A Political History of the State* (Tuscaloosa: University of Alabama Press, 2001), 185–89; see also Thornton, *Dividing Lines*, 144, 318–19, 655. In a preceding article in this volume, we have encountered Miller Bonner as the leader of the Black Belt bloc in the state Senate during the first Graves administration.

9. J. J. Green to Chauncey Sparks, July 11, 1942; Sparks to Green, July 15, 1942; Green to Sparks, July 21, 1942; Sparks to Carl W. Bear, September 9, 1942; Bear to

Green, October 6, 1942; Wilbur H. Hollins to Sparks, December 10, 1942, all in SG 12491, folder 8; *Pittsburgh Courier*, February 3, 1945, clipping in SG 12501, folder 3, Governor's Correspondence, ADAH.

10. Chauncey Sparks, Inaugural Address, SG 12527, folder 1, Tuskegee Institute Founder's Day Address, SG 12527, folder 3, CME Convention Address, SG 12527, folder 8. See also Sparks to D. Ward Nichols, January 25, 1944; W. D. Hargrove to Sparks, May 8, 1944; C. Wesley Gordon to Sparks, May 27, 1944, all in SG 12400, folder 14; John Temple Graves to Sparks, May 6 and May 7, 1944; Sparks to Graves, May 9, 1944, SG 12501, folder 5; Sparks to J. Forney Johnston, June 9, 1945, SG 12501, folder 3, all in Governor's Correspondence, ADAH.

11. Chauncey Sparks, CME Convention Address, SG 12527, folder 8 (quotation); Statement of Governor Sparks on US Supreme Court's white primary decision, April 3, 1944, SG 12490, folder 8; John H. Bankhead to Sparks, August 31, 1944; Robert P. Patterson to Sparks, September 1, 1944; Frank M. Dixon to Sparks, August 31, 1944; N. Duke Kimbrough Jr. to Sparks, August 27, 1944; Talmadge Winn to Sparks, August 24, 1944; Sam Erle Hobbs to Sparks, wire, August 26, 1944; Ernest D. LeMay to Sparks, September 13, 1944; Sparks to Horace Wilkinson, August 31, 1944, all in SG 12491, folders 5, 6; Champ Pickens to Sparks, February 15, 1943; R. F. Finkley to Sparks, February 16, 1943; Harry M. Ayers to Sparks, August 31, 1943, all in SG 12491, folder 9; James E. Chappell to Sparks, April 8, 1943; Sparks to Chappell, April 10, 1943, SG 12501, folder 5; George Bliss Jones to W. R. Ragland, March 7, 1946, SG 12515, folder 5; R. T. Nelson to Sparks, February 27, 1946; A. H. Harris to Sparks, January 31, 1946; Lillian P. Long to Sparks, October 29, 1945, SG 12515, folder 6; Sparks to Dr. J. C. Foshee, December 11, 1946; Henry Husing to Sparks, November 29, 1946; and Text of Associated Press interview with Governor Sparks on the adoption of the Boswell Amendment, November 8, 1946, SG 12521, folder 31, all in Governor's Correspondence, ADAH; Harvey H. Jackson, sketch of Sparks in Webb and Armbrester, eds., *Alabama Governors*, 190–93.

12. Mrs. Belzora S. Ward to James E. Folsom, January 21, 1947; Robert Durr to Folsom, March 17, 1947, SG 13422, folder 1; Durr to Folsom, September 23, 1947; Folsom to P. L. Brownlow, February 11, 1948; Ira B. Thompson to Gilbert S. Derr, March 25, 1948, SG 13441, folder 5; Thompson to V. G. Appleby, August 4, 1948; Robert Durr to Folsom, August 30, 1948; Folsom to Durr, September 1, 1948, SG 13441, folder 6; W. H. Drinkard to Mrs. W. H. Duke, May 23, 1946; Mrs. Duke to Folsom, October 26, 1948; Mrs. Duke to Folsom, November 12, 1948; Ira B. Thompson to Mrs. Duke, November 22, 1948; Thompson to Henry Hannan, September 29, 1948, SG 13461, folder 5; Thompson to Sen. John C. Stennis, September 3, 1948; J. J. Green to Folsom, August 15, 1949; E. D. Nixon to Folsom, June 6, 1949; A. C. Maclin to Folsom, June 2, 1949; Bankhead Bates to Folsom, June 8, 1948; O. H. Finney Jr. to E. D. Nixon, June 8, 1949; Clara Hard Rutledge to Folsom, January 4, 1949, SG 13461, folder 6; Press Release, January 3, 1949; W. C. Patton to Folsom, January 7,

1949; Minutes of Organizational Meeting of Negro Higher Education Committee, January 14, 1949; Minutes of Committee Meeting, March 12, 1949; Rev. J. R. Wingfield to Folsom, January 14, 1949, SG 13450, folder 6; Minutes of Meeting of Negro Higher Education Committee, March 26, 1949, and attached statistics, SG 13450, folder 7; Minutes and Final Report of Negro Higher Education Committee, April 20, 1949, SG 13450, folder 8; Ira B. Thompson to Alberta Sierras, November 30, 1949; Thompson to Mrs. W. H. Duke, January 12, 1950; Folsom to T. A. Langford, June 9, 1950, SG 13473, folder 7; O. H. Finney Jr. to John G. Hosey, May 17, 1949; Hosey to Folsom, May 18, 1949; E. J. "Gunny" Gonzales to Finney, May 28, 1949; Gonzales to Finney, June 7, 1949; Gonzales to Finney, June 18, 1949; Gonzales to Folsom, July 15, 1949; George D. Patterson Jr. to Folsom, July 12, 1949; Ralph R. Britain to Folsom, June 21, 1949; O. H. Finney Jr. to J. Milton Schnell, June 24, 1949; J. Milton Schnell and Mrs. D. C. Randle to Folsom, July 10, 1949; Gonzales to Finney, July 21, 1949; Finney to Gonzales, July 27, 1949; Gonzales to Finney, August 2, 1949; Gonzales to Finney, August 13, 1949; Ira B. Thompson to John G. Hosey, November 18, 1949; Charles S. Lanier to Folsom, November 23, 1949; Gonzales to Thompson, December 1, 1949; Willie Louis Dick to Folsom, December 3, 1949; Finney to Dick, December 6, 1949; J. D. Culp to Thompson, December 5, 1949; Emory O. Jackson to J. Howard McGrath, December 10, 1949; N. C. Fulmer to Haygood Patterson and Dan Thomas, December 10, 1949; Emory O. Jackson to Folsom, December 6, 1949; Thompson to Jackson, December 14, 1949; O. H. Finney to Haygood Patterson and Dan Thomas, December 14, 1949; Sam S. Douglass to Folsom, January 4, 1950; Robert Thrasher to Folsom, December 19, 1949, all in SG 13473, folder 13; Thornton, *Dividing Lines*, 163–64, 167. On Folsom, see George E. Sims, *The Little Man's Big Friend: James E. Folsom in Alabama Politics, 1946–1958* (Tuscaloosa: University of Alabama Press, 1985), and Carl Grafton and Anne Permaloff, *Big Mules and Branchheads: James E. Folsom and Political Power in Alabama* (Athens: University of Georgia Press, 1985). In an earlier article in this volume, we have encountered "Bud" Boswell as a zealous advocate of the Redeemer element's expulsion movement of 1929.

13. A full account of these events is in Thornton, *Dividing Lines*, 20–96. The next article in this volume explores the legal questions surrounding the Bus Boycott.

14. This misunderstanding limits the usefulness, for instance, of Glenda E. Gilmore, *Defying Dixie: The Radical Roots of Civil Rights, 1919–1950* (New York: Norton, 2008).

9
Rosa Parks and the Law

Racial segregation first came to public transportation in Montgomery, Alabama, in the summer of 1900. There had been a racial incident on a streetcar in Augusta, Georgia, in May of that year. A black man had killed a prominent young white man there in the course of an altercation over a seat. As a result, a white mob had lynched the black man, and the Augusta City Council had adopted an ordinance in June requiring the racial segregation of trolley seating.[1] In the meantime, within days of the Augusta incident, Montgomery alderman John D. Finley, an attorney, had responded to it by introducing a proposed ordinance requiring the trolley lines in his own city to reserve half the seats in each streetcar for whites and half for blacks. Montgomery's three trolley lines denounced this proposal as simply unworkable, and as a result of their opposition, the city council rejected Finley's ordinance by a vote of five in favor to six against.

The *Montgomery Advertiser* was an enthusiastic proponent of Finley's idea, however, arguing that it would prevent violent encounters such as the one in Augusta, and under the *Advertiser*'s editorial prodding, Finley revised the ordinance and reintroduced it. His new proposal eliminated the racial reservation of seats. Instead it required streetcar conductors to assign all passengers to seats in such a way as to separate the races. It made the refusal of a passenger to take the seat the conductor assigned a misdemeanor. But it provided that no passenger could be moved from his seat unless there was a vacant seat in the area for his race to which he could have moved. These changes satisfied the trolley companies. The council therefore adopted the revised Finley ordinance unanimously on August 6, and Mayor Edwin B. Joseph, an insurance agent, signed it into law on August 10.

August 12 was a Sunday, and essentially every black clergyman in Montgomery used his sermon that morning to denounce the new ordinance. The result was that on Monday, August 13, black trolley passengers began a boycott of the streetcars. By August 16 the trolley lines reported their receipts down by 60 percent, and on September 20 they said that receipts were down by a fourth during the boycott's first month. The boycott continued throughout 1901 and into 1902. By that time, though, the trolley lines apparently had passed quiet instructions to their conductors to turn a blind eye to violations of the ordinance. Under these circumstances, blacks slowly drifted back to riding, and the boycott gradually ended.[2]

The trolley companies' lack of enforcement of the new law did not go unnoticed by some whites, however. In late 1905, a firm headquartered in Lynchburg, Virginia, gained control of all three of Montgomery's trolley lines and petitioned the city for an exclusive franchise. The discussions over the franchise revived the question of the segregation ordinance. In return for the grant of the franchise in April 1906, the trolley company promised, among other things, to begin enforcing segregation more vigorously. By August, however, there had been no noticeable changes, and Alderman John F. Jones, a clerk in the Montgomery Fair department store, therefore introduced a new segregation ordinance requiring completely separate streetcars for blacks and whites. In October, over the trolley company's strenuous protests, the council adopted Jones's proposal. Mayor William M. Teague, a wholesale hardware merchant, vetoed the ordinance, echoing the trolley company in saying that it imposed an excessive financial burden on the company. But the council overrode Mayor Teague's veto with only one dissent.

The company thereupon sent a formal letter to the mayor announcing that it could not and would not comply with the new ordinance's terms. The mayor, determined to embarrass his council opponents, then ordered police to arrest any trolley employee who defied the new plan. It went into effect on the morning of November 23, and by noon fifty-four arrests had been made, the operation of the trolley system had come to a complete halt, and the city was in an uproar. But that afternoon, City Court judge Anthony D. Sayre granted the company a temporary injunction against the further enforcement of the Jones ordinance, and trolley operations resumed.

These events brought the company's Lynchburg president, R. D. Apperson, and its general counsel, John D. Horsley, rushing to Montgomery to negotiate with the angry city aldermen. Apperson proposed a plan of segregation that he said had worked well in Lynchburg: the reservation of the front four rows of seats on each streetcar for whites, the back four for blacks, and each race using the middle seats closest to its section when needed. Conductors were to have police power to reseat passengers to preserve segregation, and the reserved sections were to be kept free even if there were no passengers of the appropriate race aboard the streetcar. Alderman William J. Ryan, a dry goods store clerk, introduced Apperson's proposal as an ordinance, and the council adopted it on January 7, 1907. But on January 12, Alderman John Jones, the author of the separate cars ordinance, moved to reconsider the Ryan proposal. Railing that the Ryan ordinance gave special preference to blacks, he denounced it as discriminatory toward white people. Equally odd was the reply of Alderman J. Lee Holloway, an attorney. Holloway informed the council that Jones's idea of racially separate cars was a violation of the Fourteenth Amendment's equal protection clause. Only separate seats within the same car would pass federal court muster, he assured the aldermen. After a lengthy argument, the council repealed both Ryan's and Jones's ordinances and abandoned any further effort to legislate on this subject.

The result of this battle was to leave the city with the Finley ordinance of 1900. But the trolley company proceeded on its own to adopt as company policy the segregation plan that R. D. Apperson had brought from Lynchburg. As the squabble of 1906–7 faded into a dim local memory, the company policy soon settled into accepted practice among streetcar employees. And when the trolley system was replaced by buses in 1936, the new bus company inherited and adopted the practices that had become customary on the streetcars.[3]

Montgomery's buses had thirty-six seats. The front ten (the two facing bench seats and the first row of parallel seats) were reserved for whites and the back ten for blacks. The white reserved section was kept clear even when there were no whites on the bus. The middle sixteen seats (four rows) had no fixed racial designation. It was the responsibility of the bus driver, taking on the role of the streetcar conductor, to adjust the racial ratio of these seats to accord with the changing composition of the ridership as the bus proceeded along its route. In all these ways, the bus company policy accorded with the proposals that R. D. Apperson had suggested to the city council at the end of 1906.

On at least two crucial points, however, the bus company's seating practices differed from the Finley ordinance of 1900 that remained the city's only regulation governing segregation on public transportation. The ordinance provided that the driver was to assign seats to the two races only when there were members of each race on board. But the bus company ordinarily kept the first ten seats reserved for whites even when there were no whites on the bus. And the ordinance provided that a passenger's refusal to move when ordered to do so by a driver was unlawful only if there was a vacant seat to which the passenger could move. But the bus drivers in fact often compelled black passengers to stand in order to accommodate boarding whites. In both of these practices the bus company actually was violating the terms of the 1900 ordinance, as a result of its dimly remembered efforts to satisfy the city council during the dispute of 1906–7.

If this situation had not been complicated enough, at the end of World

War II the Alabama legislature added new confusion. In 1945 the legislature adopted a statute compelling all bus companies to provide segregated seating, terminals, and ticket windows and instructing the Alabama Public Service Commission to administer these requirements in the same manner as it administered the Alabama Motor Carrier Act of 1939. The statute contained none of the exceptions of the Montgomery city ordinance; every passenger had to sit wherever, and move whenever, the bus driver ordered. But the Alabama Motor Carrier Act of 1939 specifically provided that it did not apply to municipal bus lines, and the terms of the 1945 statute clearly seemed to be talking about intercity buses. Then in 1947 the legislature passed another act authorizing, but not requiring, bus companies to segregate bus seating and terminal facilities. This statute contained no reference to the Motor Carrier Act, but like the 1945 act it referred to facilities only relevant to intercity bus operations. And because its provisions were merely permissive, rather than mandatory, a bus company would have had to have taken formal action to adopt its terms, something that the owner of Montgomery's bus company, National City Lines of Chicago, apparently had never done.[4]

If these new state laws applied to Montgomery's municipal bus line, then they had superseded the city ordinance of 1900, and the ordinance's exceptions had become inoperative. But if the state laws were not applicable, then the provisions of the city ordinance were still in force, and significant aspects of the bus company's practices were in conflict with them. The result was that the precise legal powers and duties of Montgomery's bus drivers in the early 1950s were quite obscure.

The practice of bus segregation in Montgomery's coastal neighbor, Mobile, at the same time was much more straightforward. Under an ordinance adopted by the Mobile City Commission in April 1917, that city had neither any racially reserved seats nor any unseating of passengers once they were seated. Whites seated from the front and blacks from the back, and the line of division was wherever they met. It was readjusted only by the departure of passengers as they reached their destinations.[5] This plan was used also in a number of other southern cities, including Atlanta. But its use in Mobile was particularly significant for blacks in Montgomery because the Montgomery and Mobile bus companies were both divisions of National City Lines. Beginning in October 1952, therefore, Montgomery's black Women's Political Council—a club composed primarily of female faculty members at Alabama State College—began pressing the bus company and the city commission to consider adopting the Mobile pattern of seating segregation. They raised the question again in meetings in December 1953, and March 1954. And in May 1954, the president of the Women's

Political Council, Alabama State English professor Jo Ann G. Robinson, wrote to Mayor William A. Gayle to warn that, unless some positive response was forthcoming, black organizations were contemplating a boycott of the buses.[6]

The matter was still a very sore point for blacks as the city election campaign of 1955 began. On February 23, 1955, all candidates for the city commission appeared at a public meeting before a committee of the black Progressive Democratic Association, and association chairman Edgar D. Nixon, who was the president of the Montgomery local of the Brotherhood of Sleeping Car Porters and one of the most prominent leaders of Montgomery's black community, handed them all a questionnaire seeking their positions on a range of issues of concern to blacks. The very first question asked the candidates' opinion of adopting the Mobile plan of bus seating. Then, in the midst of the campaign, came the arrest and trial of Claudette Colvin.

Colvin, a high school student, was returning home on the afternoon of March 2. She was seated far back in the bus, just forward of the rear door, when a white couple sat down across the aisle from her. The bus driver therefore ordered her and the pregnant black woman seated next to her to stand, and when she refused, he called the police. As Colvin was carried weeping from the bus, she apparently kicked one of the arresting officers. At her trial before Juvenile Court judge Wiley C. Hill, therefore, she was charged with violation of the city bus segregation ordinance and with assault and battery on the policeman. But because all seats had been filled, the requirement of the city code that there have been another seat to which she could have moved meant that she was not guilty of that count. Circuit Solicitor William F. Thetford met this difficulty by moving to amend the complaint to charge instead a violation of the 1945 state statute. Colvin's young attorney, Fred D. Gray, who had been admitted to the bar only six months earlier, objected that the statute applied only to intercity bus lines. But Judge Hill overruled the objection, found Colvin guilty on both counts, declared her a juvenile delinquent, and placed her on probation. She appealed to circuit court. But at her circuit court trial, Solicitor Thetford dropped the segregation charge and pressed only the charge of assault and battery. On this count her conviction was sustained.[7]

The Colvin trial led to a new round of negotiations between black leaders and bus company and city officials over the Mobile seating plan. But no agreement was forthcoming. And the city elections produced the defeat of the racially liberal commissioner of public affairs, Dave Birmingham, who had integrated the city police force, by a strong segregationist, Clyde C. Sellers, who had made the Progressive Democratic Association's questionnaire a principal campaign issue. By the summer and fall of 1955, therefore, blacks increasingly despaired of gaining reforms through the political process and searched for an alternative way to compel white leaders to take their concerns seriously.[8]

It was in this context that Rosa Parks was arrested on December 1. Mrs. Parks, born Rosa Louise McCauley in 1913, had grown up on her grandfather's farm near Pine Level, in the southern part of Montgomery County. In 1924, her mother arranged for her to move into Montgomery to live with cousins so that she could attend a private school for black girls. Known as Miss White's School, this extraordinary institution had been created by Alice L. White and Margaret Beard, New England Congregationalist missionaries, in 1886. Under Miss White's tutelage, Rosa McCauley began training for a career as a stenographer and typist. She was also taught considerable skill as a seamstress and, perhaps most important of all, a strong sense of dignity and self-worth.

On completion of Miss White's, which ran through the eighth grade, Rosa decided to seek a high school degree. At this time, Montgomery did not provide a public high school for blacks. Rosa enrolled in Alabama State College's laboratory high school, which required tuition payments from its students, but financial constraints forced her to leave school after the eleventh grade, in 1930. In December 1932, she married Raymond A. Parks, a barber who was ten years her senior, and with his assistance she resumed her schooling. Finally, in 1933, she received her high school diploma, against considerable odds, at the age of twenty.

Only a tiny percentage of blacks in Montgomery—6 percent of them in 1940, the first year for which the statistic is available—were high school graduates in this period, and even fewer had Rosa Parks's typing and shorthand skills. But she found herself unable to obtain employment commensurate with her education and talent. Secretarial jobs for blacks were virtually nonexistent in the South; there were only 140 black typists or stenographers in the entire state of Alabama in 1940, as against 8,491 white ones. And employment of any description was scarce in Montgomery at the bottom of the Depression. Mrs. Parks went through a series of menial jobs—as a helper at Saint Margaret's Hospital, as a domestic, as a presser at a tailor shop. She worked at Maxwell Air Force Base for a time during World War II and briefly tried her hand at selling insurance for a black-owned company in 1946. By 1955 she, her husband, and her mother were all living in a small apartment in a public housing project, Cleveland Courts, and she was employed altering ready-to-wear clothes at the city's principal department store, the Montgomery Fair.

In the meantime, Mrs. Parks developed an increasing hostility toward the racial barriers that were in part to blame for her plight. In 1934 her husband had joined the Montgomery branch of the NAACP, and in 1943 she joined him as a member. There her secretarial skills were much needed and appreciated. She was quickly elected the branch's secretary, and in 1947 she was put in charge of the NAACP's newly opened office in downtown Montgomery. These duties were entirely on a volunteer basis; they paid nothing. But through them she became a good friend of Edgar D. Nixon, who lived only a few blocks from her public housing apartment and was the NAACP branch president from 1945 to 1950, and she enthusiastically embraced Nixon's militant crusade for equal rights. She attended an NAACP leadership training conference in Jacksonville, Florida, in the spring of 1946, at which she met director of branches Ella J. Baker and assistant special counsel Robert L. Carter. As a result of the conference she professed herself "very much inspired." In October 1947, she served on a three-person nominating committee at the Alabama state NAACP convention that arranged to have Nixon chosen state president. She was again a delegate to the state NAACP convention, meeting in Mobile in 1948, and gave a speech in which she "denounced the stand of some [blacks] for feeling proud of their home or the South when Negroes every day are being molested and maltreated. No one should feel proud of a place as long as Negroes are intimidated," she insisted. The convention thereupon elected her secretary of the statewide conference, in addition to her duties with the Montgomery branch. In 1949 she was forced by her health to resign the two offices, to the great distress of Nixon and of the national NAACP headquarters in New York. But by 1952 she had resumed the position of secretary of the Montgomery branch, and in 1954 she was also elected corresponding secretary for the Second Congressional District of the NAACP's Alabama Coordinating Committee for Registration and Voting; her friend Edgar Nixon was chosen district chairman. She also became adult adviser of the Montgomery branch's NAACP youth council, formed in 1953, and in this position she arranged in the spring of 1955 to have Claudette Colvin describe to the members the circumstances of her arrest for violation of the bus segregation ordinance. About 1953, too, Edgar Nixon introduced her to the white progressive leaders Clifford and Virginia Durr, and in the summer of 1955, Mrs. Durr arranged to have Mrs. Parks invited to a two-week-long interracial conference at the Highlander Folk School, a radical Tennessee institution specializing in the training of community organizers. Some of the South's most active racial reformers also participated in this conference. Throughout the early 1950s as well, her NAACP position allowed her to be fully informed about the years of quiet negotiations between blacks and city officials regarding the seating regulations on Montgomery buses; indeed, she herself served on several of the delegations that met with white authorities to discuss this matter. Thus the woman who took her seat on the Cleveland Avenue bus on the evening of December 1, 1955, was far more knowledgeable about efforts being made to eliminate racial discrimination in Montgomery than all but a tiny handful of the city's residents, white or black.[9]

When Mrs. Parks boarded the Montgomery City Lines bus at Court Square, she took her seat in the first row of the black section. At the time, the bus was divided into ten seats for whites and twenty-six for blacks. Two blocks later, at its stop in front of the Empire Theater, the bus was nearly completely filled. All seats were taken, as was all standing room in the white section, but some standing room remained in the rear of the black section. Bus driver J. Fred Blake therefore decided to readjust the racial division to fourteen white and twenty-two black seats, by clearing the first row in the black section. This step opened four seats and two standing-room spaces for the whites who were waiting to board. If Blake had not taken this action, none of the waiting whites could have been accommodated, even though there was standing room available in the rear. On the other hand, since all the seated blacks would have to stand, the 1900 city ordinance in fact authorized them to refuse his order. The order was legal only under the 1945 state statute, if it applied to municipal buses. The other three blacks on the row of seats all got up, but Mrs. Parks, with her awareness of the long series of negotiations over the adoption of the Mobile seating plan, refused and was arrested.

At her trial before Recorder's Court judge John B. Scott on December 5, the city faced the same problem with the Finley ordinance of 1900 that the state had faced at the Colvin trial nine months earlier. City Prosecutor D. Eugene Loe attempted to meet it in much the same way that Solicitor Thetford had. The city code also contained a section making it "unlawful for any person to commit any offense in the city which is declared by a law of the state to be a misdemeanor." Prosecutor Loe moved to amend the city's complaint by alleging a violation of this section, rather than of the bus segregation section that had been specified in the original complaint, and then asserting that Mrs. Parks had violated the 1945 state statute. Fred Gray, her attorney, once again argued that the state statute did not apply to city buses, but Judge Scott overruled his objection, found Mrs. Parks guilty, and fined her ten dollars and costs. Gray appealed to circuit court. In March 1956, after a trial before Circuit Judge Eugene W. Carter without a jury, Mrs. Parks's conviction was affirmed, and she then appealed to the Alabama Court of Appeals.[10]

In the meantime, the one-day boycott of the buses that had been called by black leaders for the day of Mrs. Parks's Recorder's Court trial to demonstrate support for her, had proven so successful that black leaders urged continuation of the boycott until the city commission and the bus company accepted the Mobile seating segregation plan. In negotiations during December 1955, and January 1956, the newly formed black organization the Montgomery Improvement Association (MIA) pressed the black seating proposal. But the commission rejected it, and the bus company maintained that it could take no action without the commission's approval. Finally, and quite reluctantly, the MIA's executive board at the end of January authorized the filing of a federal court suit seeking to declare bus segregation unconstitutional. Fred Gray filed the suit on February 1, in the name of a number of black women, Claudette Colvin among them, who had suffered incidents on the buses. Rosa Parks was not included among the plaintiffs because Gray feared that the fact that her prosecution was then pending in the state courts might create legal difficulties.[11] In June, a three-judge federal court ruled 2–1 that both the Montgomery ordinance and the two state statutes violated the US Constitution's Fourteenth Amendment. Montgomery's judges Richard T. Rives and Frank M. Johnson constituted the majority, while Birmingham's Judge Seybourn H. Lynne dissented. In November, in a brief per curiam order, the US Supreme Court affirmed this ruling, and buses were integrated on December 21, an event that was followed by a flurry of shootings and bombings.[12]

The complicated legal questions surrounding the Montgomery bus segregation ordinance would never receive any clear judicial resolution. In February 1957, the state Court of Appeals dismissed Mrs. Parks's appeal of her conviction. Writing for a unanimous court, Presiding Judge Robert B. Harwood held that, because Fred Gray had failed to create a bill of exceptions to Judge Scott's rulings at Mrs. Parks's original Recorder's Court trial, it left the Court of Appeals with nothing to review. A general statute regulating criminal appeals had dispensed with assignments of error, but the waiver did not apply to appeals from convictions for violating municipal ordinances, which were only quasi-criminal and were instead governed by the rules for civil appeals, Harwood wrote. Therefore, the fact that Mrs. Parks had been convicted under the provision of the city code incorporating state misdemeanor statutes, rather than under the state statute itself, became the crucial factor in the court's dismissal of her appeal. Because of this holding, the court never reached the issues of the applicability of the state law to municipal bus lines or the exceptions specified in the city ordinance. And of course, because of the US Supreme Court ruling in the federal court case, these questions were effectively moot by this time anyway. Nevertheless, it does seem clear that Mrs. Parks had actually been entitled to an acquittal under city and state law, even if the constitutionality of the segregation regulations had not been questioned.[13]

In November 1957, as a part of a general settlement of the various prosecutions surrounding the Bus Boycott, Mrs. Parks's attorneys agreed to withdraw her appeal to the Alabama Supreme Court of the ruling of the Court of Appeals, and she paid her fine.[14] In the meantime, she had lost her job as a seamstress at the Montgomery Fair department store, and she and her family had decided to move to Detroit, Michigan, to join her brother. The complexities surrounding her prosecution and the specifics of the Mobile plan of bus seating quickly faded in the public memory, and within a few years most Montgomerians, in common with most Americans, came to think of the Bus Boycott as a movement to obtain the racial integration of the buses.

But this perception is misleading, particularly because it obscures the essential localism that is a defining characteristic of the boycott, as of virtually all of the events of the civil rights movements in the South—because the structure of the white supremacy that the movements were contesting was inherently local—and instead converts it into a mere local manifestation of national developments. If that were an accurate way of understanding these events, it would leave us with no way effectively to distinguish those communities that produced significant direct action movements from those that did not. Broad national developments did have an impact on Montgomery, where the Bus Boycott occurred, but they had no greater impact there than, for example, in Meridian, Mississippi, or Columbus, Georgia, cities of comparable size and with comparable racial climates, where no direct action movement emerged, then or later. If, however, we recognize that segregation was not a single, uniform phenomenon, that the structure of bus segregation, for instance, was very different in Mobile and Montgomery; and if we recognize not only the particularities of local ordinances, but also the central importance of local politics—how crucial to the emergence of the Montgomery Bus Boycott, that is, was Clyde C. Sellers's defeat of Dave Birmingham in the municipal election of March 1955—then we take a long step toward explaining why mobilization occurred in some places and not in others.

Such an account deprives us of a vast national civil rights movement, sweeping across America like an increasingly irresistible tide in the decade from 1955 to 1965—a portrait of this period that is essentially mythical.[15] But it substitutes something else: a way to understand the profound significance of the local in the lives of people and in the fabric of history, and therefore an appreciation of the capacity of ordinary, and even humble, residents of obscure places to shape their destiny in decisive and world-historical ways.

Notes

This article initially appeared, in a somewhat different form, in the fall 2005 issue of the Montgomery County Historical Society *Herald*, and is reprinted here with the kind permission of the Montgomery County Historical Society.

1. On the Augusta incident, see W. Fitzhugh Brundage, *Lynching in the New South: Georgia and Virginia, 1880–1930* (Urbana: University of Illinois Press, 1993), 200.

2. *Montgomery Advertiser*, July 3, 10, 24; August 4, 7, 16, 18, 1900; *Montgomery Journal*, July 3, 10; August 7, 13, 14, 15, 16, 18, 1900; *Huntsville Republican*, September 22, 1900; Montgomery City Code of 1952, Chapter 6, Section 10–11; August Meier and Elliott Rudwick, "The Boycott Movement against Jim Crow Streetcars in the South, 1900–1906," *Journal of American History* 55 (March 1969): 756–75.

3. *Montgomery Advertiser*, October 2, 9, 16, 18, 23; November 22, 23, 24, 25, 29; December 1, 23, 1906; January 2, 3, 4, 5, 8, 13, 14, 22, 1907; January 6, 1957.

4. Case File, Aurelia S. Browder v. William A. Gayle, Exhibit A: "Legal Requirements concerning the Segregation of Races on City Buses," in Southeastern Regional Federal Records Center, East Point, Georgia; Acts of Alabama, Session of 1939, pp. 1064–90, at p. 1066; Acts of Alabama, Session of 1945, p. 731; Acts of Alabama, Session of 1947, pp. 40–41; Code of Alabama 1940, Recompiled 1958, Title 48, Section 301 (31a, 31b, 31c) [Subsection 31a is the 1945 act and subsections 31 b and c are the 1947 act]. The seating policy described in the text was the bus company's official one. In practice the policy seems to have varied somewhat from driver to driver and route to route. See Trial Transcript, Martin Luther King, Jr. v. State of Alabama (Records of the Alabama Court of Criminal Appeals, Office of the Clerk, Supreme Court Building, Montgomery), pp. 360–486, 510–47, and Trial Transcript, Browder v. Gayle (above), pp. 58–69.

5. 1921 Supplement to the Mobile City Code of 1907, pp. 280–81; Mobile City Code of 1947, Chapter 20, Article 1; Mobile City Code of 1955, Chapter 10, Sections 4–9. The preceding article in this volume contains a fuller account of the origins of bus segregation in Mobile.

6. (Montgomery) *Alabama Journal*, October 28, 1952; Montgomery *Examiner*, October 30, 1952; (Montgomery) *Alabama Tribune*, April 2, 1954; *Montgomery Advertiser*, April 6, 1954; Trial Transcript, King v. State, pp. 141, 256–57, 348–59; Jo Ann G. Robinson to William A. Gayle, May 21, 1954, in File 2279, Records of the District Attorney's Office, Fifteenth Circuit, Montgomery County Courthouse.

7. *Montgomery Advertiser*, February 18, 24, 25; March 1, 6, 16, 20, 1955; (Mont-

gomery) *Alabama Journal*, March 18, 19, 1955; *Birmingham World*, March 22; May 6, 10, 1955; Trial Transcript, Browder v. Gayle, pp. 17–20 and Case File.

8. Trial Transcript, King v. State, pp. 240, 256–57, 344–46, 539–40. On the background of the city election of 1955, see my *Dividing Lines: Municipal Politics and the Struggle for Civil Rights in Montgomery, Birmingham, and Selma* (Tuscaloosa: University of Alabama Press, 2002), 20–56.

9. Montgomery County, Colored Marriages, Book 33, p. 16 and Book 48, p. 327 (Montgomery County Courthouse); U.S. Census of 1940; Montgomery City Directories of 1937, 1946, 1954, 1956; Montgomery Branch, List of New Members, 1934; Rosa L. Parks to Mary White Ovington, March 8, 1944; Rosa L. Parks to Lucille Black, March 11, 1946; Minutes of the Convention of the Alabama Conference of NAACP Branches, October 3–5, 1947, pp. 4, 7, 10; Minutes of the Convention of the Alabama NAACP Branches, October 8–10, 1948, pp. 2, 10; Edgar D. Nixon to Lucille Black, May 1, 1949; Lucille Black to Edgar D. Nixon, May 10, 1949; Gloster B. Current to John L. LeFlore, December 7, 1951; Newsletter of Southeastern Regional Office of the NAACP, vol. 1, no. 2 (Spring 1955): 1; Ruby Hurley to Gloster B. Current, December 28, 1955, all in NAACP Papers, Library of Congress, Washington, DC; Birmingham *World*, July 27, 1954; Candace Stone, "Community Prayer Service, May 3, 1956, Central Christian Church, Anderson, Indiana," p. 9, in Hazel Gregory Papers, Martin Luther King Center for Social Change, Atlanta, Georgia; Twenty-Third Annual Report of the Highlander Folk School (October 1, 1954–September 30, 1955), 1, in Labadie Collection, University of Michigan Library, Ann Arbor; author's interview with Virginia F. Durr, May 2, 1979; and Hollinger F. Barnard, ed., *Outside the Magic Circle: The Autobiography of Virginia Foster Durr* (Tuscaloosa: University of Alabama Press, 1985), 278–79; Rosa Parks with Jim Haskins, *Rosa Parks: My Story* (New York: Dial Books, 1992), 2–66, 71–113. On Alice L. White and her school's curriculum, see US Department of the Interior, Bureau of Education, *Negro Education: A Study of the Private and Higher Schools for Colored People in the United States* (Washington, DC: Government Printing Office, 1917), 2: 77–78, and Helen Christine Bennett, "Two Practicing Christians," *American Magazine* 77, no. 5 (1914): 61, 63. The Highlander conference that Mrs. Parks attended was held from July 24 through August 8, 1955. Myles Horton, Septima Clark, and other staff members led it, and participants in addition to Mrs. Parks included Irene Osborne of the American Friends Service Committee, Dr. Herman Long of Fisk University, Dean Charles Gomillion of Tuskegee Institute, Dr. Frederick D. Patterson of the Phelps-Stokes Foundation, and a former president of Tuskegee Institute, Fred Routh of the Southern Regional Council, and the liberal South Carolina attorney John Bolt Culbertson.

10. Case Record, Rosa L. Parks v. City of Montgomery, Records of the Alabama Court of Criminal Appeals, Office of the Clerk, Supreme Court Building,

Montgomery; Montgomery City Code of 1952, Chapter 1, Section 8; (Montgomery) *Alabama Journal*, December 5, 1955; *Montgomery Advertiser*, December 6, 1955. Fred Gray's statement in his memoirs that Mrs. Parks was charged with disorderly conduct, rather than with violating the segregation laws, is erroneous (Fred D. Gray, *Bus Ride to Justice: Changing the System by the System* [Montgomery: Black Belt Press, 1995], 50, 56).

11. On the initiation of the Bus Boycott and the negotiations during its first months, see my *Dividing Lines*, 61–88. On the filing of the federal court suit, see also Stewart Burns, ed., *Daybreak of Freedom: The Montgomery Bus Boycott* (Chapel Hill: University of North Carolina Press, 1997), 94, 128–30, 133–35.

12. Browder v. Gayle, 142 F. Supp. 707, 352 U.S. 903. On the violence following the integration of the buses, see my *Dividing Lines*, 93–96.

13. Parks v. City of Montgomery, 38 Ala. App. 681.

14. For the general settlement of the boycott prosecutions, see *Montgomery Advertiser*, November 27, 1957.

15. The next article in this volume contains a fuller discussion of this point.

10

The Montgomery Freedom Rider Riots of 1961

The election of a racial liberal to the Montgomery City Commission in 1953, and his persuasion of his two colleagues on the commission—both of whom were fairly moderate on racial questions—to accept the hiring of black policemen in the spring of 1954, precipitated a political crisis in Montgomery. The racial liberal, Dave Birmingham, was defeated in the city elections of 1955 by an extreme segregationist, Clyde C. Sellers. And though the moderate Mayor, William A. Gayle, survived, and another moderate was elected to join them as the third commissioner, both of the moderates were swayed by Sellers's victory into adopting somewhat harder-line positions on suggestions of racial reform.[1]

Because of these developments, it became clear to black leaders that blacks could not obtain from the new commission what were, now that the integration of the police force had been effected, their two chief goals: the appointment of a black member of the city Parks and Recreation Board, and the modification of the seating plan on city buses to allow the pattern of segregation in use in Montgomery's coastal neighbor Mobile, under which blacks, once seated, could not be unseated to make additional room for whites. The political failure of March 1955, turned Montgomery's black leaders toward an effort to influence the commission outside the electoral context. As a result, after the arrest of Mrs. Rosa L. Parks on December 1 of that year for her refusal to vacate her seat for a boarding white, black leaders agreed upon the idea of a boycott of the buses as a way of influencing the now less responsive commissioners.

But the Bus Boycott, because it was such a public effort at "intimidating," as whites saw it, the political structure, actually had the effect of driving the commissioners into extreme intransigence. All three of them joined the newly formed White Citizens' Council—until then an organization that all but the most frenzied white elements had held in contempt, but which by the spring of 1956 was the largest single organization of any kind in Montgomery County. And this new white intransigence begat a new black militancy. Through the first two months of the Bus Boycott, the black leadership had rejected any suggestion that they seek racial integration on the buses. They continued to press only for the adoption of the Mobile plan of seating segregation. But at the beginning of February 1956, after the bombing of the homes of two of the boycott's leaders, Martin Luther King Jr. and Edgar D. Nixon, blacks were finally driven to file suit in federal court seeking to have bus segregation declared unconstitutional, even though doing so necessarily required the abandoning of their earlier request for a more acceptable pattern of segregation.

Meanwhile, racial moderates among the city's businessmen had been seeking to negotiate a compromise. But their effort was not merely a failure. It brought them an intense outpouring of harassment and hostility from the newly powerful Citizens' Council. Thus by the spring of 1956, three months into the boycott, all negotiations ceased, and the bus dispute now was turned over to the courts—the blacks depending on their federal court integration suit, and the whites having indicted the black leaders in state court for violation of the Alabama Anti-Boycott Act of 1921.[2]

When bus integration finally came to Montgomery just before Christmas of 1956, therefore—as a result of a decision by the US Supreme Court in the suit filed by blacks in February—it came to a city completely polarized. The Montgomery that emerged from the Bus Boycott at the end of 1956 was virtually unrecognizable as the city that had elected a liberal commissioner of public affairs in 1953 and had voluntarily integrated its police force in 1954. And the sequel was predictable: sniper shootings into the integrated buses that badly wounded a black passenger and a series of dynamite bombings in the early weeks of January 1957, which did extensive damage to black homes and churches.

Moderate businessmen, who had been impelled into silence the preceding spring, exerted themselves once more in the face of this violence, and under heavy pressure from them, police actually succeeded in breaking the bombing cases and in obtaining the indictment of the ringleaders. The violence, it turned out, had been centered in a Ku Klux Klan klavern closely connected with the Montgomery Labor Council, the voice of organized labor in the city. The chief conspirator was Eugene S. Hall, a leader of the printers' union local and also the former editor of the Citizens' Council's newspaper, the *States Rights Advocate*. But the prosecution of the first two bombers to be brought to trial produced a massive outpouring of white sympathy for them. Two rival campaigns to pay their legal expenses were held, one by the Citizens' Council and one by the Klan, with volunteers going from door to door throughout the white community. The defendants' principal attorney was the city's best criminal lawyer, a first cousin of US senator Lister Hill. They were acquitted, despite their confessions and clear and irrefutable evidence against them. And after the trial was over, Montgomery's two circuit judges took the highly unusual step of issuing a public statement congratulating the jury on its verdict and saying they agreed with it. These events had the effect of essentially completely silencing moderate opinion among Montgomery's whites. It was not to be heard again for four years.[3]

During the years from 1957 to 1961, white Montgomery slipped into a surreal dimension in which only extremist views were acceptable. As moderate opinion disappeared, the uniformity of segregationist rhetoric among whites encouraged the peculiar notion among segregationist true believers that they were winning the battle—and winning because they had succeeded in preventing any cracks in forming in the solid white phalanx. The Citizens' Council devoted much of its effort, therefore, to suppressing white dissent. In a resolution adopted in January 1959, the council said, "We believe that any person who speaks, writes, or in any way advocates or works for anything short of total and complete segregation will be ostracized, and will earn and will receive the condemnation of the public. . . . We feel sure that an aroused and informed public will make it unprofitable and uncomfortable for any person to remain in our community if he is not willing to support the will of the community in this matter."[4]

Moreover, the events of these years lent themselves to encouraging the notion among the segregationists that victory was within their grasp. As a result of a suit filed in state court against the National Association for the Advancement of Colored People by Attorney General John M. Patterson in the midst of the Bus Boycott, the NAACP had been barred from operating in Alabama, and legal maneuvers in the case kept it out for more than eight years, until October 1964. In the gubernatorial election of May 1958, each candidate to succeed the Populist governor James E. Folsom sought to outdo all the others in the strength of his devotion to segregationist dogma. And the candidate the most extreme segregationists supported, Attorney General Patterson, was elected in a startling upset over the two front-runners, circuit judge George C. Wallace and state senator Jimmy Faulkner. Patterson thereupon appointed the Citizens' Councils' state president, Sam Martin Engelhardt, both as state highway director and as state Democratic Party chairman. In January 1959, Montgomery's City Commission ordered all thirteen of its city parks and its city zoo closed and sold, rather than integrate them as a federal court had ordered. Thus no further integration came to the city during this period.[5]

In the Montgomery municipal elections of March 1959, Mayor Gayle and Commissioner Sellers were both defeated for reelection for having committed the crime of losing in the Bus Boycott. Mayor Gayle's victorious opponent, former commissioner Earl D. James, had attacked him for having been willing to negotiate with the boycotters in the boycott's early weeks. And the extreme segregationist Commissioner Sellers was defeated by a segregationist even more extreme, L. B. Sullivan, a man with ties to the Ku Klux Klan.[6] The principal charge Sullivan made against Sellers is indicative of the new level of extremism in the city's life and had important implications for Sullivan's handling of the Freedom Rider riots. We should therefore pause to examine it.

In the summer of 1958, Martin Luther King's closest associate and friend in the city's black leadership, the Reverend Ralph D. Abernathy, had had an affair with one of his female parishioners, and in late August had been attacked by her outraged husband, Edward Davis, who had discovered their relationship, apparently when information about it was passed on to him by Montgomery police. As a result of their altercation, Davis was brought before Recorder's Court, and Abernathy was summoned as the principal witness. While waiting on the sidewalk just outside the courtroom for this hearing to begin, Martin Luther King was arrested by a policeman for loitering. He was brought to trial, convicted, and fined ten dollars. King refused to pay, announcing that he preferred to go to jail in order to dramatize the extraordinary injustice of these proceedings. Commissioner Sellers thereupon had paid King's fine in order to deprive King of the considerable publicity that his going to jail would certainly have given him. Sellers told reporters, "I cannot permit him to use the facilities of the City of Montgomery," by which he meant a cell in the city jail, "for his own selfish purposes." But Sellers's logic proved too subtle for most segregationists. In the campaign of 1959, Sullivan called Sellers's action "using kid gloves in the handling of racial agitators," and Sellers found himself unable to overcome the charge. Sullivan warned, "In dangerous times like these, with our Southern traditions in grave peril, the people of Montgomery need more than the wishy-washy leadership we have had in the past." Segregationists believed that they were winning by interdicting any compromise. It followed that any attempt to mollify moderate opinion was actually evidence of the weakness on the part of white officials that had permitted blacks to imagine equality.[7]

In February 1960, the sit-ins came to Montgomery, as thirty-five students from Alabama State College sought service at the snack bar in the basement of the Montgomery County Courthouse. But this crisis seemed only to prove the new strength of the segregationists. Governor Patterson demanded and received the expulsion of nine of the leaders of the sit-in, including Bernard Lee, later to become one of Martin Luther King's closest aides and confidants. Demonstrators from Alabama State protesting these expulsions were attacked, along with a number of innocent bystanders, by whites wielding baseball bats, led by one of the two bombers who had been acquitted in 1957, "Sonny" Kyle Livingston. These attacks went unpunished, despite photographs of them that were printed in the newspapers, and were actually hailed in certain quarters. The Montgomery *Home News*, a weekly Klan organ, exulted, "The crisp crack of a hickory bat on a Negro head snapped the people out of their apathy into the realization that the steady, cold siege against their way of life was now breaking out in an obviously Communist-inspired racial strife." Governor Patterson also obtained the firing from the Alabama State faculty of the distinguished historian and civil rights activist Lawrence D. Reddick, on questionable grounds of communist associations in his youth, and later that summer Patterson forced the resignations of twenty other faculty members sympathetic to civil rights, including the Bus Boycott leader Jo Ann G. Robinson. Finally Patterson and the state board of education suspended, and then compelled into retirement, the college's elderly president, H. Councill Trenholm. Trenholm was replaced by the college's more pliable business manager, Levi Watkins, and Patterson and Watkins then installed firm measures to prevent the teaching of integrationist perspectives in the classroom. In the meantime, as a result of quite insignificantly false statements about these proceedings, which were made in a fund-raising advertisement printed in the *New York Times* on March 29, Commissioner L. B. Sullivan and Mayor Earl James were each awarded $500,000 in damages for libel in state court, and the automobiles and other property of four black Alabama ministers who were listed as endorsing the advertisement, including the Reverends Ralph Abernathy and Solomon Seay of Montgomery, were seized and sold at auction in order to satisfy the judgments. This verdict was to be reversed by the US Supreme Court in one of the landmark decisions of American constitutional law, *New York Times v. Sullivan.* But that reversal did not come until 1964, and the ministers were never able to recover their property. For the time being, therefore, it appeared that the sit-in challenge had eventuated in a general segregationist triumph.[8]

Moreover, even the segregationists' one clear defeat during this period reinforced their sense of the correctness of their tactics. In late May of 1960, Martin Luther King, at Governor Patterson's instigation, was brought to trial for state income tax evasion. The evidence was so unconvincing that even an all-white Montgomery jury returned an acquittal. But here, too, it seemed to segregationists that if they could just keep any whites from deviating from the hard segregationist line, as the jurors had in this case, whites did have ample weapons with which to defeat and to crush the integrationist menace.[9]

Thus by the beginning of 1961, it seemed to segregationists that their hard-line campaign had succeeded in halting in its tracks the forward march of integration, which had appeared at the end of the Bus Boycott four years before to be about to create a breakthrough. It was into this situation that the Freedom Riders rode in May 1961.

The idea for the Freedom Riders came from CORE, the Congress of Racial Equality. CORE had been organized in Chicago during World War II. In 1946 the US Supreme Court, in the case of *Morgan v. Virginia*, had decided that segregation on interstate bus lines was an unconstitutional burden on interstate commerce. The ruling, however, was almost universally ignored by bus companies in the South. Therefore, in April 1947, sixteen CORE members had undertaken an integrated journey south from Washington, DC, to try to force the implementation of the *Morgan* decision. They got as far as the college community of Chapel Hill, North Carolina, before being taken from the bus, arrested, and jailed.

Although this 1947 effort had accomplished nothing, it remained in the institutional memory of CORE. In December 1960, the US Supreme Court decided the case of *Boynton v. Virginia*, in which it held that segregation in bus terminal restaurants and facilities violated the nondiscrimination provisions of the National Motor Carrier Act of 1935. Like *Morgan* before it, this decision was simply ignored everywhere in the South. Therefore, CORE came up with the idea of another journey to demonstrate that terminals were not actually complying with the ruling.[10]

The riders set out from Washington, DC, at the beginning of May 1961, and despite minor incidents in Charlotte, North Carolina, and Rock Hill and Winnsboro, South Carolina, they had made it as far as Anniston, Alabama, before a mob attacked the group traveling aboard Greyhound just outside the city, burned their bus, and very nearly incinerated all the passengers. Later that same day, in Birmingham, the group traveling aboard Trailways was severely beaten by a gang of some eighty Ku Klux Klansmen. Birmingham police failed to intervene in the beatings for fifteen minutes, under an agreement with the Klan. At this point, the CORE Freedom Riders, bruised and battered, abandoned their ride and went on to New Orleans by airplane.[11]

But one of the original Freedom Riders, John Lewis, a twenty-one-year-old black student at the American Baptist Seminary in Nashville, Tennessee, and a native of rural Pike County, Alabama, refused to abandon the effort. He contacted acquaintances among activist college students who the year before had conducted sit-ins in Nashville, and at his urging, seventeen black and three white volunteers from Nashville's Tennessee Agricultural and Industrial College and Fisk University joined him in Birmingham, and on their own decided to launch a new Freedom Ride, south toward Montgomery.[12]

Initially, neither Greyhound nor Trailways was willing to take the group of demonstrators, because of the danger to drivers and buses. But as a result of negotiations with Attorney General Robert Kennedy, Governor Patterson agreed to guarantee the safety of the bus as far as the Montgomery city limits, and with this commitment, the students left Birmingham aboard Greyhound on May 20. At the Montgomery city limits, the state Highway Patrol escort left the bus. It was now the responsibility of Montgomery city police. Highway Patrol director Floyd Mann believed that he had received firm assurances from Commissioner L. B. Sullivan that police would preserve order when the bus arrived. But Sullivan, because his political power rested on the support of segregationists, could not afford to seem sympathetic to the Freedom Riders. He knew well how easily a segregationist opponent could turn against him any action such as extending police protection to demonstrators. He knew, because he had used just such an issue to defeat Clyde Sellers in 1959.

The bus was met at the Greyhound terminal in downtown Montgomery by an angry mob of some two hundred whites, most of them Klansmen, led by Claude V. Henley, a service manager at a local automobile dealership, who was both a Klansman and, until just weeks before, a member of Montgomery's volunteer reserve police unit. Police refused to respond to repeated frantic calls from the bus station; in fact, city police—as opposed to state Highway Patrolmen—did not arrive in force for almost two hours. Twenty persons were injured, two of them quite seriously: James Zwerg, a white native of Appleton, Wisconsin, who was an exchange student at Fisk, and William T. Barbee, a black seminarian from Nashville. Also injured was Attorney General Kennedy's personal representative on the scene, John Seigenthaler, a Nashville newspaperman; he was beaten and lay unconscious on the sidewalk for more than a quarter of an hour. Finally, Floyd Mann arrived to check on the situation and, discovering that he had been betrayed by Sullivan, summoned a contingent of sixty-five Highway Patrolmen who managed to begin restoring order after about an hour and a half. Mann personally saved the life of William Barbee, and apprehended his assaulter, Thurman E. Ouzts, an unemployed glazier and dump-truck operator. A black bystander later testified that in the midst of the melee, he had overheard Mann ask a Montgomery policeman, "Why didn't you call Sullivan?" and had heard the patrolman reply, "The men he would send out probably would have joined the mob."[13]

Throughout this developing crisis, the Kennedy administration had been extremely reluctant to intervene. Governor Patterson had been one of the very first public figures in America to endorse John Kennedy's campaign for the presidency. And Patterson's endorsement of Kennedy in June 1959—more than a year before the Democratic national convention—had cost him the support of a significant number of extreme segregationists. In addition, Patterson had cooperated closely with Kennedy in the staging of the ill-fated Bay of Pigs invasion of Cuba only a month earlier; four Alabama Air National Guardsmen had lost their lives in this operation. Thus both John and Robert Kennedy very much wanted to leave matters in Alabama to Patterson. Patterson, however, took no action, and even refused to receive the Kennedys' telephone calls. Finally, driven to the initiative by Patterson's refusal to cooperate, the president that night ordered the dispatch of four hundred US marshals to Montgomery. They began arriving in the city the following morning, May 21, under the command of future US Supreme Court justice Byron R. White.[14]

As it turned out, the president's action had come none too soon. That evening, a large white mob surrounded the black First Baptist Church in which Martin Luther King and Ralph Abernathy were holding a rally in support of the Freedom Riders. It appears that a substantial part of this mob was composed of thrill-seeking undergraduates at Huntingdon College, a white Methodist liberal arts college in the city. As the mob pressed forward to test the marshals' cordon around the church, King desperately telephoned Robert Kennedy from the office in the church basement to tell him that the situation looked critical. At that point, Governor Patterson finally acted, declaring martial law in the city and mobilizing the National Guard. This action eventually restored order, though not without several shooting incidents and the fire bombing of two homes later that evening. The Freedom Riders were able to leave Montgomery on May 24; some returned to Nashville to resume classes and others traveled on to Jackson, Mississippi, where they were jailed without further incident.[15]

Although among the darkest days in all of Montgomery's history, the final weeks of May 1961, proved to be the great turning point in the city's struggle to emerge from the nightmare of extremist domination into which it had been plunged by the white community's response to the Bus Boycott. In the first place, the seriously negative national publicity the city received—and quite deservedly—as a result of its handling of the riots, forced moderate white opinion back into the open for the first time since the bombings of January 1957. Business progressives voiced their fear that publicity of this kind would make more difficult their efforts to persuade northern industry to locate in the area. And even though they were ordinarily quite unsympathetic to black aspirations for racial equality, many of them showed themselves genuinely appalled by the rioting, as they had been, as well, by the bombings four years earlier. In the second place, the succession to the presidency of the city's principal civil rights organization, the Montgomery Improvement Association, of the Reverend Solomon Seay Sr.—who replaced Ralph Abernathy in December 1961, when Abernathy moved to Atlanta—gave the crucial position of black leadership in the city to a man deeply committed to quiet negotiation and compromise, just as prominent moderate whites were recovering their own willingness to seek a modus vivendi. In the third place, federal authority—in the form of the Justice Department and of the federal courts—at this time, and in no small part directly in response to these events, began more and more to discover for itself and to reveal to segregationists the extent of its capacity for coercion. As it did so, white supremacists' confidence in their power to determine the shape of race relations entirely by themselves began to erode. Their belief that they were winning the battle gave way increasingly to sullen resignation. The interaction of these three phenomena would transform the life of the city.

The business community's response to the violence began to take form on the evening of May 20, at the very same time that the Kennedy administration was deciding in Washington to send the US marshals to the city. Winton M. "Red" Blount, a prominent construction executive who would later become postmaster general in the cabinet of Richard Nixon, summoned more than one hundred of the city's business and professional leaders to a meeting at the offices of the chamber of commerce. Blount attempted to persuade those present to endorse a strong condemnation of that morning's outrages, but his effort came up against the feeling, general among Montgomery's whites, that the violence had occurred only because of the Freedom Riders' wanton provocation. T. B. Hill, a segregationist attorney and a first cousin of US senator Lister Hill, forcefully argued this position. But Blount managed to turn the tables on Hill by inviting him to draft a resolution that he could support. The result was a compromise that eighty-seven of those attending were willing to sign. It expressed resentment of the Freedom Riders, "who publicly announced their intention of coming into our community for the avowed purpose of violating our time-honored and respected laws," but it went on to affirm that "we do not under any circumstances approve or condone mob action on the part of any faction, and we do hereby call upon the law enforcement agencies of our city, county and state to take all necessary action and precautions to maintain and preserve law and order in our community."

On the morning of May 22, following the second riot of the night before, the chamber of commerce's board of directors formally endorsed this resolution, and later that day the Rotary and Kiwanis Clubs also adopted it. That afternoon the white Montgomery Ministerial Association approved somewhat stronger resolutions, and on May 23 the Junior Chamber of Commerce passed resolutions including the specific statement that, "We regret the failure of our law enforcement officials to move against Saturday's mob with sufficient speed and force to prevent violence." Finally, on May 25, the thirty-seven members of the board of directors of the Alabama State Chamber of Commerce—again at the urging of Blount, who was the state chamber's president-elect—adopted the most unqualified resolutions of this series. They affirmed that all laws and court decisions, "however distasteful to any group, can and must be enforced by lawfully constituted agencies of government," and that mob violence "can never be justified, even in the face of unwarranted and extreme provocation"; and they warned that acts of violence "damage the good name of our state and create an image harmful to its best interests and its business and industrial development." They called "upon all local and state officials to preserve law and order in Alabama under all conditions and at all costs."

The *Montgomery Advertiser* lent vigorous editorial support to these efforts. On May 23, in the face of the widespread white conviction that the riots were only a predictable response to the provocative Freedom Riders, *Advertiser* editor Grover C. Hall Jr., attacked Governor Patterson's and Commissioner Sullivan's handling of the disorders. He called the governor the "chief author" of the city's racial troubles, and he lectured white Montgomery that the mobs "were not duly quelled and that failure is ours alone. In fact, the mobsters were encouraged. . . . The people have got to understand that leaving matters to mobs is calamity." This editorial received the grateful endorsement of the black Interdenominational Ministerial Alliance. On May 28, Hall hailed the succession of resolutions against mob action adopted by the various white community groups. In the five years since the Bus Boycott, he noted, "organized originators of public opinions such as civic clubs were silent and passive in the teeth of local violence. This left the field to the loud mouths and pinheads, and Montgomery's name was smutted up to an extent that may take a very long time to wash out. But at last, a week ago, the conditions here degenerated to the point of necessary shock and alarm." Although he acknowledged that the initial chamber resolution "was guarded" because of the hesitation of "timid" and "uncertain" elements among the businessmen, "Nevertheless, the resolution was a milestone in the melancholy five-year tale of race relations blunders on the part of white leadership. It was a turning point, an assertion of leadership and intervention in the destinies of this city." And on May 31, Hall lashed out editorially at the city's more conservative social leaders, "magnificoes of civic clubs and pillars of social rectitude," who though they would not dream of joining a mob or of letting their children do so, were nevertheless quite happy to have the city's thugs rough up the Freedom Riders.[16]

The power of the segregationist social leaders Hall thus attacked did not disappear merely because of the reemergence of the moderates from hiding. A prime example of the sort of influential community figures who were quietly pleased that the Freedom Riders had been beaten was Hall's own colleague William J. Mahoney Jr., the archsegregationist managing editor of the city's evening daily, the *Alabama Journal*. Mahoney fulminated in his newspaper column against whites who focused their condemnation on the rioters, rather than the Freedom Riders, "who came into this state deliberately to foment trouble, to defy the laws of this state, and to further unhinge the emotions of two peoples who had learned to live together in tolerance if not always in harmony." And he protested, "Every decent person hates violence, but once it has come, be sure of your loyalties. Be sure that, in your hatred of violence, you don't indict your own side and join the ranks of an enemy that has been showing its true colors—red and black—ever since Earl Warren's court started legislating."[17]

Nevertheless, despite the considerable social consequence of many white supremacists and the bluster and bullying of many more, and despite an active hostility to the civil rights demonstrators that spread across the entire spectrum of white opinion, the business progressives, having at last found the courage to launch their moderate project, now earnestly pressed it. On May 22, some thirty business and professional leaders met with Mayor James for more than two hours. From this meeting dates the reintroduction into city politics of a coherent and determined white moderate voice. Thereafter, such meetings apparently continued frequently.

On May 29—the day that martial law ended in Montgomery—Attorney General Kennedy filed with the Interstate Commerce Commission in Washington a petition asking the commission to compel the integration of all facilities in all bus and train terminals in the United States. The ICC granted this petition on September 22, to take effect on November 1. On that date, Montgomery's two bus stations and its train station were peacefully integrated. In the meantime, the Civil Aeronautics Board had sued the Montgomery airport in federal court to compel the integration of that terminal as well, and it was integrated without incident in January 1962.[18]

The quiet integration of the bus, train, and air terminals convinced Solomon Seay that the time had come to attempt to open communications with the moderate white leaders. Immediately after the desegregation of the airport, Seay dispatched a lengthy letter to prominent Montgomerians of both races, emphasizing his hope that further racial progress could now come through confidential negotiations. The city did possess, he had come to see, "the potential leadership for peaceful progress in human relations," even though in past years that leadership had been "pent-up by fear and mistrust." He urged that "all difficult or strained relations in the community should be brought to a conference table for argument and reason." And he pledged that the MIA would turn to demonstrations or court suits "only when peaceful relations have not been attainable through negotiation."[19]

These were precisely the sorts of sentiments that the white business progressives wanted to hear, and unpublicized discussions quickly commenced. By April 9, Seay was sufficiently encouraged that he decided to renew what had been one of the MIA's initial requests in the Bus Boycott. On that date, he wrote to Montgomery City Lines to ask if they might now be ready to consider hiring black bus drivers. After a series of meetings, the bus company agreed, and the two organizations then went together to the City Commission to tell them of their plans. Commissioner Sullivan belligerently denounced the proposal, shouting that blood would run in the streets if blacks were hired. He lamented that the commission was legally powerless to revoke the bus company's franchise. Despite this reception, however, the company remained true to its agreement, and on July 6, Montgomery's first two black bus drivers, Allen Pierce and Thomas Jackson, commenced work.[20]

Also in April, the MIA gave its support to a federal court suit by a group of black high school students who had earlier been denied admission to the white Montgomery Public Library, that sought the integration of both the library and the Museum of Fine Arts, which was located in the same building. On August 8, US district judge Frank M. Johnson Jr., granted an injunction ordering the integration. The White Citizens' Council demanded that the library and museum now be closed, as the parks had been in 1959. The segregationist pressure on the City Commission to maintain its consistency in the face of this new integrationist challenge was immense. But this time the response of racial moderates, both in public letters to the editor and in private meetings with the commissioners, was equally vigorous. Faced with this newly evident division among their white constituents, the commissioners eventually voted to leave the library and museum open, but they ordered that all tables and chairs be removed from the library so that patrons of different races would not be able to sit together. The library was then peacefully integrated, if on a standing basis, on August 13. The commissioners' compromise made them objects of no little ridicule outside the city, but in truth it represented a substantial achievement. Not only had the moderates found the courage to face down the segregationists in public debate, but the City Commission, despite its efforts to hide behind the library furniture, had in effect cast its lot with the moderates.

There can be no doubt that before the Freedom Rider riots and the consequent reemergence of moderate opinion into the open, the commission would have closed the library and museum. In the intervening year, the city clearly had embarked upon a new course.[21]

A principal reason for this development is unquestionably the erosion of the segregationists' earlier confidence that they could prevail. The Interstate Commerce Commission's order of September 22, 1961, compelling the desegregation of all bus and train terminals throughout the United States, was the very first federal action to seek to bring integration to an entire class of institutions everywhere at once. All of the previous decisions of the Supreme Court, despite their general implications, had actually integrated only the specific institutions that were party to the suits. Segregationists therefore ordinarily saw no change in the patterns of daily life in their communities. The ICC order, therefore, constituted the first real blow to the segregationists' belief that they were winning the battle; it was the first clear evidence that integration inevitably held the initiative, that the federal government had, if it would but use, the weapons with which to overwhelm the segregationists' defenses. This process of discovery, which Montgomery's segregationists shared with white supremacists throughout the region, was conjoined in the city itself with the renewed willingness of Montgomery's white moderates following the Freedom Rider riots to speak out and to urge less obdurate attitudes and actions upon the City Commission. This reemergence of the moderates was so important because it deprived the uncompromising enemies of integration of their essential comforting myth, that they spoke for an undivided white community.

The Freedom Rider riots, then, appear in retrospect to have been an authentic turning point in the city's life because they constituted, as a result of the revivification of the white moderate constituency and as a result of the breadth of the ICC order, the beginning of the process by which, eventually, the segregationists were convinced that continued resistance was useless. The increasing zeal with which the federal government sought to advance the cause of civil rights, and the growing willingness of the local politicians to respond to the new ad hoc alliance of business progressives and black leaders, began relentlessly to deprive the segregationists of the sense that the tide of events was flowing their way. Divested of its intellectual and perceptual supports, their intransigence turned gradually but inevitably to resignation.

These events allow us to see the complicated interaction between the national and the local that formed the civil rights movement. As the Freedom Riders sped southward toward Montgomery on the morning of May 20, very likely not a single one of them had ever heard of L. B. Sullivan or Floyd

Mann, "Red" Blount or Solomon Seay, whom their actions were about to summon into world history. The Freedom Riders thought of themselves as seeking to impose national standards on an aberrant region, of which Montgomery was merely an incidental representative. The story of the civil rights movement is too frequently told from that same perspective. It is a misleading perspective in the first place because it obscures the extent to which the South's patterns of white supremacy, though uniquely embedded in statute, were far more common in practice in the rest of the nation than Americans at the time often acknowledged to themselves. But it is misleading also because it obscures the very great diversity in the patterns of white supremacy and in the structures of power from community to community within the South itself. And yet that diversity crucially shaped the course and the outcome of the civil rights movement.

The achievement of the civil rights movement certainly rested upon the fact that, in the years following World War II, the dramatic mobilization of elements of the black population in the South was, for the first time since Reconstruction, able to provoke sympathetic federal intervention. As I have observed already, the South did not possess within itself the capacity to save itself, because of the diversity and complexity of southern life, since any fundamental reform of race relations in the region would necessarily affect an almost infinite variety of interests. The strength of segregation thus was bound up with the pluralism of southern society, and like the Gordian knot, it could yield only to external pressure, whether in the form of court order or of executive or legislative action. Nevertheless, the diverse patterns of race relations in southern towns and cities, not to mention the quite different structures in the countryside, determined the forms that the new order would take, once the transformation could no longer be avoided, and it varied as much from community to community as the older one had.

We see this interaction at work in Montgomery during the Freedom Rider crisis. The intervention of the Kennedy administration, the Interstate Commerce Commission's order, and the subsequent federal court injunctions all were essential to moving the city forward, but the community's response evolved from existing municipal rivalries and relationships, and so took unique form. A portrait of the civil rights movement that fails to capture how greatly its outcomes differed from place to place fundamentally distorts its history. Just as segregation expressed itself in different forms in different communities, so too did integration. To tell the story of the civil rights movement without attending to the extraordinary variety of both its municipal and rural expressions and consequences is, therefore, not to tell it at all.

Notes

This article was a paper delivered, in a somewhat different form, to the annual meeting of the Alabama Historical Association in Florence, Alabama, on April 28, 1984. It has not previously been published, but its substance was incorporated into my *Dividing Lines: Municipal Politics and the Struggle for Civil Rights in Montgomery, Birmingham, and Selma* (Tuscaloosa: University of Alabama Press, 2002).

1. On the background of the Montgomery municipal elections of 1955, see my *Dividing Lines*, 20–53.

2. On the failure of the negotiations in the boycott's first months, see ibid., 53–88. The preceding two articles in this volume explain more fully the operation of bus segregation in Mobile, and how it differed from the practices in Montgomery.

3. Ibid., 88–96; Browder v. Gayle, 142 F. Supp. 707, 352 U.S. 903.

4. *Selma Times-Journal*, January 21, 1959; Montgomery *Home News*, February 5, 1959; Thornton, *Dividing Lines*, 96–99.

5. NAACP v. State ex rel. Attorney General, 265 Ala. 356, 699, 349; 268 Ala. 531; 271 Ala. 331; 274 Ala. 544; 277 Ala. 89; NAACP v. Jones, 268 Ala. 504; NAACP v. Alabama, 357 U.S. 449, 360 U.S. 240, 377 U.S. 288; NAACP v. Gallion, 190 F. Supp. 583, 290 F.2d 337, 368 U.S. 16; NAACP v. Flowers, 217 F. Supp. 70; Gilmore v. City of Montgomery, 176 F. Supp. 776, 277 F.2d 364; Thornton, *Dividing Lines*, 101–3, 108–9, 613, and on the doctrines of the Citizens' Councils, see also 400–405.

6. Thornton, *Dividing Lines*, 109–12.

7. Ibid., 109–10; Johnson Publishing Co. v. Davis, 271 Ala. 474.

8. Thornton, *Dividing Lines*, 113–17; Montgomery *Home News*, March 3, 1960; Dixon v. Alabama State Board of Education, 186 F. Supp. 945, 294 F.2d 150, 368 U.S. 930; New York Times v. Sullivan, 273 Ala. 656, 376 U.S. 254; Abernathy v. Patterson, 295 F.2d 452; Parks v. New York Times, 195 F. Supp. 919, 308 F.2d 474, 376 U.S. 949.

9. Thornton, *Dividing Lines*, 117–18.

10. August Meier and Elliott Rudwick, *CORE: A Study in the Civil Rights Movement* (Urbana: University of Illinois Press, 1975); Morgan v. Virginia, 184 Va. 24, 328 U.S. 373; State v. Johnson, 229 N.C. 701; Boynton v. Virginia, 364 U.S. 454.

11. Thornton, *Dividing Lines*, 240–50. Raymond Arsenault, *Freedom Riders: 1961 and the Struggle for Racial Justice* (New York: Oxford University Press, 2006), is an excellent general study of the events explored here; see also Catherine A. Barnes, *Journey from Jim Crow: The Desegregation of Southern Transit* (New York: Columbia University Press, 1984), for their background.

12. John Lewis describes his early years in John Lewis with Michael D'Orso, *Walking with the Wind: A Memoir of the Movement* (New York: Simon and Schuster, 1998). On the Nashville sit-in movement, see David Halberstam, *The Children* (New York: Random House, 1998).

13. *Montgomery Advertiser*, May 20, 21 (quotation), 23, 24, 26, 27, 28, 30; June 1, 2, 3, 1961; (Montgomery) *Alabama Journal*, May 15, 16, 17, 18, 19, 20, 23, 25, 26, 27, 29, 30, 31, 1961; Lewis v. Greyhound Corp., 199 F. Supp. 210; U.S. v. U.S. Klans, 194 F. Supp. 897; Excerpt Transcripts, U.S. v. U.S. Klans, and Trial Transcript, Lewis v. Greyhound Corp., in Federal Records Center, East Point, Georgia.

14. On the president's reluctance to intervene, see (Montgomery) *Alabama Journal*, May 23, 1961; *New York Times*, May 24, 1961; draft of wire from John F. Kennedy to Alabama congressional delegation, May 22, 1961, in Robert F. Kennedy Papers, Kennedy Presidential Library, Boston, Massachusetts (transcript in Birmingham Public Library). On Patterson's endorsement of Kennedy and its consequences for the governor, see *Selma Times-Journal*, June 17, 29; July 2, 15; August 10, 1959; October 19, 1960; and *Montgomery Home News*, June 18, July 23, August 13, December 24, 1959; January 14, 1960. On the Alabama Air National Guard in the Bay of Pigs invasion, see *Montgomery Advertiser*, March 17, 1998. On Patterson's reluctance to cooperate with Kennedy and the dispatch of the US marshals, see (Montgomery) *Alabama Journal*, May 17, 19, 1961; *Montgomery Advertiser*, May 20, 21, 22, 1961; transcripts of telephone conversations between Robert F. Kennedy and John M. Patterson, May 20, 21, 1961; Robert F. Kennedy to John M. Patterson, telegram, May 20, 1961; memorandum to Robert F. Kennedy, n.d. [May 20, 1961], all in Robert F. Kennedy Papers.

15. *Montgomery Advertiser*, May 22, 23, 24, 1961; (Montgomery) *Alabama Journal*, May 22, 23, 24, 25, 1961; Robert F. Kennedy to Floyd Mann, telegram, May 21, 1961; transcript of telephone conversation between Robert F. Kennedy and Montgomery assistant police chief E. P. "Tiny" Brown, May 21, 1961; Robert F. Kennedy to John M. Patterson, telegram, May 21, 1961; William Geoghegan to Robert F. Kennedy, May 22, 1961, all in Robert F. Kennedy Papers. See also Lewis with D'Orso, *Walking with the Wind*, 169–74.

16. *Montgomery Advertiser*, May 21, 23, 24, 26, 28, 31, 1961; (Montgomery) *Alabama Journal*, May 23, 25, 26, 1961. On T. B. Hill, see *Montgomery Advertiser*, May 5, 1982. Blount gives his own sparse account of these events in Winton M. "Red" Blount with Richard Blodgett, *Doing It My Way* (Lyme, CT: Greenwich Publishing Group, 1996), 88–90.

17. (Montgomery) *Alabama Journal*, May 22, 1961.

18. *Discrimination in Operations of Interstate Motor Carriers of Passengers*, 86 MCC 743; U.S. v. City of Montgomery, 201 F. Supp. 590.

19. Seay prints the entire text of his letter in his memoirs: Solomon S. Seay Sr., *I Was There by the Grace of God* (Montgomery: Seay Educational Foundation, 1990), 225–31.

20. Montgomery Improvement Association to James H. Bagley, April 9, 1962; Solomon S. Seay Sr., to Bernard W. Franklin, July 9. 1962, both in Hazel Gregory

Papers, Martin Luther King Center, Atlanta, Georgia; Seay, *I Was There by the Grace of God*, 234–35, 241.

21. Cobb v. Montgomery Library Board, 207 F. Supp. 880; *Montgomery Advertiser*, March 16, April 28, June 22, July 25, August 8, 9, 10, 11, 12, 13, 14, 16, 17, 18, 19, 21, 23, 1962.

Conclusion

My comments at the end of the preceding essay may perhaps leave the reader with the impression that I think synthesis in history is impossible, or at least unhelpful. Quite the contrary; it is my hope that the bringing of these articles together may offer synthetic possibilities. To clarify this point, let me conclude with some more general reflections.

In the first place, because my scholarly interests have spanned both the nineteenth and the twentieth centuries, periods that in the history profession are usually regarded as separate fields, I have come to think of this division, particularly in southern history, not only as artificial but also as tenebrific. Far from being distinct subjects of inquiry, the later periods grow organically from the earlier ones, and putting them into conversation helps to make logical sense of each of them, clarifying how the periods are linked by the common intellectual and political forces on which they draw. I trust that the articles collected here have worked to throw light on some of these interconnections.

A second implication of this collection speaks to the intellectually rather embattled subfield of political history. Too many political historians tell their stories as if politics were merely a product of the social and economic forces that surround it, thus becoming too readily complicit in rendering their field epiphenomenal. Politics certainly interacts with the society and the economy it represents, of course, and on many occasions socioeconomic considerations have causative primacy. But on other occasions the structures of political and legal institutions or the commitments of political ideology and conviction are themselves the causative forces, and shape the society, the economy, and indeed cultural sensibility and religious faith. In the South, as I have sought to describe it here, the inherited ideologies of antebellum two-party competition and the power of the twentieth century's one-party system gave form to all social experience. The failure to recognize their significance may be profoundly misleading. In his portrait of Alabama in his great *Southern Politics in State and Nation* (1949), for instance, V. O. Key correctly identifies the importance of the "friends and neighbors vote" in the mid-twentieth century, but fails to understand the deeper institutional constraints that gave it its force in Alabamians' lives. He thus tends to discount the continuity of class conflict expressed in white Alabamians' voting at that period.

I suspect that no reader has missed a third implication of this volume, my conviction of the necessity of a close examination of local conditions and circumstances for a correct understanding of American history. That necessity proceeds from a recognition that even events that Americans experience in common are perceived and interpreted from the particular context in which each American lives, including inevitably many other events and assumptions that other Americans have not shared. America is a vast and diverse federation; the very acceptance of the existence of regional distinctiveness is testimony to the power of that fact. But though the grouping of states into regions is often conceptually useful, the state in a federal system has its own unique experience. No one, surely, would confuse the political culture of Arizona with that of New Mexico, or Louisiana's with Arkansas's, though they are neighbors and share regional histories. And yet, as several of the articles in this volume seek to argue, the state does not really impose itself fully on the life of its communities. In Alabama, residents of the Black Belt think about their world in very different ways from residents of the hill counties; and similar distinctions may be made within every state. And more than that, within communities, racial, religious, ethnic, and gender groups have all experienced their lives in ways that give unique shape to their perspectives, often at the level of unexamined but unshakeable assumption. These observations may seem commonplace, but the history of America is very often written without genuine attention to them. I believe that taking state and local history seriously can work to reveal American history for the patchwork of rival perceptions that it is.

A fourth implication of this volume, on the other hand, may initially seem to be at war with the one I have just emphasized. For I also think that this collection works to reveal the Americanness of the American South. In the 1840s and 1850s, Northern enemies of slavery increasingly came to believe that the existence of slavery in the Southern states had made the region an essentially un-American one. It was an allegation that most white Southerners deeply resented, but that Southern nationalists soon began to embrace. And following Southern secession and defeat in the Civil War, the notion became nearly universal in both South and North, and was extended to characterize the postemancipation South as well. But to my mind it is false.

If anything, the antebellum period saw the South more fully integrated into the life of the nation than at any subsequent time. Southern leaders—

Thomas Jefferson and John Marshall, Andrew Jackson and Henry Clay—were national luminaries, and their ideas gave indispensable substance to Americans' emerging understanding of themselves and their project, in all sections. Nor was the free states' rejection of slavery a very long-standing one. It is perhaps too seldom emphasized that, of the twelve states represented at the Constitutional Convention, eight were slave states and only four were free states. It is true that, by the mid-nineteenth century, slavery had become an exclusively Southern commitment. But the same is most certainly not true of white Southerners' racism. Rather, white Southerners' racial animus was quite generally shared in all parts of the Union, and formed one of the bonds that held the states together.

That racism actually continued to be characteristic of the overwhelming majority of white Americans throughout the late nineteenth and the first half of the twentieth centuries. If after the turn of the twentieth century, it was expressed in formal statute only in the South, that fact reflected not a greater racial animus on the part of white southerners but rather a response to the particular political structure of the region. The rise of the one-party system after the end of Reconstruction, and the adoption of thoroughgoing black disfranchisement at the end of the nineteenth century, do represent developments that marked the South off from the rest of America, as slavery had in the first half of the nineteenth century. But the statutory requirement of segregation, which was an outgrowth of the conflicts surrounding these developments, differed from the racial discrimination almost universal elsewhere in the United States at this time only in being embodied in law, not really in its substance.

I offer this discussion as preface to the point I wish to make. One of the most fallacious and exasperating deductions that some scholars have drawn from their belief in the un-American character of southern society, is the notion that racial ideology so united whites as effectively to eliminate or to mask class, cultural, or religious divisions among them. It is certainly true that, in the years between Reconstruction and disfranchisement, the Redeemer element labored tirelessly to manipulate white racial fears in order to maintain white solidarity; "drawing the color line," they called it. But the Greenbackers, the Farmers Alliance, and the Populists stand as clear evidence that this effort was not really very successful. Indeed, it was their too frequent failures with these maneuvers that moved the Redeemers to turn to disfranchisement. And both in the antebellum era and through the twentieth century, political life was constantly roiled by profound conflicts of class, religion, and culture. It is my hope that the essays collected here help to demonstrate that fact. Racial divisions unquestionably were a central part—indeed, the most consequential part—of southern social enmities, but divisions of class and culture were as real in the region as in the rest of America, and the ideologies through which all of these divisions were understood were thoroughly American. Nor is my claim for the Americanness of the South at war with my emphasis on the necessity to focus on the particularities of local experience. Rather, it is exactly by a sensitive recovery of local perspectives that one is able to see beneath what may seem at first glance to be some eccentric or parochial controversy, to discover its deeper social meaning for those engaged in it. Moreover, the examination of such controversies helps us to understand the great variety of circumstances in which the more general ideologies may become active and the complex and quite unexpected ways in which social divisions and attitudes may express themselves when refracted through differing cultural lenses. It is the path to a subtle understanding of our nation's diversity.

A colleague has recently said of my body of work that it seeks primarily to engage two animating issues of American political life: the nature of our republic and the mechanisms of political change. I accept this characterization and think that the essays collected in this volume all reflect, in one way or another, this persistent quest. Throughout my scholarly career, with my native Alabama frequently my laboratory, my work has sought, at the broadest level, to analyze key transition points in the political history of the American South, from the 1840s and 1850s to the 1950s and 1960s. The essays here all constitute parts of that enterprise. I hope very much that readers may have found them enlightening contributions.

Index

Abernathy, Ralph D., 202, 203, 206, 207
Alabama, 10, 15, 16, 19, 30, 33, 35, 44, 45, 55–57, 59, 60, 62, 64, 216, 217, 219
Alabama, University of, 140, 149, 165, 173, 175
Alabama A&M University, 173, 177
Alabama State College, 173, 177, 189–91, 202, 203
American Baptist Seminary, 204
American Friends Service Committee, 197
Ames, Jessie Daniel, 171
Anderson, John C., 125
Anniston, Alabama, 136, 204
Anti-Boycott Act of 1921, Alabama, 200
Anti-Saloon League, 125, 126, 128, 131, 133, 137, 140, 153
Appalachia, 2, 3, 12–14, 75, 81
Apperson, R. D., 187, 188
Appleton, Wisconsin, 205
aristocracy, southern, 2, 5, 6, 13, 20–22, 71–74, 87, 88, 159
Arizona, 217
Arkansas, 6, 134, 217
Ashland, Alabama, 144, 148, 149
Atlanta, Georgia, 156, 189, 207
attorneys and secession, 16, 21, 75–76
Auburn University, 173
Augusta, Georgia, 186
Autauga County, Alabama, 92

Baker, Ella J., 192
Baldwin County, Alabama, 77
Baltimore, Maryland, 1
Bankhead, John H., 77, 132
Bankhead, John H., Jr., 127, 140, 141
banks, 6–8, 11, 15, 21, 31, 72, 78, 80
Barbee, William T., 205
Barbour County Alabama, 74, 109
Barnett, Ross, 148
Bavaria, 110
Bay of Pigs, Cuba, 206
Beard, Margaret, 191
Bell, John, 3, 19, 92
Bell, Middleton R., 75, 84, 90
Bethea, Tristram B., 73, 78, 119
Bilbo, Theodore, 148, 169
Birmingham, Alabama, 116, 128, 135, 137, 140, 149, 150, 154, 155, 170, 171, 173, 174, 176, 177, 194, 204, 205
Birmingham, Dave, 190, 195, 199
Birmingham News, 131
Black Belt, Alabama, 73, 84, 85, 87, 95, 98, 123, 125, 129, 130, 136, 137, 142–44, 152, 165–67, 175–78, 183, 217
Black Codes, 71, 78–80, 82, 86, 88
Black, Hugo L., 127, 129, 132, 134, 140, 143, 144, 148–63
Black, LaFayette, 148
Blake, J. Fred, 193
Blakely, Battle of, 98
Blease, Cole, 169
Blount County, Alabama, 75, 131
Blount, Winton M. "Red," 207, 208, 212
Bonner, J. Miller, 129, 172, 183
Boston, Massachusetts, 5

Boswell Amendment, 136, 177
Boswell, Edward C. "Bud," 136, 177, 185
Boykin, Frank, 127, 153
Boynton v. Virginia, 204
Bragg, Walter L., 119
Brandon, John W., 75
Brandon, William W., 26, 135
Breckinridge, John, C., 3, 19, 92
Brockton, Massachusetts, 138
Brookley Air Force Base, 164
Brooks, Nathan L., 74, 84–87
Brotherhood of Sleeping Car Porters, Montgomery, 190
Brown, Cyrus, 140
Brown, E. B. M., 111
Brown, J. Bascom, 151
Brown, Lonnie, 167
Bryan, William Jennings, 133, 142, 148
Buckner, Simon B., 142, 148
Burt v. State, 96–98
Butler, Benjamin, 1
Byrd, William M., 95, 97–101, 105, 107

Caffey, Henry M., 73
Cahaba, Alabama, 99
Calhoun County, Alabama, 74, 95
Calhoun, John C., 13
California, 15
Calloway, Jeff, 131
Camden, Alabama, 172
Canada, 114
Canby, E. R. S., 107
Cannon, James, 133
Carmichael, Albert A., 177
Carmichael, Archibald H., 126, 128, 145
Caroline, 99
Carpetbaggers, 28, 29, 87, 88, 114, 118
Carrollton, Alabama, 79
Carter, Eugene W., 193, 201
Carter, James E. "Jimmy," 148
Carter, Robert L., 192
Castens, James W., 74
Chamber of Commerce, Alabama, 208
Chamber of Commerce, Montgomery, 207, 208
Chambers County, Alabama, 94, 132
Chapel Hill, North Carolina, 204
Charleston, South Carolina, 114
Charlotte, North Carolina, 204
Cherokee County, Alabama, 75
Chicago, Illinois, 166, 176, 180, 189, 204
Chicago, University of, 166
Childers, W. S., 146
Choctaw County, Alabama, 83, 90, 94
Civil Aeronautics Board, US, 209
civil rights movement, xiii, 166, 167, 174–82
Civil War, 6, 36, 56, 68, 72, 74, 78, 98, 106, 110, 111, 114, 160, 161, 217
Civil Works Administration, US, 175
Clansman, The, 170
Clark, Septima, 197
class conflict, southern, 2, 5, 6, 11–14, 18, 20–22, 32–38, 46, 55, 71–73, 81, 82, 86–88, 126–28, 133, 140, 142, 143, 148, 152–54, 158–60, 176, 177, 217–19
Clay, Henry, 17, 100, 218
Clay County, Alabama, 144, 148
Clayton, Henry DeLamar, II, 123, 125
Clayton Antitrust Act, 125
Cleveland Courts, Montgomery, 191
Cobbs, Hamner, 171
Cobbs, James, 97
Coffee County, Alabama, 94, 175
Coleman, Walter L., 111, 112, 114, 116
Colored Methodist Episcopal Church (CME), 174
Columbia University, 170
Columbus Enquirer-Sun, 131
Columbus, Georgia, 195
Colvin, Claudette, 180, 190, 192–94
Communist Party, 181, 203, 209
Confederacy, 3, 4, 36, 68, 72, 74, 95, 98, 99, 106, 110, 114, 161
Congress of Racial Equality (CORE), 166, 204

conscription, civil war, 3, 110
Constitutional Convention of 1865, Alabama, 76, 84, 92–95, 96, 99, 100, 102, 103, 107, 108
Constitutional Convention of 1867, Alabama, 100, 101, 106, 109, 112
Constitutional Convention of 1875, Alabama, 122, 165
Constitutional Convention of 1901, Alabama, xii, 123, 125, 130, 132, 134–37, 141–43, 146, 152, 165, 176–78, 216–18
Constitutional Convention, US, 155–58, 218
convict lease system, 127, 130, 150
Cooper, Aaron B., 74, 78
Cooper, Thomas B., 75
Coordinating Committee for Registration and Voting, Alabama, 192
Court of Appeals, Alabama, 193–95
Craft, Walton H., 164, 179, 180
Craig, William, 74
Crenshaw County, Alabama, 130
Culbertson, John Bolt, 197
Cullman, Alabama, 175

Dallas County, Alabama, 74, 99, 101, 167
Dargan, Edmund S., 95
Darwin, Charles, 155, 160
Davis, Edward, 202
Davis, Gardner H., 74
Davis, W. C., 129, 139
Dawson, N. H. R., 98, 99
debt, state, 59–64, 68
Decatur, Alabama, 141
Democratic Party, 3, 6, 11–14, 16, 18, 19, 21, 22, 31, 45, 49, 61, 63, 64, 72, 76, 95, 100, 101, 110, 112–20, 122, 123, 125, 128, 134–43, 147, 151, 152, 159–61, 163, 173, 201, 206, 216
Demopolis, Alabama, 125
Dent, S. Hubert, 137, 138
Detroit, Michigan, 195
Dixiecrats, 151, 152, 172, 175
Dixon, Frank M., 170–73, 175, 178
Dixon, Thomas, 170
Doster, Charles S. G., 84
Dothan, Alabama, 136, 141
Dothan Eagle, 131
doublechoice primary, Alabama, 128, 136, 137, 139–42, 145
Douglas, Stephen A., 3, 19, 92, 100, 101
Douglas, William O., 158
Drake, John N., 74, 76, 80, 90
Draper, Hamp, 135
DuBois, W. E. B., 71
Dunning school of historians, 38, 61
Durr, Clifford J., 192
Durr, Virginia F., 192

Edwards, William H., 75
Elba, Alabama, 75
Eliza, 99
Ellis, L. Handy, 129, 175
Elmore, John Archer, 111
Elyton, Alabama, 112
Emancipation Proclamation, 2, 92–94, 98–104, 106, 107
Empire Theater, Montgomery, 193
Engelhardt, Sam Martin, 201
Ervin, Sam, 148
Esdale, James, 130, 150
Eufaula, Alabama, 137, 165, 172
Evans, Hiram, 127, 144

Faber, Ellnora, 110
Faber, Henry E., 110, 111, 113–18, 120
Fair Employment Practices Committee (FEPC), 171, 175
Farmers' Alliance, 160, 218
Faubus, Orval, 148
Faulkner, James "Jimmy," 201
Fayette County, Alabama, 75
Feagin, William F., 151
Federalists, 5
Felder, Adam C., 84, 90
Ferdinand (Smith), 96, 98, 100, 109

Finley, John D., 186, 188, 193
Finney, O. H., 178
First Baptist Church (black), Montgomery, 206
Fisk University, 197, 204, 205
Fite, Arthur F., 141
Fitzpatrick, Benjamin, 31, 92, 93
Florence, Alabama, 79
Florida, 30, 31, 33, 35, 36, 56, 57, 59–62, 70, 146
Flowers, Walter W., 165
Folsom, James E., 148, 152, 170, 175–78, 201
Foster, John T., 90
Fourteenth Amendment, US Constitution, 83–85, 87, 156, 188, 194
Franklin County, Alabama, 74
freedom, meaning of, 6, 7, 9, 11, 12, 17–20, 22, 159, 218, 219
Freedom Rider riots, 202, 204–12
Freeman, Zenas F., 74
free soil, 19–22

Gayle, George W., 99
Gayle, William A., 190, 199, 201
Geneva County, Alabama, 136, 177
Genovese, Eugene D., 18, 26
George, Walter F., 146
Georgia, 6, 30, 32–34, 36, 47, 48, 55, 56, 63, 64, 66, 68, 76, 77, 131, 146, 156, 169
Georgia, University of, 140
Gibson, A. M., 75
Glasscock, Thomas O., 112, 113
Goldbugs, 142, 148
Gomillion, Charles, 197
Goodwin, F. LeBaron, 74
Goodwyn, R. Tyler, 129
Goodwyn-Rogers runoff bill, 129, 133, 136, 137, 142
Gough, Jerry B., 101, 106
Grady, Henry, xii
Graves, D. Bibb, 126–30, 136, 137, 139, 140, 143, 145, 150, 151, 170–72, 175, 183
Gray, Fred D., 190, 193, 194
Green, J. J., 173
Greenbackers, 143, 218
Greene County, Alabama, 74, 98
Greensboro, Alabama, 77, 171
Greyhound bus lines, 204, 205
Gunter, William A., Jr., 125, 134, 136, 140, 151

Hackney, F. Sheldon, xii
Hale County, Alabama, 137
Hall, Eugene S., 200
Hall, Grover C., 131, 133, 134, 151
Hall, Grover C., Jr., 208, 209
Harding, W. P. G., 133
Harlan, John Marshall, II, 156–58
Harris, Crampton, 150
Harris, Sampson W., 20
Harwood, Robert B., 194
Hawthorn, J. Richard, 74
Headland Wiregrass Farmer, 131
Heflin, Harrington P., 132, 141
Heflin, John, 132
Heflin, J. Thomas, 131–36, 138–43, 150, 151, 169
Heflin, Robert S., 131
Heflin, Wilson L., 132
Helms, Jesse, 148
Helper, Hinton Rowan, 2
Henderson, Charles, 123, 144
Henley, Claude V., 205
Highlander Folk School, 192, 197
Highway Patrol, Alabama, 205
hill country, Alabama, 74, 75, 77, 81, 84–87, 95, 123, 125, 126, 130, 131, 133, 135, 136, 140, 142–45, 152, 160, 175–78, 217
Hill, J. Lister, 151, 200, 207
Hill, T. B., 207
Hill, Wiley C., 190
Holloway, Frank, 167
Holloway, J. Lee, 188
Hooper, Johnson J., 95
Hoover, Herbert, 135, 136, 141, 142
Horsley, John D., 187

Horton, Myles, 197
Houston, Texas, 134
Hubbard, David, 20
Huckabee, Caswell C., 74
Huddleston, George, 137
Hull, Cordell, 146
Hume, Richard L., 101, 106
Humphrey, William D., 74
Huntingdon College, 206
Huntsville, Alabama, 74, 76, 173

Indian removal, 8
Interdenominational Ministerial Alliance, Montgomery, 208
Interstate Commerce Commission, US, 209, 211, 212

Jackson, Andrew, 13, 17, 159, 161, 218
Jackson, James M., 74
Jackson, Mississippi, 206
Jackson, Thomas, 210
Jackson County, Alabama, 74, 81
Jacksonianism, xii, xiii, 5–7, 10–15, 17–22, 32, 61, 69, 81, 87, 88, 95, 149, 159–61, 163, 216
Jacksonville, Florida, 192
Jacobs, B. E., 117
James, Earl D., 202, 203, 209
Jasper, Alabama, 129
Jefferson, Thomas, 159, 161, 218
Jefferson County, Alabama, 93, 103, 111, 127, 131, 154, 178
Jeffries, Lafayette, 98, 100
Jeffries, Washington, 98, 100
Jews, 110, 111, 113, 114, 117, 118, 120, 121, 131, 148, 149, 153
Johnson, Andrew, 3, 71, 89, 106
Johnson, Frank M., Jr., 194, 210
Jones, Elliott P., 75
Jones, John F., 187, 188
Jones, Thomas G., 119
Jones, Walter B., 171, 201
Joseph, Edwin B., 186
Judge, Thomas J., 95, 96, 98–100, 107
Judge, Thomas J., III, 140
Judkins, John C., 74
Junior Chamber of Commerce, Montgomery, 208
Justice Department, US, 167, 207

Kennedy, John F., 206, 207, 212
Kennedy, Robert F., 205, 206, 209
Key, V. O., 216, 217
Kilby, Thomas E., 172
King, Martin Luther, Jr., 200, 202, 203, 206
Kiwanis Club, Montgomery, 207
Klender, Barbara, 1, 22
Know-Nothings, 19, 27
Ku Klux Klan, 125–32, 136–43, 145–47, 149–55, 158, 159, 161, 172, 177, 200, 202–5

LaFayette, Alabama, 132
Lapsley, John W., 99
Langham, L. L., 98, 101, 105
Lauderdale County, Alabama, 92
Lawrence, John, 75
Lawrence County, Alabama, 79, 83, 100
Ledbetter, J. W., 74
Lee, Bernard, 202
Lee, W. L., 141
Lee County, Alabama, 135
legislature, Alabama, 71–75, 77, 82, 87, 95, 115, 123, 129, 130, 136, 137, 143, 146, 152, 171, 172, 176, 177, 183, 189
LeGrand, Milton P., 115, 118
Lehman, Emanuel, 119
Lehman, Mayer, 119
Leopard's Spots, The, 170
Leslie, John W., 98, 105
Levystein, Avon, 118, 122
Lewis, John, 204
Limestone County, Alabama, 74
Lincoln, Abraham, 1, 22, 98, 99, 101, 103, 106
Linden, Alabama, 95
Lindsay, Robert B., xii, 74, 83, 115

Livingston, W. Kyle "Sonny," 200, 201, 203
local, significance of, xii, xiii, 165, 169, 170, 178, 179, 181, 182, 195, 196, 211, 212, 217, 219
Locke, Hugh, 135, 136, 140–42, 150
Loe, D. Eugene, 193
Logan, Frances L., 99, 100
Long, Herman, 197
Long, Huey, 148
Long, J. Lee, 136, 137
Louisiana, 6, 16, 19, 30–34, 36, 55, 57, 59–62, 69, 70, 217
Lowndes County, Alabama, 74, 84, 95
Lynchburg, Virginia, 179, 187, 188
Lynne, Seybourn A., 141
Lynne, Seybourn H., 194

Mabry, Albert G., 74
Macon County, Alabama, 74, 151
Macon, Nathaniel, 12, 13
Madison County, Alabama, 74, 80
Madison, James, 157
Mahoney, William J., Jr., 209
Mallory, Hugh S. D., Jr., 137–39
Mann, Floyd, 205, 211, 212
Marengo County, Alabama, 95, 97, 142, 171
Marion County, Alabama, 74, 77
market economy, 6, 8, 9–12, 14, 16, 17, 148, 149, 159, 160
Marshall, John, 218
martial law, 98–100, 107, 206, 209
Maryland, 1, 22
Maxwell Air Force Base, 175, 191
McBee, Henry, 74
McCall, Charlie, 127, 129
McCann, Joseph D., 74
McCoy, Henry R., 74
McDaniel, Henry, 142
McDowell, Charles S., Jr., 126–29, 145
McElvain, Wallace S., 103, 106
McElvain v. Mudd, 102–7
McPherson, James M., xii
McQueen, John D., 141
Menefee, W. C., 74
Mercer University, 172
Meridian, Mississippi, 195
Merit System, Alabama, 171
Mexican-American War, 6, 15, 72, 160
Michigan, University of, xiii
Miller, B. Meek, 151
Ministerial Association, Montgomery, 208
Mississippi, 6, 19, 30, 33, 35, 44–46, 56–60, 62, 66, 169
Mitchell, Americus C., 74
Mobile, Alabama, 95, 96, 127, 134, 151, 153, 164, 179–81, 189, 190, 192–95, 199, 200
Montgomery, Alabama, 110–22, 125, 127, 134, 136, 137, 140, 151, 171–73, 179–81, 186–95
Montgomery Advertiser, 126–28, 130–32, 134, 137–41, 151, 153, 175, 186, 208, 209
Montgomery Alabama Journal, 209
Montgomery Bus Boycott, 180, 181, 193–95, 199–204, 206, 208, 210
Montgomery County, Alabama, 73, 78, 90, 129, 151, 191, 199, 202
Montgomery Fair department store, 187, 191, 195
Montgomery Home News, 203
Montgomery Improvement Association, 180, 181, 194, 207, 210, 211
Montgomery Labor Council, 200
Montgomery Museum of Fine Arts, 210, 211
Montgomery Public Library, 210, 211
Moore, John G., 75, 77, 94
Morgan, John Tyler, 101
Morgan County, Alabama, 74
Morgan v. Nelson, 101–4
Morgan v. Virginia, 204
Morse, Joshua, 83, 84, 94
Moses, Adolph, 111, 117, 121
Moses, A. J., 114
Moses, Alfred, 114, 117, 118
Moses, Levi, 114

Moses, Mordecai L., 110, 113, 114, 117–22
Mother's Day, 134
Motor Carrier Act of 1935, National, 204
Motor Carrier Act of 1939, Alabama, 189
Moulton, Alabama, 100
Mudd, William S., 93, 103
Mullin, Atticus, 138, 139
Munter, Marcus, 117
Musgrove, L. Breckinridge, 127
Myers, M. H., 111

Nashville, Tennessee, 13, 204–6
National Association for the Advancement of Colored People (NAACP), 173, 180, 181, 192, 201
National City Lines, 180, 189, 210
National Guard, Alabama, 206
Nelson, Richard M., 101
Newark Trust and Savings Bank, New Jersey, 119
New Deal, 142, 171, 172, 175
New Hampshire, 170
New Mexico, 217
New Orleans, Louisiana, 204
New York, 74, 77, 100, 110, 134
New York, New York, 5, 117, 119, 192
New York Times, 132, 135, 142, 203
Nixon, Edgar D., 190, 192, 200
Nixon, Richard M., 207
North Carolina, 2, 12–14, 76, 77
Nullification, 8

Opelika, Alabama, 135
open range, 9, 10, 14, 18
Osborne, Irene, 197
Ouzts, Thurman E., 205

Palmer, John M., 142, 148
Palmer, Solomon, Jr., 75
Parks, Raymond A., 191
Parks, Rosa L. (McCauley), 180, 191–95, 197, 199
Parsons, Lewis E., 92, 93
Patterson, A. G., 126, 128, 129
Patterson, Frederick D., 197
Patterson, John M., 201, 203, 205, 206, 208
Patton, Robert M., 79–83, 86, 92, 109
Peck, E. Wolsey, 100–104, 106–9
Pennsylvania, 157,
Perry County, Alabama, 74
Persons, Gordon, 175
Peters, Thomas M., 100–102, 104–7
Pettus, Edmund W., II, 125, 135, 136, 140, 141
Phelps-Stokes Foundation, 197
Phenix City, Alabama, 153
Philadelphia, Pennsylvania, 5, 166
Phillips Exeter Academy, 170
Pickens County, Alabama, 79
Pierce, Allen, 210
Pierce, John G., 77
Pike County, Alabama, 74, 204
Pine Level, Alabama, 191
Pittsburgh Courier, 173
Planters, 6, 8, 12–16, 18, 21, 31–37, 44, 71–74, 76–78, 80–82, 85–88, 92, 94, 166, 176
Plowman, George P., 75
political history, structure of, 216–19
Polk, James K., 17
Pollard, Charles T., 119
Populism, xii, 28, 29, 63, 88, 123, 130, 133 143, 148, 149, 158–61, 163, 169, 175–78, 201, 218
Potter, David M., 75
Potter, John, 75
Prattville, Alabama, 84, 110
Princeton University, xii
Prohibition, 125–28, 131, 133, 134, 137, 144, 149, 152–55, 158, 159, 161, 163
Progressive Democratic Association, Montgomery, 190
Progressivism, 125, 126, 159, 169, 170, 172, 178
Pruitt, Elihu P., 177

Public Service Commission, Alabama, 189
Pulitzer Prize, 131

Rabinowitz, Howard N., 169
race relations, 78–80, 82, 83, 85–88, 93–95, 110, 112—15, 118–20, 122, 123, 125, 132, 150, 151, 153, 164–82, 186–95, 199–203, 205–12, 218, 219
railroads, 7, 8, 13–16, 29, 56, 59, 60, 63, 64, 72, 78, 80, 112, 116, 119, 120, 164, 165, 169, 172
Raisler, Charles W., 74
Randall, James Ryder, 1, 22
Randolph County, Alabama, 74, 75, 90, 132
Raskob, John J., 136
Ray, Ben, 150, 152
Reconstruction, 4, 28, 30, 37, 38, 44–49, 56–61, 63, 64, 66, 69, 71–91, 94, 99–102, 110–22, 144, 148, 165, 169, 170, 212, 218
Reddick, Lawrence D., 203
Redeemers, 28, 60–64, 66, 88, 123, 125, 127, 129–31, 133, 134, 136–45, 147, 152, 160, 161, 163, 185, 218
Reese, James T., 74
Republican Party, 1–5, 18, 21, 22, 28, 29, 38, 44, 49, 55, 58–64, 66, 71, 75, 77, 79, 80, 82–88, 93–95, 100, 101, 103, 106, 110, 112–16, 118–20, 125, 135, 144, 148, 160
Revolution, American, 7, 159, 161
Richardson, William, 74
Rives, Richard T., 150, 151, 194
Robinson, George W., 77
Robinson, JoAnn G., 190, 203
Robinson, Joseph T., 134
Rockford, Alabama, 75
Rock Hill, South Carolina, 204
Roman Catholics, 12, 13, 127, 131–34, 138, 149, 150, 152, 153
Roosevelt, Franklin D., 142, 171, 172, 175
Rotary Club, Montgomery, 207
Routh, Fred, 197
Russell County, Alabama, 74
Ryan, William J., 187, 188

Saffold, Benjamin F., 101, 102, 107, 109
Saffold, Milton, 101
Saffold, Reuben, 101
Saint Margaret's Hospital, Montgomery, 191
Sayre, Anthony D., 187
Scalawags, 3, 93–95, 106, 112–14, 118, 120, 131
schools, public, 7, 8, 16, 29, 30, 32, 48, 55–58, 64, 69, 74, 75, 78, 95, 127, 128, 130, 150, 151, 166, 169, 172–74, 176, 191, 218
Scott, Gaston, 140, 141
Scott, John B., 193, 194
Seay, Solomon S., 203, 207, 209, 210, 212
Secession Convention, Alabama, 16, 26, 92
Seigenthaler, John, 205
Sellers, Clyde C., 190, 195, 199, 201, 202, 205
Selma, Alabama, 74, 95, 98, 101, 125, 137, 167
Selma Times-Journal, 131, 139, 167
Shelby County, Alabama, 129
Shouse, Jouett, 141
sit-ins, Montgomery, 202, 203
Slaughter, Alfred H., 90
Slavery, 2, 4, 15, 17–21, 29, 33–38, 44, 76, 77, 81, 92–106, 161, 169, 217, 218
Smith, Alfred E., 127, 131, 133–37, 141, 142, 152
Smith, Gerald L. K., 148
Smith, Hamlin J., 101
Smith, Henry F., 74
Smith, William H., 75, 112
Smith, William Russell, 96
South Carolina, 6, 9, 13, 29, 33, 34, 36, 37, 55–57, 59–62, 64, 76, 169, 197
southern history, power of, xi, xiii, 216–19
Southern Politics in State and Nation, 216, 217

Southern Regional Council, 197
Sparks, Chauncey, 164, 170, 172–75, 177–79
Stansel, Martin L., 79
States Rights Advocate, Montgomery, 200
Steadham, Winston, 74
Stockton, Alabama, 77
Stone, George W., 82, 95
Stowe, Harriet Beecher, 2
Strassburger, Albert, 111, 117, 118, 122
Student Nonviolent Coordinating Committee (SNCC), 167
subsistence, ethic of, 7–9, 11, 14, 16–18, 159
Sullivan, L. B., 202, 203, 205, 208 210, 211
Sumter County, Alabama, 92
Supreme Court, Alabama, 95–109, 116, 125, 151, 195
Supreme Court, US, 93, 149, 173, 194, 200, 203, 204, 206, 209, 211
Sykes, Francis W., 79, 83, 84, 90

Talladega County, Alabama, 74, 75, 93
Tallapoosa County, Alabama, 74, 90, 95
Talmadge, Eugene, 148, 169
Taxes, 15, 29–38, 44–48, 55, 60–64, 68, 81, 116, 117, 127, 130, 165, 171, 172, 175, 176, 178
Taylor, Richard, 98, 99, 107
Teague, William M., 187
tenant farmers, 9, 10, 48, 166, 167, 173
Tennessee, 2, 6, 13, 76, 95, 146, 192
Tennessee Agricultural and Industrial College, 204
Tennessee Valley, Alabama, 108, 144
Terry, James P., 113, 115
Texas, 6
Thetford, William F., 190, 193
Thirteenth Amendment, US Constitution, 76, 77, 80, 90, 93, 107
Thomasville Times, 142
Thompson, Holland, 112
Thompson, Ira B., 176
Thorn, Thomas, 74
Thrasher, David H., 95
Thurmond, J. Strom, 148, 172
Tillman, Benjamin, 169
Toomey, Christopher, 97
Towles, Toliver, 94
Trailways bus company, 204, 205
Trammell, Park, 146
Trenholm, H. Councill, 203
Truman, Harry S., 151, 152, 175
Tunstall, Alfred M., 137
Tuscaloosa, Alabama, 96, 100
Tuskegee Institute, 173, 174, 177, 197

Underwood, Oscar W., 127, 133
Unionism, 3, 95, 100, 101, 106
Union League, 112

Vansandt, James, 75
Vardaman, James K., 169
Vasser, L. B., 101
Virginia, 2, 6, 157, 170
Virginia, University of, 170

Walcott, Derek, xi
Waldman, Leopold, 111, 117
Walker, Abram J., 95–99, 107
Walker County, Alabama, 146
Wallace, George C., 148, 201
War Manpower Committee, Alabama, 171, 173
War of 1812, 5, 159
Warren, Earl, 209
Washington, DC, 132, 140, 142, 171, 204, 207, 208
Watkins, Levi, 203
Watson, Thomas E., xii, 169
Watts, Thomas H., 95
Weaver, Leroy G., 99
Webb, Samuel L., 145
Wedowee, Alabama, 75, 112
Weil, David, 111, 117, 118, 122
Weil, Henry, 117
Wesberry v. Sanders, 155–58
West, Mabel Jones, 137, 138

West Virginia, 2
Wetumpka, Alabama, 135
Whigs, xii, 2, 3, 7, 8, 11–14, 16–21, 31, 72, 95, 100, 160, 163, 175, 216
White, Alexander, 93, 94, 103
White, Alice L., 191
White, Byron R., 206
White Citizens' Council, 199–201, 203, 210, 211
white supremacy, 78–80, 82, 85–88, 95, 112, 115, 118, 119, 122, 151, 164–82, 186, 188, 189, 191, 193–95, 199—203, 205–12, 218
Wilcox County, Alabama, 74, 78, 98, 129, 167, 172
Wilhite, John, 75
William, 98
Williams, James, 81
Wilson, James, 157
Wilson, Woodrow, 170
Winnsboro, South Carolina, 204
Winston County, Alabama, 75
Winston, John A., 92
Winter, Joseph S., 116
Wiregrass, Alabama, 74, 81, 84–87, 123, 125, 126, 130, 131, 133, 135, 140, 143–45, 152, 160, 175–77
Women's Christian Temperance Union, 125
Women's Democratic Club, Alabama, 137
Women's League for White Supremacy, Alabama, 137, 138
Women's Political Council, Montgomery, 189
women's suffrage, 134
Wood, Gordon S., 155, 157
Woodliff, Augustin L., 75
Woodward, C. Vann, xii, 28, 169
World War I, 127, 154, 159, 170
World War II, 151, 166, 170–72, 177, 180, 181, 189, 191, 204, 212

Yale University, xii, 150
Yancey, William Lowndes, 76, 95
yeomen, white southern, 2–5, 9–11, 13–22, 27, 28–31, 33, 34, 37, 38, 45, 46, 49, 55, 58, 59, 61, 63, 66, 74, 75, 77–81, 85–87, 123, 125–28, 131, 134, 138, 140, 142, 148, 149, 152, 153, 160, 176–78
Young, John H., 173
Young America, 21, 22, 34, 69, 72, 160

Zwerg, James, 205